Stalking the Black Swan

STALKING

the

BLACK SWAN

RESEARCH AND DECISION MAKING IN
A WORLD OF EXTREME VOLATILITY

Kenneth A. Posner

⅄ Columbia Business School
Publishing

Columbia University Press
Publishers Since 1893
New York, Chichester, West Sussex
Copyright © 2010 Columbia University Press

Library of Congress Cataloging-in-Publication Data

Posner, Kenneth A.

   Stalking the black swan : research and decision making in a world of extreme volatility / Kenneth A. Posner.

      p.   cm. — (Columbia Business School Publishing)
Includes bibliographical references and index.
ISBN 978-0-231-15048-4 (cloth : alk. paper) — ISBN 978-0-231-52167-3 (ebook)
1. Investment analysis.   2. Investments—Forecasting.   3. Business cycles.   4. Recessions.
I. Title.   II. Series.

HG4529.P67   2010
332.63'2042—dc22

2009041215

Columbia University Press books are printed on permanent and durable
acid-free paper.

This book is printed on paper with recycled content.

Printed in the United States of America

c 10 9 8 7 6 5 4 3 2 1

References to Internet Web sites (URLs) were accurate at the time of writing. Neither
the author nor Columbia University Press is responsible for URLs that may have expired
or changed since the manuscript was prepared.

ACKNOWLEDGMENTS

I'd like to thank the people who have worked for me over the years, without whose effort I would have produced very little research: Andy Bernard, David Brown, Andrew Chen, David Cohen, Michael Courtian, Camron Ghaffari, Melini Jesudason, Tony Kim, Athina Meehan, Mita Nambiar, Miriam O'Brien, Suzanne Schiavelli, and Vivian Wang.

I owe gratitude to a number of people at Morgan Stanley (including alums), from whom I learned many valuable lessons over the years: David Adelman, Richard Berner, Mike Blumstein, Mayree Clark, Bob Dewey, Betsy Graseck, Chris Hart, John Havens, Eric Hemel, Trevor Harris, Vlad Jenkins, Tom Juterbock, Marty Leibowitz, Bill Lewis, Henry McVey, Mary Meeker, Vikrim Pandit, Ruth Porat, Tomer Regev, Steve Roach, Norm Rosenthal, Alice Schroeder, Dennis Shea, Art Soter, Byron Wien, and Alan Zimmermann. I owe similar debts to many clients, too.

The following people were kind enough to review drafts of various chapters and offer comments (they are not responsible for the content): David Adelman, Robert Aliber, Doug Bendt, Peter Burns, Max Bazerman, Harry Davis, Bob Dewey, Emanuel Derman, Trevor Harris, Brian Hayes, Vlad Jenkins, Michael Mauboussin, Alex Pollock, Richard Posner, Tomer Regev, Steve Sexauer, Carol Tavris, Jim Wiener, Byron Wien, Mark Zandi, and two anonymous reviewers.

I am obliged to Myles Thompson of Columbia University Press for suggesting this project, as I had long planned to write a book, and his encouragement got me started. Fred Miller did a great job editing the manuscript.

My family—Sue, Emeline, and Philip—put up with long hours, not only during my career as an analyst, but also while I was writing the book. I am grateful for their love and support.

By ratiocination, I mean computation.

—Thomas Hobbes, 1588–1679

If I had to bet on the best long-term predictor of good judgment among [a group of political and economic forecasters], it would be their commitment—their soul-searching Socratic commitment—to thinking about how they think.

—Philip Tetlock, *Expert Political Judgment*, 2005

The premise of this book is that the practice of fundamental research can help decision makers adapt to a world of "Black Swans," the seemingly improbable but highly consequential surprises that turn our familiar ways of thinking upside down. Most commonly associated with the work of Benjamin Graham and David Dodd, fundamental research is the study of causal variables underlying the performance of companies, industries, or economies, with the goal of predicting future developments. The research strategies in this book build upon that heritage, but they have been updated for the growing importance of computer technology, and they have a special focus on volatility. To be sure, fundamental research (with or without computers) will not provide a sure-fire way to success. We are all destined to be surprised far more often than we would like. Nonetheless, this book shows how fundamental research can help us forecast *some* Black Swans, recognize the possibility of others *just a little bit earlier*, and when surprise is unavoidable, *react more quickly* and (one hopes) mitigate the losses (possibly catastrophic) that result from misjudgments during periods of extreme volatility.

This book is based on my experience as a Wall Street analyst, but it is aimed at a much broader audience. As a senior analyst at a major investment bank, I covered the so-called "specialty finance" sector consisting of firms like Countrywide, Fannie Mae, CIT Group, Sallie Mae, MasterCard, Discover, American Express, and Providian Financial. A decade's worth of experience with this controversial group culminated in a ground-zero view of the mortgage, housing, and capital markets crisis that erupted in 2007. My experiences are directly relevant to investment professionals, such as analysts, traders, portfolio managers, risk managers, and chief investment officers, and possibly to retail investors. But the Black Swan phenomenon also takes wing in businesses and professions outside the securities industry. This book should be useful to senior executives, corporate strategists, regulators, and policymakers throughout the business world and in the intelligence community, the social sciences, journalism, and research in other fields—to anyone who must analyze, react, and strategize in the face of sudden change.

The capital markets crash of 2008 has taught more people to appreciate the idea of the Black Swan. Popularized by Nassim Nicholas Taleb, the Black Swan refers to a highly improbable event that seemingly could not have been anticipated by extrapolating from past data. Taleb references Europeans' surprise on discovering the Australian black swan (*cygnus atratus*): they had believed that all swans by definition were white (*cygnus cygnus*) because these were the only kind they had ever seen. In the markets, Black Swan events are marked by sudden shifts in the level of volatility affecting stocks, sectors, and sometimes the entire economy, producing price shocks of multiple standard deviations, at least as measured by the sense of risk prevailing before the storm. Of course, students of the markets have long recognized that the volatility of financial returns has a slippery quality. Benoit Mandelbrot, the founder of fractal science, observed that financial markets had fatter tails than implied by the normal (or bell-shaped) distribution. Taleb warned that people tend to underestimate risk, especially when armed with statistical models built on normal curves. His criticism of financial risk management and, more broadly, his warnings to beware the Black Swan proved timely.[1] Mistakes during the crash of 2008 suggest that some decision makers missed his message or did not know how to implement it. That is where this book comes in: it offers a pragmatic approach to research, analysis, and decision making for an environment punctuated by episodes of extreme volatility.

The idea of the Black Swan should not be reserved for infrequent global shocks; rather, Black Swans occur at different scales all the time. Many now associate the concept with the recent downturn, widely regarded as the most severe since World War II, the kind of shock we all hope is infrequent. But there are plenty of smaller, more mundane swans, whipsawing individual stocks and sectors, even when the rest of the market is calm. (There are numerous examples in the chapters that follow). These surprises have several sources, including the inherently difficult-to-forecast complexities of the fundamental world, the collective behavior of people in markets, and the feedback effects between fundamentals and markets.

In formulating the strategies in this book, I have tried to place the principles of fundamental research on a more scientific foundation. Some of the old rules, like value investing, do not necessarily work when Black Swans are operating. Yes, there is much good sense in the value discipline. But the logic has failed in certain areas, such as in the insistence on valuation rules of thumb (like price-to-book ratios), uncritical assumptions about the mood swings of "Mr. Market," or even "magic formulas" that are supposed to produce superior results—an approach that Graham himself dismissed.

To take fundamental research to the next level, I have tried to update the field's commonsense principles for recent advances in finance theory, quantitative investing, and artificial intelligence, borrowing insights from Fischer Black, David Shaw, Marvin Minsky, Judea Pearl, and Herbert Simon, among others. To be clear, I am not an academic or a "quant." But as a practicing analyst, I was always interested in using advanced computer modeling to improve my forecasts (as some of the stories that follow will show). I have seen how powerful analytics can produce a competitive edge. I have also seen analytics go dangerously wrong. When surprise strikes, it is no use blaming models. We live in an information-intensive environment, so decision makers must seek out the right balance between human intuition and computer analysis.[2] Basing fundamental research on the same scientific principles as fully quantitative disciplines strikes me as important, because with the ongoing growth in computational power, the two approaches may eventually converge.[3]

This book does not include any complicated math, but the reader will encounter probability trees, the basic tool for thinking probabilistically and an aid to making explicit our subjective estimates when peering into the future. Chapters 2 and 7 show how to use probability trees to map out multiple scenarios for a set of critical causal variables. Chapters 3, 4, 5, and 6 use probability trees to illustrate how we should react to new information, as well as intuitive mistakes people sometimes make. Chapter 8 covers Monte Carlo analysis, the ultimate in computer-powered probabilistic reasoning.

The book is organized into three parts. The first focuses on *uncertainty*: what are its sources, and how can one make accurate predictions in a volatile world? The three chapters in this section cover the process of generating and testing hypotheses, thinking in scenarios, and finding the right level of confidence to make decisions.

The second part is about *information*. It shows how to zero in on critical issues, react accurately to new data, and obtain useful information from parties with strategic interests, such as corporate managers.

The final part of the book covers *analysis*. It showcases high-powered analytic techniques that can help resolve complex fundamental questions—and that can also be misused. The book ends with a discussion of judgment, a critical component of any decision, and the main defense against certain kinds of Black Swans.

Here is a more detailed road map:

Part I—Uncertainty

Chapter 1: Forecasting in Extreme Environments. The first chapter starts with some of the main sources of excessive volatility: complex fundamentals, imitation among traders, and the interaction between markets and fundamentals, which can produce positive feedback effects. While forecasting in extreme environments is a daunting exercise, the basic approach involves generating and testing hypotheses, the basics of the scientific method. Most investors understand the importance of hypotheses. But maximizing accuracy requires two steps that real-world decision makers sometimes miss (especially outside of controlled laboratory conditions): calibrating models with the market and identifying catalysts to test hypotheses. The discipline of calibration and catalysts can prevent costly mistakes, as we will see in a story about Fannie Mae in late 2007, when signs of trouble were emerging but before the company's ultimate fate was sealed.

Chapter 2: Thinking in Probabilities. This chapter introduces the probability tree as a basic but versatile tool that helps in confronting uncertainty.

This tool can translate judgments about critical issues into stock-picking decisions, calibrate subjective assessments of risk with market volatility, and identify asymmetric outcomes. The case study turns back the clock to 2001, when a subprime credit card issuer called Providian offered me an early taste of extreme volatility.

Chapter 3: The Balance Between Overconfidence and Underconfidence, and the Special Risk of Complex Modeling. If extreme volatility is how the markets register surprise, then we may surmise (with hindsight) that investors were too confident. Indeed, it has become commonplace for psychologists and behavioral economists to assert that people are overconfident. Chapter 3 discusses the nature and limitations of human confidence as an emotional signal for decision making, including the risk that abundant information and sophisticated modeling may produce a special kind of false confidence. However, the behavioral critique takes us only so far, because without confidence no one would make decisions. Too little confidence can also be a problem; to make accurate decisions, one must search for the right balance. Further, in competitive businesses, where resources are limited, decision makers need to find that balance as quickly and efficiently as possible. In this chapter I recount successful recommendations based on limited information with unsuccessful calls based on advanced analytics. The chapter also reveals how flaws in modeling subprime credit risk contributed to the mortgage and housing crisis of 2007.

Part II—Information

Chapter 4: Fighting Information Overload with Strategy. One reason people are surprised by episodes of extreme volatility is that the world contains more information than any person, team, or organization can process. Information overload is a fundamental reality of the modern world. True, ever more powerful computers assist us in organizing and analyzing information. Unfortunately, any computational device, human or silicon, is subject to physical and mathematical limitations, so computers cannot solve the problem of information overload. This chapter highlights the difference between acquiring information under an active strategy and reacting passively. The active strategy focuses on critical issues and combines intuitive reactions to new information with conscious decisions about how to allocate limited resources. A case study contrasts the information strategy of a hedge fund that anticipated the subprime mortgage crisis of 2007 with the strategy of a mutual fund that did not.

Chapter 5: Making Decisions in Real Time: How to React to New Information Without Falling Victim to Cognitive Dissonance. If we had more time to react, then perhaps extreme volatility might be manageable. But a fast-changing world puts a special kind of stress on the human cognitive system. Terms such as *cognitive dissonance, change blindness,* and the *boiling frog syndrome* refer to the trouble people sometimes have changing their minds until the evidence is overwhelming—at which point it may be too late. Case studies from my research include examples of successfully reacting to new information, as well as mistakes.

Chapter 6: Mitigating Information Asymmetry. Access to management teams is high on many investors' wish lists, because rarely does anyone have more information about a business than the people running it. However, trying to acquire proprietary information from management teams (or other expert sources) can be difficult—and even counterproductive. The challenge lies in the *information asymmetry* between managers and investors. This chapter describes how to monitor a company's message for signs of internal contradiction, echoing the concept of cognitive dissonance discussed in Chapter 5. The chapter also explains how the right questions can elicit useful information.

Part III—Analysis and Judgment

Chapter 7: Mapping from Simple Ideas to Complex Analysis. With hindsight, Black Swans may seem simple. Beforehand, it is not clear whether one factor will dominate, and if so, which one. Analysts use models to manipulate multiple variables across various scenarios. But modeling introduces its own source of complexity. The goal in "mapping out" a problem is to link the model's output to a handful of critical issues in a way that maximizes accuracy and minimizes complexity. This chapter will illustrate the practice of mapping with stories about MasterCard and American Express, two high-profile competitors in the global payments sector whose stocks produced surprising outcomes.

Chapter 8: The Power and Pitfalls of Monte Carlo Modeling. Monte Carlo modeling is a high-powered analytic technique used extensively in science, engineering, and financial *"quant"* applications. Monte Carlo models solve problems by generating thousands or millions of random scenarios, serving up probabilistic estimates for problems too complicated to work through by hand, sometimes with eerily accurate results: I will recount how my research team used Monte Carlo modeling to estimate litigation risk at American Express and value Fannie Mae's stock at a time when the company was not publishing current financial statements. However, every model has its limits. Monte Carlo models produce dangerously unreliable results if the analyst does not understand the correlation between variables, which requires a sound grasp of underlying causal relationships. This chapter will explain how incorrectly analyzing correlation contributed to the 1998 failure of Long-Term Capital Management and, just a few years later, to the collapse of a new market in *"correlation trading,"* which involved hundreds of billions of dollars worth of collateralized debt obligations.

Chapter 9: Judgment. Whether intuitive, conscious, or computer powered, analysis of any sort faces physical, mathematical, and human limitations. For this reason, successful decision making requires a final step, which we call judgment. More than just weighing the pros and cons, judgment involves thinking about—and when necessary changing—the process by which we analyze information and arrive at decisions. You see judgment at work when a decision maker weighs the output of a sophisticated computer model against intuitive insights. You also see it when executives evaluate their corporate strategy in light of changing competitive conditions.

Judgment is a critical defense against the Black Swans that arise when too many people follow the same style of analysis and decision making without recognizing that their collective behavior can bring about a break with past trends. This chapter illustrates the perils that can arise when this kind of recognition is lacking, including profiles of the "Quant Quake" of 2007, a risk management backfire that cost credit card issuer MBNA its independence, and the inherent flaw in the Basel II regulatory capital regime that unleashed a global banking crisis.

Because collective behavior is hard to quantify, judgment is more art than science. Further, the unpredictability of collective behavior is one of the main causes of market swings—and thus a reason that we will likely never banish the Black Swan. Rather than hoping we could, the more constructive attitude, in my view, is to learn to live with the phenomenon of extreme volatility. This means making realistic predictions and staying quick on your feet, ready to react accurately to surprises. To help decision makers with these tasks is the purpose of fundamental research, and this book.

Part I

Uncertainty

Chapter 1

Forecasting in Extreme Environments

Ideas, sentiments, emotions, and beliefs possess in crowds a contagious power as intense as that of microbes.

—Gustave Le Bon,
The Crowd: A Study of the Popular Mind, 1896

What I call the attitude of reasonableness or the rationalistic attitude presupposes a certain amount of intellectual humility. Perhaps only those can take it up who are aware they are sometimes wrong, and who do not habitually forget their mistakes. It is born of the realization that we are not omniscient, and that we owe most of our knowledge to others.

—Karl Popper, *Conjectures and Refutations*, 1963

I learned that individual opinions (my own as well as the next man's) are of little value—because so frequently wrong.

—Humphrey Neill, *The Art of Contrary Thinking*, 1997

A "society of solipsists," where members could seek only first-hand knowledge, would be profoundly crippled.

—Christopher Cherniak, *Minimal Rationality*, 1986

Black swans are but one manifestation of the uncertainty with which we peer into the future, mindful that other people are trying to do the same thing and that the interaction of opinions and decisions can affect the very future outcomes we are trying to foresee. Investors have strong incentives to make accurate forecasts in the face of this kind of uncertainty. So do decision makers in most any field characterized by competition, cooperation, or other forms of collective action.

This chapter describes some of the main sources of extreme volatility and how to make better forecasts in challenging times. We consider three sources of volatility. First, volatility arises because the fundamental world is complicated and has nonlinear characteristics, which means that some events are about as predictable as the weather or earthquakes. Second, the nature of collective behavior can produce sudden shifts in consensus thinking, because people imitate each other in forming opinions. Third, markets do not simply reflect fundamental value; they also interact with the fundamental world, in some cases producing positive feedback effects that can lead to extreme outcomes. For these reasons, analysts face severe limits in forecasting fundamentals for even the simplest businesses, let alone industry developments or macroeconomic trends. That does not mean our swan-stalking quest is impossible. To surmount these challenges, it will help to take a close look at the scientific principles of forecasting.

Forecasting starts by identifying hypotheses and building models. Regardless of whether a model is intuitive, the outcome of conscious reasoning, or developed with a computer, forecasting relies upon a set of the principles that make up the scientific method. But outside the laboratory, it is easy to get sloppy, especially in fluid environments, where numerical data are not available for statistical tests. In my experience, real-world decision makers sometimes overlook two critical steps: calibrating models with the market and ensuring that hypotheses will be tested by upcoming information, what traders call "catalysts." A simple rule of thumb is to agree with the consensus outlook unless you can point to a catalyst to test a different view. Of course, no rule is guaranteed to work all the time, but this one might help you avoid the disastrous losses that often accompany episodes of extreme volatility. Illustrating these points is a stock-picking story involving Fannie Mae during late 2007, just a few months before the government seized it and placed it into conservatorship.

Fannie Mae: The Gathering Storm

This story does not show how to "predict a Black Swan." But it does demonstrate how the discipline of forecasting, with an emphasis on calibration and catalysts, can help avoid disaster. When operating during periods of extreme volatility, survival is the first priority.

During its waning days as a publicly owned institution, Fannie Mae presented me with a dilemma. Today we know that the U.S. Treasury placed Fannie Mae into conservatorship over fears that the company might suffer a fatal liquidity crisis. As of mid-2009, its stock traded under $1 per share. But in the early summer of 2007, this dismal fate was not yet apparent. The stock was trading in the $50s, and I was recommending it with an overweight rating. My investment hypothesis centered on what appeared to be lucrative returns in its business of guaranteeing mortgages against default, where the high fees it collected had more than compensated for the occasional loss on a bad loan. Such a profitable business was explained, I thought, by the duopolistic market position of Fannie and its sibling, Freddie Mac, as both firms enjoyed special benefits in their government charters, which essentially precluded competition. On the basis of my earnings forecast and valuation model, I thought Fannie's stock was worth close to $70.

Why had investors lost sight of the value of this business? Perhaps because the company was not producing current financial statements, an obvious concern for any analyst who wanted to study the numbers. The lack of financials was the consequence of an accounting debacle in 2004 that had forced out management and required a multibillion-dollar restatement. My hypothesis about the value of the company's guarantee business would soon be tested, because by year-end 2007 the company would resume current reporting status. This event would encourage analysts to focus on the stock, and I thought they would recognize the value of the guarantee business. So far, so good: I had a hypothesis and a catalyst. Of course, there were risks, too. Like everyone else, I expected the U.S. housing market to slow and Fannie's credit losses to rise, but those were already factored into my earnings forecast and valuation (or so I thought).

As the summer progressed, clouds gathered on the horizon. Starting in July, liquidity in the market for mortgage securitizations began to dry up and the riskier bonds backed by subprime loans stopped trading. This was something of a surprise: I had anticipated widening spreads on these bonds, but I had not expected a halt in trading. Liquidity had not been an issue since the global currency crisis of 1998, when Russia's default and the Long-Term Capital Management debacle temporarily threw the capital markets into disarray.

But by August, problems in the capital markets had deepened; soon, even the highest-rated tranches of the subprime securitizations stopped trading. The nation's largest mortgage originator, Countrywide, suffered a run on the bank. This was not a good sign.

Despite these omens, Fannie Mae's stock held in the mid-$50s. After all, the company did not depend on securitization markets. Rather, it competed against them. Over the last few years, when booming home prices had catalyzed an explosion in subprime lending, the company had ceded almost half its market share to mortgage lenders that sold their increasingly risky loans into the securitization markets. Now with these markets in chaos, Fannie and Freddie were the only game in town. Their unique status as government-sponsored enterprises (GSEs) allowed them to raise debt at narrow spreads over U.S. Treasury rates, and in past crises, investors had flocked to the comparative safety of GSE debt, widening their cost advantage even further. There was no reason to think that capital-market volatility would imperil Fannie's fundamentals. To the contrary, the company stood to raise prices and gain market share.

I drafted a report outlining the case for long-term revenue and earnings growth that would reiterate my overweight recommendation. The company had just raised its fees for guaranteeing mortgages against default, so the only question was how quickly new loans with high fees would cycle into the portfolio, replacing old loans and thus pushing up revenues. This took simple math, and I was confident in the projections. My report also included a new forecast of credit losses. I had analyzed Fannie's experience in the California housing market downturn of the early 1990s, taking into account differences in products and market conditions between then and now. My analysis suggested that Fannie's credit losses would rise but not necessarily become problematic.

My clients, however, showed little willingness to extrapolate credit losses from past cycles. "Analysts are underestimating Fannie's losses," one client warned me. She would not go into specifics and hung up before I could probe her reasoning. This reaction irritated me, because I had put a lot of thought into my analysis and wanted to debate the details. Truth be told, the client did not sound knowledgeable. (And how could she be? As a typical buy-side analyst, she was responsible for covering the entire financial services sector.) She seemed to be merely reacting to rumors and other people's opinions.

The deepening chaos in the capital markets indicated that a Black Swan might be beating its wings nearby. Today we know what the correct decision was going to be, but I did not have the advantage of hindsight in late 2007. How should I have decided what to do with Fannie Mae?

Sources of Extreme Volatility: Nonlinear Fundamentals

Before concluding this story, we need to delve deeper into volatility and how to analyze it. Economists and scientists have theorized extensively about volatility. A practitioner does not need to understand the math behind these theories, but appreciating the sources of extreme volatility helps one cope with it. I divide the sources of "extreme" volatility into three categories: the complexity of the fundamental world, the nature of collective behavior in the markets, and the potential for positive feedback between the two (Exhibit 1.1). Forecasting results for a company or industry typically involves simple, linear models. But as we all know, the fundamental world is more complicated, a fact appreciated by natural scientists, who grapple with butterfly effects, self-organized criticality, and other nonlinear processes.

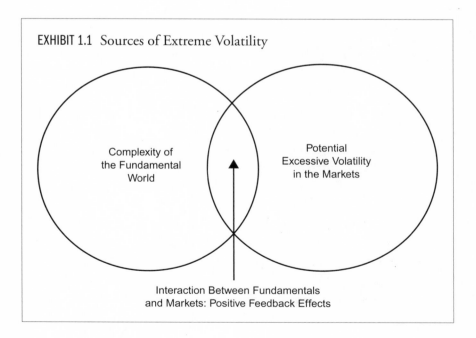

EXHIBIT 1.1 Sources of Extreme Volatility

Complexity of the Fundamental World

Potential Excessive Volatility in the Markets

Interaction Between Fundamentals and Markets: Positive Feedback Effects

Butterfly Effects and Weather Forecasting

Weather forecasters have long been aware of nonlinearities in the atmosphere, a phenomenon often expressed by the term *butterfly effect*. Thanks to the movie *Jurassic Park*, many people are familiar with the idea, namely, that an event as insignificant as a butterfly flapping its wings over the Indian Ocean might lead—through a set of complex interactions—to a hurricane forming over the Atlantic. If similar effects influence the world of business and economic fundamentals, then it may often be impossible to forecast the long-term. The logical implication: start by focusing on the short-term.

To be sure, many people hold long-term investing in higher regard than short-term trading. But during periods of extreme volatility, this stance may be unrealistic. Weather forecasters have made progress in improving their short-term accuracy with better models and more granular data, and this should be the goal for analysts who are struggling with volatility in other sectors.

The term *butterfly effect* was coined by Massachusetts Institute of Technology (MIT) scientist Edward Lorenz in the early 1960s, when he was developing computer models to simulate the weather. Lorenz discovered something strange with his output when, for convenience, he tried to restart a simulation at the midpoint of its last run. To do so, he typed in the ocean surface temperature (the variable in question) from the last simulation run as the starting point from which the program was to resume its calculations. However, he discovered that after a few periods, the new simulation began to diverge from the old one, even though the same code was operating on the same input. Then it dawned on him that he had typed in the temperature to only 3 decimals, forgetting that the computer conducted calculations to 6 decimals. This tiny difference eventually accounted for a massive divergence in output (Exhibit 1.2). The technical term for this phenomenon is *sensitive dependence on initial conditions*.[1]

Fifty years after Lorenz coined the term, butterfly effects continue to vex weather forecasters. Studies of their work have found that accuracy degrades rapidly after the first twelve hours, and skeptics question whether there is any long-term predictive skill at work in the trade.[2] However, the short-term accuracy of weather forecasting has improved in recent years.

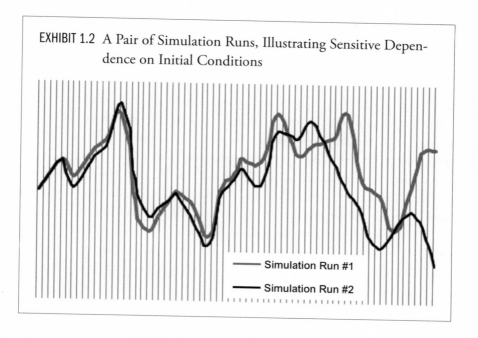

EXHIBIT 1.2 A Pair of Simulation Runs, Illustrating Sensitive Dependence on Initial Conditions

Simulation Run #1

Simulation Run #2

According to the American Meteorological Society (AMS), from 1987 to 2004 the nominal lead time for tornado warnings increased from less than 5 minutes to 13 minutes. In 2006, the average track error for hurricane forecasts made 48 hours in advance was as accurate as 24-hour forecasts a decade ago. The lead times for winter storm watches in 2006 averaged 17 hours, a 70% increase over 1999. The AMS data also show gains in monthly and trimonthly forecasts.[3] A study by scientists at the European Center for Medium-Range Weather Forecasts found a one-day gain in the predictability of atmospheric pressure in the Northern Hemisphere over the last decade: today's 4- and 5-day forecasts are about as accurate as 3- and 4-day forecasts a decade ago. Similar gains in the Southern Hemisphere have been achieved in just the last 3 years.[4]

What has happened? New technology and better information are addressing the issues Lorenz found in his simulations. Higher-resolution data reduce the error inherent in the starting point for weather modeling, as if Lorenz had restarted his simulation with 4 or 5 decimals instead of 3. Satellite-borne instruments collect greater quantities of data about current conditions, including microwave radiance, humidity, and surface wind speed—especially important for the Southern Hemisphere, given limited data collection over the ocean from other sources. In addition to better data, more sophisticated computer modeling has improved forecasting skills.[5]

Butterfly effects appear to affect predictions about business fundamentals, too. Skeptics have long criticized economic forecasting, arguing that economists show no statistically valid skill in making long-term forecasts, let alone in predicting turning points in the economy. In contrast to the science of meteorology, there has been no measurable improvement in the accuracy of economists' forecasts over the past 30 years.[6] Similar criticisms apply to the published forecasts of securities analysts. I can empathize. My long-term forecasts often proved incorrect, not only because of surprises at individual companies, but also because of macro events, like the global currency crisis of 1998, the popping of the technology stock bubble, the 9/11 terrorist attacks, recession, deflation scares, Federal Reserve monetary policy, and of course the great housing market boom and bust.

Given such challenges, analysts should borrow a page from weather forecasters: improve forecasting accuracy by focusing first on the short-term. And like Lorenz, watch for when predictions start to diverge, a signal that it is time to rebuild or recalibrate the model. The long-term outlook is still important, but it can also be expressed as a series of short-term predictions, whose accuracy should be closely monitored. The Fannie Mae story will highlight the importance of understanding the short term.

Extreme Distributions: Predicting Earthquakes and Avalanches

Turbulent weather is one apt metaphor for the difficulty in forecasting the fundamental world. But there are other kinds of nonlinear forecasting challenges, some of which may resemble avalanches or earthquakes: tranquility reigns for long periods and is followed abruptly and unpredictably by extreme outcomes.

To describe the dynamics of avalanches, scientists use the term *self-organized criticality*. If you drop grains of sand one by one on top of a sand pile, sooner or later one of the grains will trigger an avalanche. But it is very difficult to predict which grain, unless you understand how the incremental weight from each new grain alters the stresses inherent in the existing pile, leading to the critical point.[7] Self-organized criticality describes the seismic pressures that produce earthquakes. While scientists understand something about the frequency of earthquakes of different magnitudes, unfortunately, despite much study, they cannot predict the timing of individual earthquakes.[8]

In some situations, analysts and decision makers may have no better luck predicting sudden shocks in the business world. Think back to the failures of Bear Stearns, IndyMac, Washington Mutual, and Wachovia during 2008. These were like falling grains stacked on top of a growing pile. The bankruptcy of Lehman Brothers, which triggered the freezing up of the global capital markets, was like the grain that set off an avalanche.

Yet some earthquake-like events may be predictable if the analyst grasps the underlying causative variables. These variables include such things as management incentives, competitive pressure, and corporate strategy; they are not always as opaque as the stresses that build along a fault zone. Many of the stories in this book will demonstrate how seemingly extreme outcomes might have been better anticipated if analysts and investors had picked up on the presence of lurking causative variables. The stories also illustrate the importance of rapid and accurate reaction to new information, because not all shocks are instantaneous.

Sources of Extreme Volatility: Collective Behavior

Self-organized criticality and butterfly effects remind us that extreme volatility may arise from the inherent complexity of the fundamental world. But in dealing with securities prices, extreme volatility may also surface from within the market itself because of the ways in which people interact with each other in forming opinions. Some regard this as irrational behavior, on a par with mob psychology. Others think of it as a rational process of forming and updating opinions. Regardless of how it is described, collective behavior can produce extreme outcomes. Thus the swan hunter must keep an eye on his peers.

One of the leaders of the behavioral finance movement, Yale professor Robert J. Shiller, argues that stocks are "excessively volatile," meaning that price moves are bigger than business fundamentals warrant. He comes to this conclusion by comparing the volatility of stock prices to the volatility of dividends. Why are stock prices more volatile? Shiller believes excessive volatility may occur "for no fundamental reason at all." Instead, it may reflect nothing more than the effects of "mass psychology," as may happen during speculative bubbles:

> When speculative prices go up, creating successes for some investors, this may attract public attention, promote word-of-mouth enthusiasm, and heighten expectations for further price increases. The talk attracts attention to "new era" theories and "popular models" that justify the price increases. If the feedback is not interrupted it may produce after many rounds a speculative "bubble," in which high expectations for further price increases support very high current prices. The high prices are ultimately not sustainable, since they are high only because of expectations of further price increases, and so the bubble eventually bursts, and prices come falling down. The feedback that propelled the bubble carries the seeds of its own destruction, and so the end of the bubble may be unrelated to news stories about fundamentals.[9]

Shiller is articulating the classic theory of bubbles. One of the preeminent economic historians of bubbles, Charles Kindelberger, described how the enthusiasm surrounding new businesses or technologies could attract unsophisticated classes of investors into the market. According to one aspect of his theory, prices rise until the supply of new buyers is exhausted, at which point prices collapse.[10] This phenomenon was evident in the Internet and technology boom of the late 1990s, in which the growing participation of retail investors in the market could be seen in the newfound popularity of day trading and in larger family holdings of stocks and mutual funds.

History is full of bubbles that appear to have been inflated by unsophisticated investors. In 1720, the South Sea Company was licensed by the British government to issue stock in order to purchase and retire existing British debt. The South Sea Company's stock soared from an initial price of £128 to a peak of £1,050 before collapsing in midsummer. During its rise, the stock attracted all sorts of new investors to the market: women, poets (Alexander Pope), scientists (Isaac Newton), the King of England, the Prince of Wales, over 100 peers, 300 members of Parliament, people from all social classes, and foreign speculators.[11]

If we turn our attention to the more recent past, we find evidence of an influx of new investors in the boom and crash of the U.S. housing markets. According to the U.S. Bureau of the Census, the U.S. home ownership rate increased from 66.2% in 2000 to 68.9% at its peak in 2007. This change does not seem big enough to indicate an enormous wave of new home buyers. However, speculative investors were more active in the housing market than people realized at the time. According to government surveys, investors accounted for around 15% of new mortgages, up from prior levels of around 7%—a meaningful change. But these surveys appear to have missed those investors who masqueraded as owner-occupiers in order to secure more favorable mortgage terms, sometimes with the complicit encouragement of loan officers or brokers. A survey by the National Association of Realtors indicated that investment properties and second homes made up as much as 40% of total home sales at their peak in 2005. If so, the housing market saw a massive inflow of new investors, much like Internet stocks in the 1990s or the South Sea Company's stock in 1720.

New investors were also crowding into the global securities market. As time went by, it became clear that managers of collateralized debt obligations (CDOs) were buying up enormous volumes of securities backed by mortgages. CDOs were a new structure set up to purchase an ostensibly well-diversified pool of securities, which the CDO funded by issuing its own securities. To be sure, CDO managers were professionals, not retail investors. Nonetheless, in the eyes of other professionals, the CDO managers seemed unsophisticated. At a 2006 industry conference, I recall hearing mortgage security analysts openly question how well CDO managers understood the nature of the securities they were buying. The CDO managers argued that mortgage security yields were attractive when compared with yields of comparably rated corporate bonds. In this regard, however, they were mistaken. The rating agencies were careful to point out (if asked) that their ratings were not consistent across different types of securities, because the nature of the risks in different asset classes was not comparable. In other words, a BBB-rated mortgage-backed security did not necessarily present the same level of risk as a BBB-rated corporate bond. That nuance was missed by CDO managers, who continued to acquire investment-grade-rated tranches of mortgage-backed securities with great enthusiasm until the market finally collapsed (Exhibit 1.3). (In Chapter 8 we will discuss how the enthusiasm for CDOs also reflected inaccurate estimates of correlation.)

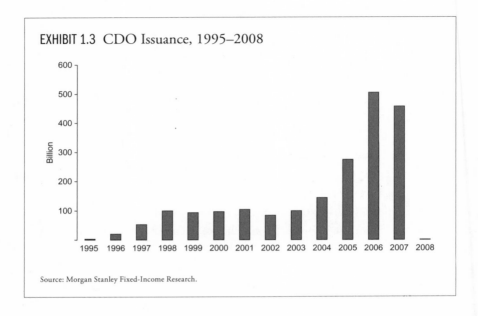

EXHIBIT 1.3 CDO Issuance, 1995–2008

Source: Morgan Stanley Fixed-Income Research.

Imitation and Mob Psychology

At their heart, bubble theories are about imitation, as new classes of investors attempt to profit from strategies that have already enriched their peers. Behind many bubble theories, one detects distaste for imitation, a presumption that these episodes reflect irrational attitudes and the worst of human behavior. Indeed, there is a long history of educated persons distrusting crowds. The 19th-century French social psychologist Gustave Le Bon published a famous study of mob psychology, in which he described the "law of the mental unity of crowds":

> An agglomeration of men presents new characteristics very different from those of the individuals composing it. The sentiments and ideas of all the persons in the gathering take one and the same direction, and their conscious personality vanishes. A collective mind is formed. . . . [12]

Le Bon thought crowds were in a state of "expectant attention, which renders suggestion easy," much like a state of hypnosis, such that the first idea that arises "implants itself immediately by a process of contagion in the brains of all assembled." He does not seem to have been a fan of mob behavior, observing that "in crowds the foolish, ignorant, and envious persons are freed from their sense of insignificance and powerlessness, and are possessed instead by the notion of brutal and temporary but immense strength."

Imitation can also take place through peer pressure. In the 1950s, the psychologist Solomon Asch demonstrated how group attitudes could pressure individual decisions. In a series of tests, subjects were shown cards with lines of different lengths and were asked to identify the lines with equal lengths. By themselves, test subjects did so with an error rate of less than 1%. However, in a group setting, the dynamics changed. When other members of the group, who were secretly following the researcher's instructions, unanimously pointed to the wrong line, the test subjects went along with the crowd roughly 37% percent of the time. Some test subjects went with the majority nearly all the time. Exit interviews revealed that these subjects interpreted their difference from the majority as a sign of personal deficiency, which they believed they must hide by agreeing with the group. These kinds of results appear to support Shiller's arguments that market bubbles and other forms of extreme volatility arise from the natural tendency of humans to imitate each other, in some cases for reasons that seem irrational.

However, peer pressure has its limits. Asch found that about one-quarter of the subjects were completely independent and never agreed with the group. Further, when even one other member of the group dissented from the otherwise unanimous view, the pressure on the test subjects to conform was substantially reduced, and their error rate dropped by 75%.[13] Therefore, we should be careful about assuming that imitation is necessarily widespread or irrational.

Imitation as Rational Herding

In some situations, imitation is entirely rational. After all, many kinds of animals move in herds for protection against predators, and many kinds of predators hunt in packs. In these cases, imitation (one animal following the next) is a form of coordination that appears to have been a successful evolutionary adaptation. Imitation is also one of the underlying principles of economics: profits are supposed to attract new competition.

Similarly, imitation among traders or investors can be perfectly rational. Would it not be logical to buy a stock if a smart investor convinced you of the company's growth prospects through sound arguments supported by data and research? It might be rational to buy the stock even if you had not heard the arguments but knew that the investor had a superior track record. If many traders buy a stock because of some smart investor, they may push up its price. But the consensus view supporting the new, higher price could be described as "fragile," in the sense that rather little information or analysis underlies it. Everyone is depending on the smart investor. If the smart investor gets it wrong and the fundamentals disappoint, the other investors might dump their shares, because they really know little about the company. In this case, the stock might gap down—a small example of extreme volatility, a mini-bubble and crash involving a single stock, but produced by a rational form of imitation.[14]

One might argue that traders should analyze fundamental information before making decisions, but there is no a priori reason to favor information about fundamentals over information about other investors. Furthermore, traders do not have unlimited time or resources, so they cannot analyze everything.

Imitation as Phase Shifts

Some scientists think they can explain the pattern of exponential price changes in bubble markets by modeling imitation among traders.[15] They compare the shift from normal to bubble markets to "phase shifts" in materials—for example, when water transitions to steam at the boiling point. A popular model for phase shifts is the so-called Ising model, developed by the German physicist Ernst Ising, which is based on interactions among adjacent particles. To explain the magnetic properties of a piece of iron, for example, an Ising model may represent a three-dimensional lattice of iron atoms with different magnetic spins. At high temperatures, the spins are disordered, and the metal has no coherent magnetic field (Exhibit 1.4). But as the temperature drops below a certain threshold, the magnetic spin of each atom starts aligning with those of its neighbors. As the spins snap into alignment across the entire piece of iron, a sudden phase shift occurs, producing a uniform magnetic field.

With a little effort, one can imagine using an Ising model to describe how traders align their opinions. In normal markets, traders likely imitate each other to some extent, but they also form differing views, and a healthy debate accompanies changes in market prices. However, in extraordinary times, the propensity to imitate may rise to an unusually high level, possibly because of a wave of enthusiasm surrounding some new technology—the classic catalyst for a bubble. Once this propensity passes a critical threshold, the opinions of

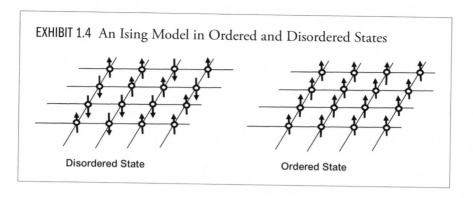

EXHIBIT 1.4 An Ising Model in Ordered and Disordered States

Disordered State

Ordered State

traders might snap into alignment with each other, much like the magnetic spins in iron atoms. At this point, the market could be going through a "phase shift" into a bubble market, where everyone has the same view.

The Ising model provides a metaphor for many forms of collective activity. The 19th-century English financial journalist Walter Bagehot (founder of *The Economist*) wrote that "credit, the disposition of one man to trust another, is singularly varying. In England, after a great calamity, everybody is suspicious of everybody; as soon as that calamity is forgotten, everybody again confides in everybody."[16] Thus one could think of liquidity and certain aspects of the credit cycle as "phase shifts" in collective opinion.

Other models of social interaction may be relevant to how groups of people form opinions. Consider the waves of traffic congestion that percolate down interstate highways, often with no visible origin. According to researchers into "traffic physics," the phase shift from high-speed coherent flow to a pattern of stop-and-go traffic can result from nothing more than minor driver error, such as loss of concentration and abrupt braking.[17] If Ising, traffic flow, or similar models are relevant metaphors for human coordination, then one should be prepared for abrupt phase shifts in consensus views as a potential source of extreme volatility, and these may reflect or even amplify whatever surprises emerge from the world of fundamentals.

Feedback, Feedforward

Shiller used the term *feedback* to describe imitation, as new sets of investors copy the strategies already employed by others and, in the process, push up prices too high. Nobel Laureate Herbert Simon used the term *feedforward* to describe how investors may anticipate each other's *future* actions. Simon cautions that feedforward can lead to "an infinite regress of outguessing," as "each actor tries to anticipate the actions of the others (and hence their expectations)"—and that this may in turn have "unfortunate destabilizing effects, for a system can overreact to its predictions and go into unstable oscillations."[18]

Fischer Black, economist, Goldman Sachs partner, and coauthor of the famous Black-Scholes option pricing model, came up with a feedforward explanation for the 1987 stock market crash. Many blamed the extreme volatility of October 1987—including a single-day decline in excess of 20%—on portfolio insurance programs, according to which investors adopted algorithmic rules for selling stocks if they fell below a certain price. The idea behind portfolio insurance was to limit downside risk by enforcing a disciplined transition into cash as prices fell. The problem with this strategy is that if everyone tries to sell at once, stocks might suddenly gap down. This sounds like a fair description of what happened in 1987. Indeed, portfolio insurance was soundly discredited.

However, a number of economists questioned whether portfolio insurance by itself explained the crash.[19] Fischer Black was in this camp. Rather than blaming the execution of portfolio insurance strategies, he argued that the crash was sparked by the dawning realization among investors as to just how widespread portfolio insurance had become. Smart investors may have anticipated the risk that widespread execution of portfolio insurance programs could exacerbate a market sell-off. Or they may have recognized that the widespread adoption of portfolio insurance programs had emboldened investors (who wrongly felt they had covered their downside risk) to bid up market prices too aggressively. In either case, as this group started tiptoeing toward the door, the rest of the market must have caught on in a flash.[20]

Sources of Extreme Volatility: Interaction Between Markets and Fundamentals

Even if the fundamentals seem normal (as opposed to nonlinear) and the markets appear rational (not driven by mass psychology), extreme volatility may still arise, for the reason that the markets and the fundamentals may interact to produce positive feedback effects. What starts as a normal, predictable outcome may become amplified into an extreme shock. The financier and philanthropist George Soros coined the term *reflexivity* to describe the circular logic that links markets and fundamentals. He claimed to have observed powerful feedback effects in currency and credit markets and moderate effects in equities.[21]

The so-called wealth effect is one example of positive feedback. Economists estimate that for every $1 increase in consumers' stock market wealth, their spending rises by around 3 to 6 cents; this is consistent with the idea that consumers seek to spread out their consumption over time.[22] Similar effects have been estimated for consumers' home equity wealth. Higher consumer spending should, in turn, lift revenues for corporations that sell goods and services to consumers, leading to higher stock prices. Because the 3- to 6-cent coefficient is relatively small, the positive feedback effect associated with the wealth effect diminishes relatively quickly in normal environments.

The recent crisis has provided a sharp reminder of the positive feedback loop between credit markets and the real economy. The economist Hyman Minsky would not have been surprised by the subprime mortgage crash of 2007 and the ensuing global liquidity crisis. According to his *financial fragility hypothesis*, capitalist economies are inherently unstable, because the availability of credit expands during booms and contracts during busts. Easy monetary policy, new banks or unregulated lenders, improved liquidity from repackaging government debt, innovations in financial products—all these factors may expand credit. Easier credit then acts as an accelerant, helping to supercharge the boom. When credit tightens, diminished liquidity exacerbates whatever economic shock triggered the bust—by making it harder for consumers and businesses to borrow. Minsky believed that government intervention—both lender-of-last-resort operations to bail out failing banks and fiscal stimulus to prevent a deflationary spiral—was crucial during recessions in order to break the feedback cycle. In support of his arguments, he pointed to the large number of financial crises during the postwar period.[23] Recent events have led to renewed appreciation for his theory.

In extreme circumstances like the Great Depression, the savings and loan crisis of the 1980s, or the current crisis, the mass failure of banks and other financial institutions can restrict credit in a dangerous fashion. In studying the global impact of the Great Depression, Federal Reserve Chairman Ben Bernanke found a statistically significant correlation between bank panics and plunging economic output. Specifically, bank panics were correlated with a 16% decline in real gross domestic product in countries that experienced them. Financial institutions have underwriting skills and proprietary information that helps them differentiate between good and bad borrowers. When financial institutions fail, these services are disrupted, to the detriment of good borrowers and the economy as a whole.[24]

Positive feedback effects between markets and economies may be even more extreme in the foreign exchange markets. Bernanke notes how countries following the gold standard in the 1930s suffered when speculators sold their currencies, because the outflow of gold forced them to contract the money supply (in order to maintain a constant ratio of gold reserves). Tighter money helped turn a severe recession into a protracted depression.[25] Because the outflow of gold was so traumatic, these countries were vulnerable to investor expectations, thus creating a form of self-fulfilling prophecy, that is, a feedback loop between investor expectations and the real economy.

Vulnerability to investor expectations appears to be a common theme among emerging market economies. When investors lose confidence in their currencies, these countries may suffer a major depreciation and widespread financial stress among banks and corporations that have borrowed in foreign currencies. Alternatively, their central banks may defend their currencies by hiking interest rates, a move that chokes off economic growth. In studying the major global lending cycles since the 1820s, emerging markets strategist Michael Pettis found a relationship between liquidity bubbles in rich-country financial centers and credit booms in emerging markets, demonstrating global linkages between markets in one region and the real economies in other regions.[26]

Self-fulfilling prophecies can affect individual stocks. For example, a rising stock price may create the perception of a successful franchise with strong growth prospects, helping the company attract talented employees, negotiate favorable terms with trading partners, convince customers to try new products, and raise capital for investments or acquisitions. These effects could help boost earnings and add to shareholder value, thus justifying the high stock price or perhaps warranting further gains. During the technology boom of the late 1990s, creating a "buzz" and winning the minds of investors was thought to help a company win in the marketplace as well. For firms in a winner-takes-all business, a rising stock price may become a competitive advantage, perhaps a decisive one.[27]

Feedback effects may also prove dangerous, as the recent liquidity crisis has shown. A falling stock price may undermine confidence, not only among investors, but also among employees, customers, and suppliers. For financial institutions in particular, diminished confidence, if unchecked, can become fatal. The ultimate catalyst for the bankruptcy of Bear Stearns was a falling stock price, as clients pulled their accounts and stopped trading with the firm. A sharp sell-off in American International Group's stock price alarmed the rating agencies, which then downgraded the company, forcing it to post additional collateral it did not have against derivative contracts. Wachovia's sinking share price triggered a run on the bank, with businesses pulling tens of billions of dollars in deposits, forcing the company into the arms of Wells Fargo.

Leverage can intensify feedback effects. As a falling stock price drives down the market value of a company's equity, the stakes rise for its bondholders. The equity is their cushion against the risk of default, for a severe shock that eliminates the equity cushion renders a company insolvent (the company will default on its debt as soon as it runs out of cash). Thus, even a small shock to the equity makes the debt riskier, as the bondholders' cushion shrinks. With a thinner cushion, the market will demand wider spreads on any new debt issued to replace debt that matures. Higher interest costs on the new debt will in turn hurt the company's margins, pressure earnings, and further depress the equity—making the debt even riskier.[28] Another reason that debt holders become nervous as a company's fortunes wane is the possibility that the management may undertake risky projects, in effect "gambling for resurrection" at the expense of debt holders, who are left holding the bag if the projects fail. Thus even a modest impairment of equity may tip the enterprise onto a slippery slope that ends in financial distress. The slope's steepness will depend on the timing of debt maturities and the collective opinions of a company's creditors when it needs to raise funds. To the extent that these opinions are prone to the "phase shifts" of Ising models, the slope could become nearly vertical, and the company could face a binary outcome.

As an aside, some firms become vulnerable to feedback effects because of structural flaws in their securities or balance sheets. For example, sometimes firms neglect to place limits on the dilution associated with convertible debt. If the stock price declines, the debt becomes convertible into a larger number of shares, which introduces greater dilution for existing shareholders, thus placing downward pressure on the stock price. Or firms may agree to debt covenants that make a decline in the company's market capitalization an event of default. In this case, a decline in the stock price may allow lenders to accelerate the payment of debt, which could force the company into bankruptcy. In Chapter 9, we will see a company that entered into a forward commitment to buy back its own stock at a fixed price. As the stock rose, this commitment created mark-to-market gains, but once the stock began to fall, the commitment became a dangerous liability.

Forecasting in Extreme Environments

The good news is that the nature of forecasting does not change merely because of heightened volatility. It does get more difficult, however, so that it is important to ground one's forecasts in the basic principles, which derive from the so-called scientific method. David Shaw, founder of the hedge fund D. E. Shaw, known for its focus on fully quantitative investing strategies, explains the process:

> What we do [in quantitative investing] is similar to what a classical natural scientist does. You go out there and study some set of phenomena. Then, using that sort of experience-based pattern recognition and creative thought that's so hard to describe, you formulate a well-defined hypothesis about what may be going on. . . .[29]

A hypothesis is a theory or model of the world that allows one to make forecasts, and the creation and updating of such models is just a technical description of how we learn.[30] Interestingly, some economists are starting to emphasize the importance of learning in their theories of how markets operate. Tiring of the debate between those who believe markets are efficient and those who believe they are irrational, MIT's Andrew Lo is now emphasizing how market participants learn and adapt to changing environments. University of Chicago researchers Lubos Pastor and Pietro Veronesi argue that learning can explain some market quirks, such as high stock prices for young companies (which may reflect uncertainty about future growth prospects) or seemingly excessive trading volumes (which may reflect people's interest in learning whether they have stock-picking skills).[31] During episodes of extreme volatility, the ability to learn as quickly as possible is a key survival trait.

Investors are mindful of the scientific method, as can be seen in the common use of the term, "investment thesis." However, investors operate outside of the laboratory, and controlled conditions are not possible. Further, fundamental research often lacks numerical data for statistical tests and so is imprecise, making it easy to lapse into sloppy ways of thinking that fall short of scientific discipline. Failing to calibrate models and neglecting to identify catalysts are two mistakes I have observed contribute to inaccurate forecasts.

Forecast Accuracy

Forecasting accuracy can be thought of as a function of *calibration* and *discrimination*. Consider an analogy between stock picking and target shooting. Before a shooter can hope to hit the target, he must "zero in" a rifle's sights, which means adjusting (or calibrating) them for range, wind, and the imperfections of the rifle's mechanism. Once the sights are zeroed in, the bullets ought to wind up in the general ballpark of the target. Discrimination is another term for precision. A skilled marksman places the shots in a tight group, whereas the amateur is all over the place.

For any kind of forecaster, both calibration and discrimination are necessary.[32] But for investors, arguably one must start with calibration. After all, an investor whose thinking is miscalibrated might exhibit a persistent bias in judgment, perhaps consistently too pessimistic or too optimistic, too early or too late, and so forth. Biased stock pickers are like skilled marksmen with badly adjusted rifle sights: their shot groups would consistently miss the bull's-eye.

The measure of a well-calibrated forecaster is that on average her subjective probabilities for different kinds of events correspond with the actual frequencies. For example, a well-calibrated forecast of a random coin toss ought to produce an average 50% probability estimate for heads, which would correspond to the actual frequency over a long-enough series

(continued)

of flips. For this forecaster to achieve superior discrimination would require that she identify which coin flips were more likely to come up heads than others—obviously a challenge with fair coins.

Studies of managers and other decision makers have found that human judgment of probabilities is not always well calibrated with actual frequencies. For example, people sometimes overestimate the probability of especially vivid scenarios, like terrorist attacks or plane crashes, and underestimate the probability of mundane events. Curiously enough, studies looking at a number of professions and industries have found that weather forecasters produce some of the best-calibrated forecasts. Accountability and immediate feedback may help.[33]

Calibration for Fundamental Research Analysts

For fundamental researchers, calibration can be tricky because it is largely an intuitive process and because it requires an attitude of humility. Investors following fully quantitative investment strategies do not face these challenges, because they can calibrate their models by back-testing them against historical stock prices (although this does not guarantee success, as we will see in Chapter 9). In contrast, fundamental researchers calibrate their mental models by talking with other investors, hearing the critical issues people are concerned about, and watching how prices respond to new information.

The challenge for some people, particularly those with strong opinions, is that calibration requires agreeing with the crowd. People who distrust group behavior (like Shiller or LeBon) or think of themselves as contrarians will have a hard time with this attitude. Yet dismissing consensus thinking is a dangerous first step when it comes to evaluating an investment opportunity. The better approach is to start by respecting consensus thinking. After all, there is only so much a single person can understand. We learn most of what we know from other people. Indeed, it would be reckless to ignore what they think.[34]

The art of valuation is largely an exercise in calibration. If everyone agreed on a company's prospective earnings, its stock price in theory would depend on the risk premium used to discount those earnings to present value. However, in practice, the earnings outlook cannot be observed, so risk premiums cannot be measured.[35] Instead, analysts develop a general sense as to what kinds of valuation metrics are appropriate for different kinds of firms, and they start their analysis with these generic inputs.

Of course, calibrating is not going to produce exact answers about the consensus view. The market is too big for anyone to be certain of what "it" is thinking. The best we can do is come up with a theory as to how the market is thinking—in effect, a kind of *null hypothesis* against which our investment hypothesis will be tested.[36]

Furthermore, given the size of the markets and the fast pace of change, it is safe to say that calibration is going to require significant effort, especially when consensus opinions are in flux. And the task becomes even more difficult if consensus thinking is undergoing the kind of "phase shifts" discussed earlier, a signature of extreme volatility. The economist John Maynard Keynes had this challenge in mind when he wrote this famous passage:

> A conventional valuation which is established as the outcome of the mass psychology of a large number of ignorant individuals is liable to change violently as the result of a sudden fluctuation of opinion due to factors which do not really make much difference to the prospective yield [i.e., long-term return on capital]; since there will be no strong roots of conviction to hold it steady. In abnormal times in particular, when the hypothesis of an indefinite continuance of the existing state of affairs is less plausible than usual, even though there are no express grounds to anticipate a definite change, the market will be subject to waves of optimistic and pessimistic sentiment, which are unreasoning and yet in a sense legitimate where no solid basis exists for a reasonable calculation.[37]

Importance of Identifying Catalysts

Once a model is calibrated to the extent possible, the question becomes how to improve its discrimination. The goal shifts from understanding the market to finding something the market has missed. For fundamental analysts, discrimination depends on the information they can obtain, the analysis they conduct, and the hypotheses they generate. The challenge is to produce specific hypotheses with testable predictions as opposed to vague opinions.

One of the principles of the scientific method is that a hypothesis must be subjected to some kind of test. This point was central to the work of the philosopher Karl Popper, who argued that a theory could not be considered a "scientific proposition" unless it could be tested and falsified.[38] If a thesis cannot be falsified, then no data can ever prove it wrong. A "thesis" that cannot be tested is just an opinion—or worse, a dogmatic belief. In investing, the test is called a "catalyst" and refers to upcoming information that will support or contradict the investment hypothesis, moving the stock in the desired direction, one hopes, or if not, at least shining some light on the strength of the thesis.

People at cocktail parties with dogmatic views are considered bores, because no argument can shake their beliefs. For investors, unshakeable opinions are not just boring, they may be deadly—because nothing will cause them to rethink these positions until it is too late. Even for an analyst with a reasonably open mind, failure to identify upcoming catalysts can lead to a mental trap. Safe from tests, the thesis may harden into a belief, without the analyst recognizing the transition in his thinking. This state of mind leaves one ill prepared to cope with change (already a difficult challenge, as Chapter 5 will show). In periods of extreme volatility, it is likely that many investment theses will be upended—so the sooner they are tested, the better.

In quantitative disciplines, the catalyst is taken for granted, as the model's numerical output will be judged against the data it is trying to predict. Fundamental research, however, may turn on qualitative factors, like the intensity of competition, quality of management, differentiation of a product, competitive advantage of a business model, and so forth. It may take effort to imagine catalysts against which the accuracy of the thesis can be judged. Indeed, the requirement to identify catalysts forces analysts to make some kind of prediction about upcoming events.

It is easy to operate with vague opinions about long-term trends. Because these opinions are not tested in the short term, we avoid the effort and discomfiture of trying to get the short term right. However, any long-term view on value must derive from and be supported by information that is known today. Hence, no matter what the time horizon, an investor should continually test, evaluate, and revise theories based on information available in the short term. In this way, one benefits from a rapid learning cycle no matter what the outcome of individual investment theses (Exhibit 1.5).

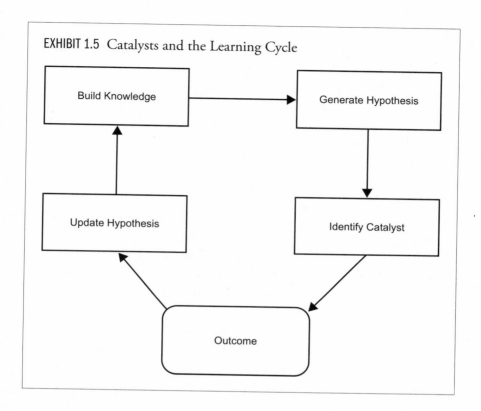

EXHIBIT 1.5 Catalysts and the Learning Cycle

Here is a rule of thumb for analysts, investors, and other decision makers: start by agreeing with the consensus on every issue, no matter how distasteful this may seem, except for those where you can articulate a hypothesis that will be tested by upcoming catalysts.

The Fall of Fannie Mae

The conclusion to the Fannie Mae story demonstrates the importance of calibration and catalysts during an episode of extreme volatility.

My client had just hung up on me. Whatever her knowledge about Fannie, she was not interested in discussing past credit cycles. As I considered her objections, I realized that my analysis would not have convinced her, even if she had been willing to listen. The problem was that the catalyst to prove me right would have been a peak in credit losses, after which investors could have bracketed the maximum risk to Fannie. Unfortunately, a peak in credit losses was a long way off, possibly one or two years, even according to my more sanguine analysis.

I struggled with the decision for several days before opting to downgrade the stock to equal-weight. There was some reluctance in my mind, as I still thought the stock was undervalued. Acknowledging that my loss forecast was little better than guesswork and that the next set of catalysts was likely to show rising credit costs and further mark-to-market losses, I wrote in the downgrade note that

> in recent conversations, investors have expressed concern to us about the risk of rising credit losses at the government-sponsored enterprises (GSEs), Fannie Mae and Freddie Mac. This concern is appropriate, in our view, as the housing market slump will translate into higher losses for all mortgage investors, even those with portfolios of high-quality prime loans like the GSEs.[39]

The downgrade was fortuitous. My forecast of credit losses was going to prove too low, and considerably so. Meanwhile, as fall approached, the company's problems multiplied. Apart from questions of credit quality, Fannie was also suffering from unexpected accounting charges in its portfolio of interest rate derivatives. Soon, investors were concerned about the need for additional capital, which might be highly dilutive to existing shareholders. By year-end, the stock was trading in the mid-$30s, down from $57 at the time of the downgrade. When the company reported troubling third-quarter results for 2007, the stock price fell 30% in a single day—an avalanche-like shift in consensus opinion about the company's risk profile, unprecedented price action for Fannie Mae shares, and a signal that the consensus might have been "fragile," in the sense previously discussed here. Presumably some of Fannie's shareholders held high-conviction views about long-term value, but others had not done enough work to have strong opinions, so as trouble mounted they cut their losses and ran.

Part of the problem for investors was the incredible complexity of Fannie's accounting, which was producing a bewildering array of charges, write-offs, and markdowns. In getting its accounting problems fixed, Fannie had subjected itself to a new set of rules, different from those that had governed past results. These write-offs reflected accounting complexities, not economic reality, I thought. So I got to work with my associate, Vivian Wang, to see if we could gain an edge in forecasting results for the fourth quarter of 2007, which were due out in January 2008. We spent several weeks studying the company's disclosures, analyzing the relationships between write-downs and factors such as changing interest rates and secondary market prices for delinquent loans. The challenge was not so much the complexity of these relationships, but rather the number of obscure line items in the financial statements that had to be understood and modeled.

One of Fannie's problems was that its derivatives were marked to market, but its loans and debt were not. So when interest rates dropped, Fannie was forced to book large losses on the derivatives portfolio, even though these were meant to hedge the value of its assets. The company's assets presumably benefited from lower interest rates, but this did not show up in the accounting results. I regarded such derivatives losses as an accounting issue, not a business model problem. Nevertheless, Vivian and I concluded that Fannie's fourth-quarter 2007 results were going to disappoint investor expectations. Specifically, we forecast a loss of $3.14 per share, as opposed to consensus estimates of a loss of $1.80.

As we studied credit-quality trends in securitized mortgages, we found that even prime loans were now displaying higher delinquencies. We built a model to project Fannie's delinquency rate as a function of what we observed in the securitized pools, and this work led us to predict further deterioration in Fannie's portfolio, which we knew would be disclosed together with fourth-quarter earnings.[40]

As the clock ticked down to the end of the fourth quarter, investor fears of a dilutive capital raise continued to mount. Vivian and I modeled several scenarios with varying levels of credit losses and thought that the company could replenish its capital base if it let its giant portfolio of securities run off. However, we did not expect to convince anyone. That would have been like shouting into the wind.

I thought the stock price (now $35) was unreasonably low. But with a sense of the consensus, I predicted that the stock would sell off further on disappointing fourth-quarter 2007 results. Accordingly, I downgraded the stock to underweight, citing mounting evidence that the housing slump was going to be worse than previously thought. I argued that if Fannie's management raised its loss guidance, "investors would be concerned about the impact of losses on operating and GAAP [generally accepted accounting principles] earnings and regulatory capital."[41]

This forecast proved accurate. The company reported a loss of $3.80 per share for the fourth quarter of 2007, in line with our estimate and well below consensus. The stock sold off to around $25. Because my thesis was predicated on fourth-quarter results as the catalyst, and because I thought the stock was worth more than where it was trading, I had no basis to maintain the underweight recommendation. Accordingly, I upgraded the stock to equal-weight in early March.[42] The stock dipped as low as $19 before rebounding into the $30s.

But concerns about housing and the economy intensified, and by summer the stock had resumed sinking. Our views on credit losses, capital, and long-term value soon proved to be incorrect. The stock sold off sharply in early July (Exhibit 1.6), and this development raised fears among holders of the company's debt, which included foreign central banks in China, Russia, and elsewhere. As Fannie's debt spreads widened, the U.S. Treasury lost confidence in the company's ability to refinance its short-term borrowings. A

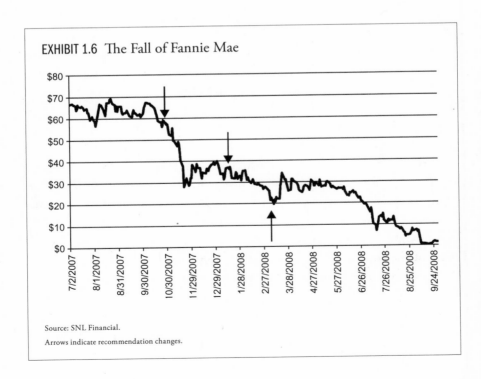

EXHIBIT 1.6 The Fall of Fannie Mae

Source: SNL Financial.

Arrows indicate recommendation changes.

liquidity crisis for the GSEs had to be avoided at any cost, because their function of guaranteeing mortgages was helping keep the housing slump from worsening even further.

The Lesson of the Story

The collapse of Fannie Mae's stock would have been unthinkable just a year or two earlier. The near-complete loss of value qualifies as a Black Swan, or if you like, it was part of the larger Black Swan that swept through the housing, mortgage, and capital markets. As the story makes clear, I did not predict this Black Swan—those who did had a better understanding of macroeconomics or mortgage underwriting quality (Chapter 4 will profile one such analyst). As much as one would like to anticipate every Black Swan, that is not possible, so the first priority is to avoid being caught by surprise. In this case, I managed to avoid potential disaster (which would have occurred had I continued to recommend Fannie's stock) and made a successful trading call. The key was the discipline of calibration and catalysts: agreeing with the consensus until you can identify a thesis that will be tested by upcoming catalysts.

In this story, my thinking became better calibrated to the market by discussing the stock with other investors. When I could not identify near-term catalysts that would support my hypothesis of moderate credit losses and adequate capital, I dropped them and went with consensus thinking, which in this case turned out to be correct. Once my thinking was properly calibrated with the prevailing consensus views, I shifted my focus to discrimination, using information and analysis to identify issues the market had not yet recognized, such as the short-term trend for earnings and delinquency rates.

During this episode, the shift to a focus on near-term forecasting might have made me appear something like a weather forecaster who looks out only a few days at a time. Conventional wisdom places a premium on the long-term outlook. But during periods of extreme volatility, such an outlook may be unrealistic because the long term could be swamped by near-term uncertainty, as indeed was the case at Fannie Mae. As volatility subsides, then the focus may extend once again to a longer horizon, but calibrating and identifying catalysts will still be important components of the forecasting process.

Chapter 2

Thinking in Probabilities

Someone who had been to business school would have recognized the charts I made on my yellow pad as expected-value tables, used to calculate the expected value of a transaction. After a while, organizing my thoughts according to these tables became second nature and I'd do them in my head. . . . The arbitrage business I learned [at Goldman Sachs] was consistent with the way I thought about life, as a process of weighing odds in a world without absolutes or provable certainties.

—Robert E. Rubin, *In an Uncertain World*, 2003

If you don't get this elementary, but mildly unnatural, mathematics of elementary probability into your repertoire, then you go through a long life like a one-legged man in an ass-kicking contest. You're giving a huge advantage to everybody else. One of the advantages of a fellow like Buffett, whom I've worked with all these years, is that he automatically thinks in terms of decision trees. . . .

—Charles T. Munger, 1994

The test of a first-rate intelligence is the ability to hold two opposed ideas in the mind at the same time, and retain the ability to function.

—F. Scott Fitzgerald, *The Crack-Up*, 1945

People naturally think in probabilities. For high-stakes decisions, getting the odds right is a critical skill—especially when Black Swans are involved. The challenge for decision makers is that Black Swans are future possibilities, not present certainties. They lurk in some future scenarios but not others. Some swans cannot be anticipated, whereas others are widely discussed and debated for years in advance.[1] For example, the media started warning about a housing bubble almost immediately after the stock market crash in 2001. Back then, the odds were remote that housing would collapse, too. By 2006, the probabilities were rising. By 2007, the housing crash had become a near certainty. The decision maker's task is to weigh the probabilities of different scenarios, neither underestimating the risks nor jumping at shadows, and to continually adjust as probabilities shift.

This chapter describes the process of thinking in probabilities. Our primary tool is the probability tree, which makes explicit the subjective probability estimates we must make when facing uncertain situations. The tree will help us refine these estimates, trace out their implications for future scenarios, and recognize the possibility of extreme outcomes. The probability tree will reappear in our discussion of intuitive errors (Chapter 3), the diagnostic power of new information (Chapters 4, 5, and 6), and sophisticated modeling techniques (Chapters 7 and 8). The probability tree does not guarantee that you will anticipate the next Black Swan, but it may help you bracket the odds of swan-like outcomes and possibly take action before disaster strikes, as the story of Providian Financial Corporation will show.

Providian's First Black Swan

Providian was a high-flying credit card company that managed to serve up not one but two Black Swan surprises. First mass marketed in the 1980s, credit cards had by the mid-1990s become the focus product for a small group of financial firms, including Providian, Capital One, MBNA, and American Express. These companies used sophisticated computer models to analyze consumer data and continually tested new card products and customer segments, looking for angles (interest rates, fees, affinity association, even envelope color) that might "lift" the response rate to targeted mailings. When they found a promising niche, the firms would employ enormous mass-mailing campaigns, which for the industry totaled billions of solicitations per year, to drum up new customers and balances. These tactics produced rapid revenue growth and rising stock prices for several years.

Like its competitors, Providian claimed that sophisticated analytics allowed it to target high-margin customer niches. Its primary focus was the so-called underserved market, a euphemism for subprime borrowers. When underwritten properly, these customers were quite profitable: They would pay high fees and interest rates, as they typically had trouble finding credit elsewhere.

Skeptics doubted claims of sophisticated analytics. But Providian and its peers traded with price-earnings multiples between 20× and 30×, well above the multiples for other financial stocks, indicative of investors' expectations for continued growth. Providian's stock had rallied from $10 at its June 1997 initial public offering (IPO) to a peak of $65 in early 1999, equivalent to an extraordinary 175% compound average annual return, in itself something of a Black Swan.

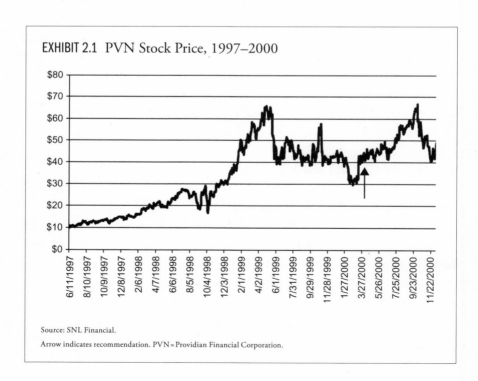

EXHIBIT 2.1 PVN Stock Price, 1997–2000

Source: SNL Financial.

Arrow indicates recommendation. PVN = Providian Financial Corporation.

However, in mid-1999, the company disclosed that it was under investigation by the Office of the Comptroller of the Currency (OCC), the national bank regulator, for allegedly deceptive marketing practices, such as failing to provide the low interest rates promised in its promotional mailings. When the news hit, the stock immediately lost a third of its value. As an analyst following credit card stocks, I was intrigued by the company's lucrative returns, in excess of 40% of equity. I thought its business model might still warrant a premium valuation. After studying the history of regulatory interventions against financial firms, I concluded that Providian would receive a "slap on the wrist" and pay a modest fine. But I did not think its business model would be jeopardized. In early 2000, I initiated coverage of Providian with a strong buy rating at $43 per share.[2] When a settlement with the OCC was finally reached, the $300 million fine was bigger than I expected, but not big enough to put a dent in the company's financial stability or growth prospects—or so I thought. The stock rallied on the news, and with the general upbeat mood of late 2000, I felt optimistic about Providian regaining new highs (Exhibit 2.1). But, of course, the world is an uncertain place.

An Introduction to Volatility and Probability Trees

It is hard to put a number on a general sense of uncertainty. Stock prices, however, allow one to be somewhat precise in measuring it. There are two ways to do this. First, one can calculate the volatility of a time series of historical prices. Second, one can estimate the expected volatility implied in the prices of options, at least for those securities for which options are traded. (Technically speaking, *volatility* refers to the standard deviation of returns over a given period, a measure of the dispersion of those returns about their mean.)

Over the course of 1999, for example, stock prices for American Express, Capital One, and Providian did not change much, ending the year more or less in the same ballpark where they had started. However, there was plenty of volatility on a daily basis (Exhibit 2.2). Providian

(continued)

EXHIBIT 2.2 PVN, AXP, and COF Stock Prices, 1999–2000

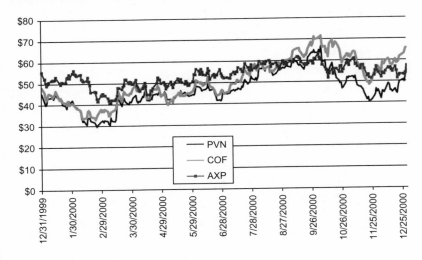

Source: SNL Financial.

AXP = American Express; COF = Capital One Financial Corporation; PVN = Providian Financial Corporation.

and Capital One shares were somewhat more volatile than the others, not surprisingly, inasmuch as these companies were smaller and less diversified, and they catered to subprime borrowers, making them potentially riskier if the economy slowed and their customers had trouble paying back loans. Subprime lending also exposed them to heightened regulatory scrutiny and political risk, because consumer activists thought the high rates and fees exploited unsophisticated borrowers.

Historical volatility shows how investors reacted to new information about the companies, their industries, and the economy during a particular period. The second chart (Exhibit 2.3) shows a histogram of daily changes in Providian's stock price during 1999. On most days, Providian's stock price did not move more than 2.5%. But on a handful of days, the stock jumped by as much as 10%. Calculating the standard deviation of these daily price changes produces a figure of around 4%. One could imagine overlaying a normal curve on top of the histogram, and about two-thirds of the daily returns

EXHIBIT 2.3 Distribution of PVN Daily Stock Price Changes During 1999

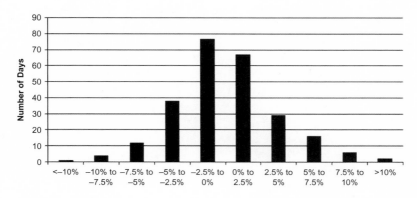

PVN = Providian Financial Corporation.

would fall between +4% and −4%, consistent with the interpretation that a +/−1 standard deviation range ought to incorporate two-thirds of the possible outcomes under a normal distribution. Expressed on an annual basis, this distribution would equate to approximately a 50% standard deviation. (Of course, I am not suggesting that the normal curve is the right distribution to describe Providian or any other financial time series, but it is a concise metric for summarizing past data.)

The volatility of a security can also be estimated from traded options, because volatility is a key input in option valuation models. Since the other inputs to these models are observable (interest rates, the strike price, the term of the option, the current price of the security), one can back out the volatility assumption that solves for the current price of the option. If we went through these calculations in the spring of 2000, we would have found that the volatility implied in Providian options was around 50%, reasonably close to the historical volatility measured above, indicating that investors did not foresee a major change in the company's risk profile.

(continued)

EXHIBIT 2.4 PVN Probability Tree: Option Market's View

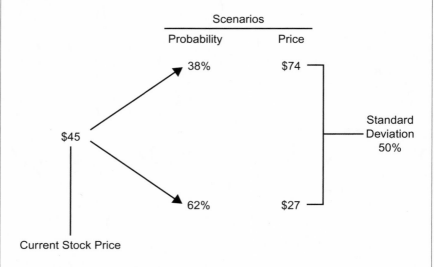

In the spring of 2001, Providian's stock price was around $45 per share. Thinking probabilistically means imagining the stock price not as a single number but rather as a range of outcomes. To start working with this idea, we will sketch a very simple probability tree with two branches, as pictured in Exhibit 2.4. On one branch of the tree, we picture the stock rising to $74, with a probability of 38%. On the second branch, the stock falls to $27, with a probability of 62%. The *expected value* of these two scenarios is calculated by multiplying the stock price in each branch by its probability and then adding the two: 38% × $74+62% × $27=$45, which by design is the current stock price. The standard deviation of these two scenarios, by design, amounts to 50%, the current level of implied volatility. I picked these values using a binomial lattice, a popular option valuation technique,[3] to illustrate the concept of 50% implied volatility when thinking probabilistically about the stock price.

The probability tree is one of the main tools this book uses to help one think through complicated situations. Also called a "decision tree," it is a basic tool for graphically representing an uncertain situation. It may have as few as one node and two branches, or it may have many of each. The basic requirements are that the branches are mutually exclusive and that the sum of the branches includes all possible outcomes, meaning that the probabilities sum to 100%. For trees with more than one node, we will generally place first (i.e., to the left) the most important variables or, in some cases, those that are likely to be resolved earlier.

Probability trees derive from so-called "influence diagrams," also called "Bayesian networks," which graphically illustrate causal relationships.[4] Corporate strategists often use multiple scenarios to help decision makers think "outside the box" about future possibilities. Our use of probability trees is related, but has one difference. Strategists do not assign specific probabilities to the branches, because their main task is to sensitize executives to other scenarios besides their base case. In contrast, we will think through the probabilities with keen attention, because nothing matters more to investors than a sound understanding of the odds.

Some investors use probability trees on a regular basis. For example, arbitrageurs betting on the outcome of mergers and acquisitions set up trees to analyze the consequences of deals closing or breaking, and they base their decisions on the expected values calculated across the branches.[5] Other investors think more generally about the upside and downside risk they envision in different scenarios, without tracing out a formal tree.

I like to set up probability trees around a small number of issues that I think are critical to the investment outcome. Focusing on critical issues allows one to avoid the noise associated with large numbers of unimportant variables. Ideally, a probability tree will be as simple as possible, with the fewest branches necessary to think through the main issues.

A Probability Tree for Providian

To illustrate the use of the probability tree, we will first set one up to reflect the market's view of Providian. This is a form of "calibration" (Chapter 1). Before we can do so, we need to identify a set of critical issues that might affect the company. To update the story, Providian's stock price had recovered from the shock when the OCC investigation was first disclosed. But despite upbeat market sentiment, the outlook was starting to seem more difficult, and in late 2000 I could point to three critical issues with Providian:

• First was the risk of impending recession. Having little understanding of the Internet boom, I felt somewhat bewildered by the meteoric rise of the NASDAQ. As it gradually dawned on me (and others) that this might represent a bubble of classic proportions, I started to wonder whether its popping would usher in a recessionary aftermath. My colleague, Dick Berner, Morgan Stanley's chief U.S. economist, had begun to warn of heightened recessionary risk.[6] Providian could get into deep trouble if its subprime customers lost their jobs and could not pay off their card balances.

• Second was the loss cycle for the credit card industry. Historically, the card industry had experienced periodic cycles, as easy underwriting led to rising losses, which in turn caused lenders to tighten standards, resulting in a decline in loss rates. Over the last several quarters, the industry had enjoyed unusually low losses, raising the question of whether losses would revert in typical cyclical fashion to higher levels, and if so, how quickly. A recession would intensify the cycle, because of job losses.

• Third was the stability of Providian's business model. The run-in with the OCC brought not only fines, but also new restrictions on marketing practices. These might hamper its continued revenue growth.

Exhibit 2.5 illustrates the causal relationships among these three critical issues and Providian's stock price—as I understood them at the time. Exhibit 2.6 transforms the influence diagram into a probability tree with three nodes (one for each critical issue) and eight scenarios. Each scenario ends with an estimated stock price, which is based on earnings projections and a valuation multiple appropriate for the nature of the scenario. For example, in one of the midcase scenarios, I estimated that Providian's stock would be worth $50 per share, assuming continued economic growth and stability in the company's business model but a problematic credit card-industry cycle. Each scenario also has a probability, an admittedly subjective estimate, which in this case was my judgment of the prevailing consensus opinion. As an aside, some people wonder how to come up with subjective probability estimates, as they may seem to be plucked out of thin air. To some extent this is true, in the sense that they most often result from intuitive judgments rather than analytic pro-

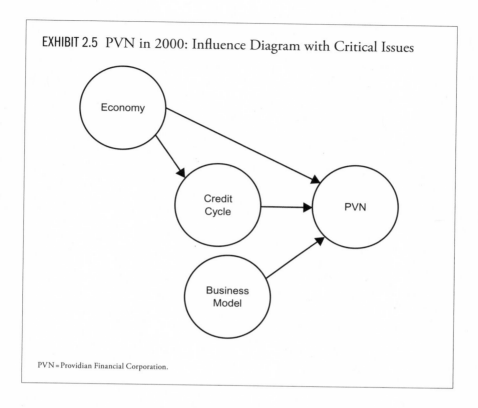

EXHIBIT 2.5 PVN in 2000: Influence Diagram with Critical Issues

Economy

Credit Cycle

PVN

Business Model

PVN = Providian Financial Corporation.

cesses. But this does not mean they are not serious estimates. According to Richard Jeffrey, philosophy professor at Princeton, "Your 'subjective' probability is not something fetched out of the sky on a whim; it is what your actual judgment *should* be, in view of your information to date and of your sense of other people's information."[7] (We will see how advanced analytic techniques can help refine probability estimates in Chapter 8.)

Summing across all of these scenarios, the expected value for Providian's stock comes to $45, the then-current stock price. The standard deviation of the stock price estimates across the scenarios is 64%, just slightly higher than the then-current level of volatility implied in Providian stock options (50%). I played around with the stock prices and probability estimates until the tree produced these values, because the purpose of this exercise was to understand the market's view of the company. In Chapter 1, we discussed the importance of calibrating our thinking with the market's—that is, making a hypothesis about how investors are valuing a stock. This probability tree

EXHIBIT 2.6 PVN Probability Tree, Calibrated with Market Price and Volatility

Critical Issues			Scenarios	
Economy	Credit Card Industry Credit Cycle	Stability of PVN Business Model	Probability	Price
60% Growth	75% Stays Good	OK	22.5%	$80
		Problems	22.5%	$65
	25% Bad Cycle	OK	7.5%	$50
		Problems	7.5%	$40
40% Recession	25% Stays Good	OK	5.0%	$35
		Problems	5.0%	$25
	75% Bad Cycle	OK	15.0%	$10
		Problems	15.0%	$5
			100.0%	

(50% / 50% splits at each Stability of PVN Business Model branch)

$45

Stock Price Implied by Probability-weighting
Each Scenario

Standard Deviation of Scenarios   64%

PVN = Providian Financial Corporation.

shows how the stock's current price and volatility might have reflected the range of scenarios investors were considering.[8]

The tree produces a wide range of potential outcomes for Providian shares, which could be worth anywhere from $5 to $80. The tree includes potential Black Swan scenarios, including the possibility of a 90% decline in the stock price to $5 per share in the worst scenario, where Providian suffers recession, a tough cycle for the card industry, and disruptions to its business model.

However, because this probability tree is by design calibrated to the market, it does not help us decide whether to buy or sell the stock. That decision depends on research, information, and analysis that might give us a different view of the range of possible outcomes and thus a different calculation of the stock's fair value. The goal of research is to improve our *discrimination*, by identifying factors that other investors have ignored or misjudged.

By mid-2001, I had come to a view different from the market's on several issues.

- First, I concluded that recession was a serious risk. The basis for this judgment was the logic of Dick's analysis, his reputation for thoughtfulness and accuracy, and the consistency between his predictions and those of the classic theories of boom-and-bust economic cycles. The catalyst to test this view would be the path of unemployment, which Dick now forecast would rise from 3.9% to 4.5%. To reflect this judgment in the probability tree, I raised the probability of recession in the first node from 40% to 50%. I kept this to a small change, because it is tough to get an edge in forecasting something as large and complex as the U.S. economy, even with the help of a talented economist.

- Second, my research convinced me that regardless of the state of the economy, the credit card industry was due for its next loss cycle. In studying the history of credit cycles, I had found that researchers had built a variety of statistical models to forecast bankruptcies, which are an excellent leading indicator of credit losses because bankruptcy allows the borrower to wipe out credit card balances and other unsecured debts. These models were generally based on commonsense predictive variables, like shocks to the labor market and aggressive growth in credit card lending. After digesting this work, I built my own model, and sure enough it called for a near-term rise in bankruptcies. I concluded the odds of a problematic credit cycle were as high as 70%, well above the 30% estimate initially used in the probability tree. In this case I was bolder in shifting my estimate of the odds away from the consensus because of the statistical significance of my model, the availability of fresh data, and the long history of research into the credit cycle. The catalyst to test this view would be the trend in bankruptcy filings, which I now estimated would rise at a double-digit pace heading into 2001.

• Finally, my review of Providian's financial results persuaded me that it was likely in worse shape than investors realized. Its cash flow was beginning to falter and interviews with senior management revealed no viable plan to replace revenue lost under the new marketing restrictions. I now saw the odds that Providian's model was in trouble at 75%, as opposed to the previous estimate of 50% in the market-calibrated model.

After making each of these changes to the probability tree, the new expected value for Providian was $29, well below the current stock price of $45 (Exhibit 2.7). And the volatility across the range of scenarios had ballooned nearly to 100%. To be sure, I did not know which scenario would play out. But according to my research, Providian's stock was riskier and likely to end up worth less than investors thought.

More Applications of Probability Trees

Before the Providian story concludes, let us review some of the probability tree's useful results.

Recognizing Asymmetric Outcomes

One of the benefits of a range of scenarios is that it may help the analyst recognize asymmetric outcomes. In our Providian tree, the odds are weighted to the downside. We see this in Exhibit 2.7, where the worst scenario has a 33.8% probability, as opposed to a 3.8% probability for the best scenario. This mismatch is a function of our assumptions about the odds of the card industry experiencing a credit cycle and Providian's business model coming under pressure.

Asymmetries like these have important implications for valuation. Positive asymmetries mean that the upside branches of the tree are likelier than the downside, or, alternatively, the value estimates associated with upside branches lie further from the mean than the downside branches do. Positive

EXHIBIT 2.7 PVN Probability Tree, After Conducting Research

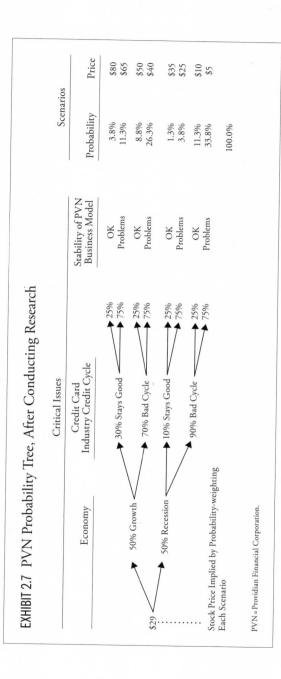

| | Critical Issues | | | Scenarios | |
Economy	Credit Card Industry Credit Cycle		Stability of PVN Business Model	Probability	Price
	30% Stays Good	25%	OK	3.8%	$80
		75%	Problems	11.3%	$65
50% Growth	70% Bad Cycle	25%	OK	8.8%	$50
		75%	Problems	26.3%	$40
	10% Stays Good	25%	OK	1.3%	$35
		75%	Problems	3.8%	$25
50% Recession	90% Bad Cycle	25%	OK	11.3%	$10
		75%	Problems	33.8%	$5
$29				100.0%	

Stock Price Implied by Probability-weighting
Each Scenario

PVN = Providian Financial Corporation.

asymmetries could include the possibility of a company being acquired at a significant premium. Or they could reflect operating leverage, in which case faster revenue growth would widen margins, producing a substantial increase in earnings. In theory, investors ought to pay higher prices for stocks of firms with positive asymmetries, because the probabilities are skewed to the upside. Similarly, investors ought to discount the stock prices of firms with negative asymmetries so as to protect themselves against downside risk.

The math behind asymmetries is known as Jensen's inequality, after the Danish mathematician Johan Jensen. Jensen's inequality is best illustrated using pictures, as shown in Exhibits 2.8 and 2.9.[9] Exhibit 2.8 shows the value of a hypothetical company as a function of revenue growth. In this case, the function is "concave," meaning that increases in the revenue growth rate translate into ever-larger increments to the stock price. This might be the case because this hypothetical company enjoys a fixed cost structure, so that higher sales cause margins to expand, producing a large benefit for the bottom line. Or perhaps there is some kind of positive feedback effect between the stock price and the company's fundamentals; for example, faster revenue

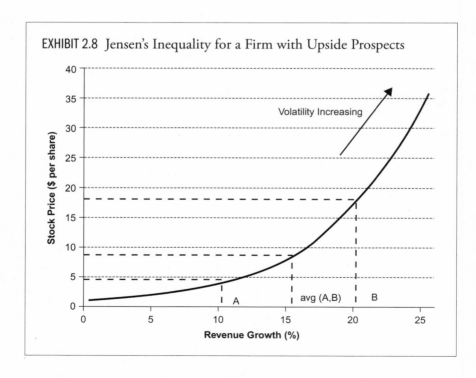

EXHIBIT 2.8 Jensen's Inequality for a Firm with Upside Prospects

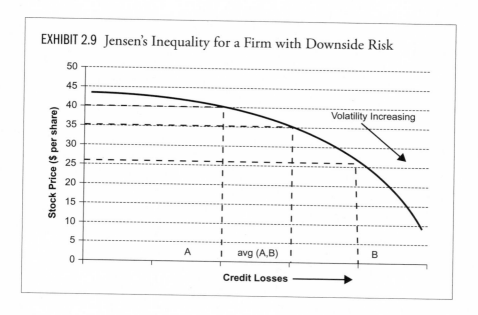

EXHIBIT 2.9 Jensen's Inequality for a Firm with Downside Risk

growth might convince investors that the company is coming to dominate a niche market and that earnings will become more sustainable as it gains a first-mover advantage.

In an uncertain world, analysts may have to consider scenarios with different revenue growth rates (labeled A and B) to bracket the range of possible outcomes. But Jensen's inequality tells us to be careful about how we draw our conclusions: if we take the average of revenue growth rates A and B as our input, the resulting stock price estimate will be lower than if we took the average of the stock price predicated on A and the stock price predicated on B. The first method produces a stock price estimate of around $8, while the second comes to $12. If the market is unsure about which revenue growth rate will prevail, then the stock ought in theory to trade at what seems like a premium valuation relative to current earnings. Furthermore, since the function curves upwards, the stock could become more volatile for higher ranges of revenue growth, and swan-like extreme outcomes might be possible. Keep this chart in mind for Chapter 7 and the story of MasterCard's IPO.

Risk factors may also produce a downward sloping function, as in Exhibit 2.9. In this case, bad outcomes for a critical issue could produce an accelerating decline in the stock price. This might happen if rising credit losses weaken earnings sufficiently to cause debt investors to reassess the equity cushion protecting them from insolvency: debt investors might then demand wider spreads on new debt that this hypothetical company would raise, further pressuring earnings and the value of its equity. As credit losses rise, the stock sells off at an accelerating pace and becomes increasingly volatile, an example of feedback effects producing an extreme outcome.

Correlations

Probability trees can help the analyst think through correlations among critical issues. Correlations can be hugely important because they tend to widen the distribution of terminal branches well beyond what normal curves would suggest, as the normal distribution assumes independence (lack of correlation) among the inputs. Notice that our probability tree for Providian assumes a higher probability of a bad credit cycle in the recessionary branches of the tree than in the other branches (90% versus 70%). This adjustment captures the correlation between recessionary unemployment and higher credit losses.

We did not assume any correlation between Providian's business model and the credit cycle. In theory, there might be a correlation. One of the underlying drivers of the credit cycle is industry-wide competitive pressure, which pushes firms to loosen underwriting standards in order to bring in lower-quality accounts, once they have exhausted the pool of high-quality borrowers. We had talked about possible pressure on Providian's business model now that it was operating under the close eye of its regulators. However, the deceptive marketing practices that regulators had objected to might themselves have reflected competitive pressure. Perhaps Providian moved down market because it was having trouble competing for prime-quality borrowers. If this were the case, then competitive pressure might contribute both to the severity of the industry-wide credit cycle and in problems with Providian's business model.

The probability tree can help us assess other forward-looking correlations, such as the "beta" between a stock and the market or other factors. We do this by comparing the scenarios in the "economic growth" branch of the tree relative to those in the "recession" branch. Taking the probability-weighted average of the growth branches, we come to a value of $47 per share. The recession branches average to $22. Clearly, our work indicates significant vulnerability to a broad downturn. Investors often calculate beta's using historical trading patterns of the stock relative to market indices. In situations where risk changes in a discontinuous pattern, historical trading patterns may offer a misleading signal.

Conclusion to the Providian Story

The probability tree shows how I ended up valuing Providian. But I did not start with that view. Initially I thought highly of the stock, consistent with my strong buy recommendation from early 2000.

Over the summer of 2000, I had begun to study historical data on bankruptcy filings for clues as to when a cycle might return, as already discussed here. This work produced the forecast model and its prediction of rising bankruptcies. However, when I talked to the credit officers of major card issuers, I found little reason for concern, leaving me unsure how much weight to place on the model. I reported to clients accordingly:

Bankruptcies have waxed and waned in a recognizable three-year cycle over the last two decades. To better understand and predict this cycle, we built a statistical model and compared it to those of consultants and independent researchers. Most models predict no more than single-digit growth in 2001. The key variables include low unemployment and modest growth in revolving credit. Our model predicts 6% growth in bankruptcies next year, a level that incidentally would not threaten consensus estimates, in our view. But we think 3% growth is more likely, because a statistical model doesn't factor in the changing face of competition. Also, chief credit officers of credit card and consumer finance companies see little sign of deteriorating credit today and are optimistic about trends going into next year. By examining weekly bankruptcy growth over the next few months, we should see early indications as to whether our outlook is on target or not.[10]

Soon enough, the weekly data revealed a troubling change in the trend: bankruptcy filings were now rising. The model had been right, the chief credit officers were wrong. As a first step toward a more cautious stance, I recommended that investors hold no more than a market weight position in credit card stocks.[11]

By January 2001, I was increasingly worried about unemployment. I still favored the specialist card operators but believed it prudent to downgrade

Providian from "outperform" to "neutral." At the time, concerns about the company's business model were not yet front and center in my mind.

> We're concerned about the risk of deceleration in growth rates, given current valuations—not credit issues per se. In our view, Providian and Capital One [which I also downgraded] are adequately reserved and have plenty of capital. We view these companies as smart and disciplined underwriters. Furthermore, we don't think their subprime portfolios pose any greater risk than that of the card industry at large. It's possible that subprime losses could be less sensitive than the industry, although we don't have a statistical basis to make that argument. If there are credit problems in the card industry, we suspect they will occur not at best-in-class competitors like PVN and COF, but rather in second-tier issuers, which are largely owned by banks and retailers.[12]

From this point, the credit card stocks sold off, and Providian fell all the way from $59 (at the time of the downgrade) to $44, shedding 25% of its market cap. I continued to warn investors that a classic consumer credit cycle was shaping up. But I thought the stocks had overreacted to this scenario. At this point, I valued Providian between $50 and $60, depending on the severity of the recession.

I still thought of the company as a skillful underwriter. True, its management did not seem to take the bankruptcy cycle as seriously as I thought they should: they assumed that filings would rise by only 10%, whereas I forecast a 25% increase. As such, I expected the company to experience somewhat higher loss rates than its management guidance. But I thought that risk was now discounted in the stock. So I upgraded Providian back to outperform on April 2, 2001, citing it as a trade for the "quick and the bold."[13] Little did I realize how quick and bold one would need to be.

Soon enough it became clear that I had made a mistake. I had the chance to visit with management early in 2001 and came away unimpressed with its new product plans, which I had imagined were a top priority, given the OCC's restrictions on its former marketing practices. Even worse were first-quarter results, reported in May 2001. Earnings seemed in line with expectations, but if one knew where to look on the balance sheet, problems were visible in an obscure line called "deferred revenues." The way the accounting worked, when the company sold a product (a credit card, an insurance policy, or some kind of membership program), the fees were initially deferred and recorded on the balance sheet, then gradually amortized into net income as revenues over the expected life of the product. The decline in the balance sheet account indicated that a large portion of revenues were coming from sales booked in the past, and new sales were not making up the difference. It now seemed that the marketing restrictions had indeed compromised the company's revenue growth. I remember discussing this observation with a client. We both thought the stock was certain to sell off violently.

But the sell-off did not happen. As luck would have it, a wave of enthusiasm about the macroeconomic environment swept through the market. Over the next few weeks, financial stocks rallied strongly, possibly anticipating a new round of interest rate cuts from the Federal Reserve. In a matter of days, Providian had soared all the way back to $60. I wasted little time in downgrading it back to neutral. Not only were Providian's results disconcerting, but the employment picture was deteriorating more severely than expected (Dick Berner was now forecasting peak unemployment at 5.1%). And bankruptcies continued to soar, a leading indicator of the losses that lay ahead for credit card issuers. My team surveyed a group of bankruptcy attorneys and found that, on the basis of activity in their practices, they expected personal filings to keep rising well into 2002.[14]

The downgrade was timely, as Providian's stock was soon to enter a near-terminal dive, making it the worst performing stock in the S&P 500 in 2001. First, it became apparent that the company had changed the methodology for calculating credit losses— without bothering to disclose this fact to the market. In other words, credit losses were worse than initially reported. Next, the chief executive officer was dismissed. Then the company reported huge losses. It lost access to the securitization and unsecured debt markets. The rest of the senior management team was let go. A turnaround specialist was brought in. Amid fears of a fatal liquidity crisis, the stock slid to $2.01 per share on November 5, 2001. From nearly $60 per share in July, it had fallen by over 96% in 4 months (Exhibit 2.10). Based on the 1-year implied volatility of 50% that we had measured earlier in the year, a 4-month 96% decline would have equated to a 5-standard deviation event—a hopelessly remote outcome, and a classic example of a Black Swan affecting a single stock.

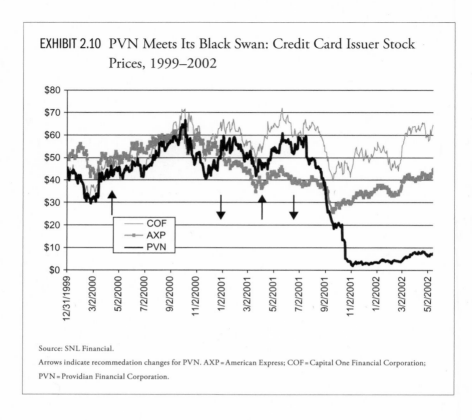

EXHIBIT 2.10 PVN Meets Its Black Swan: Credit Card Issuer Stock Prices, 1999–2002

Source: SNL Financial.

Arrows indicate recommedation changes for PVN. AXP = American Express; COF = Capital One Financial Corporation; PVN = Providian Financial Corporation.

The Lesson of the Story

The probability tree helped me avoid a Black Swan event. To be sure, I did not precisely forecast Providian's shocking demise. There were not enough public data on which to base such a dire forecast. Rather, I identified the risk factors and weighted them with probabilities that seemed appropriate for the information at the time. This approach allowed me to anticipate problems somewhat earlier than the rest of the market.

In retrospect, I had an edge over other investors in understanding the critical issues for Providian. This, combined with quick reactions to new information and some luck, allowed me to make some successful recommendations. But there is a lesson in the stock hitting bottom below even the worst scenario in the probability tree. Remember the possibility that two of the critical issues, namely the industry credit cycle and the stability of Providian's business model, might have been correlated? In fact, they were. The underlying issue was competition, which lay at the heart of both the industry cycle and Providian's shortcomings (Exhibit 2.11). Whatever the company's competitive advantage might have once been, it had dissipated to the point that without the aggressive marketing programs the OCC had censured, Providian could no longer produce the growth investors expected.

In later years I had the chance to debrief members of the management team. I learned that the root cause of the company's problems was senior management's apprehension about acknowledging pressure on revenue growth, fearing a negative reaction from investors. So they proceeded to book large volumes of new business over the Internet, without first testing the quality of the accounts. The quality turned out to be poor.

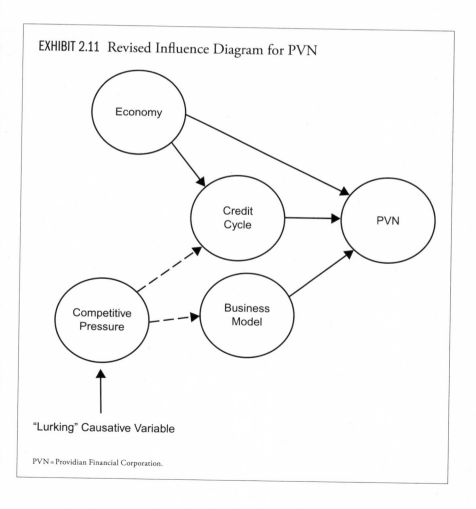

EXHIBIT 2.11 Revised Influence Diagram for PVN

PVN = Providian Financial Corporation.

That was not the end of the Providian story. With the stock in the low single digits, my team analyzed the company's cash flow and concluded that it had enough liquidity to survive. Screwing up my courage, I upgraded the stock to outperform at $6 and reiterated the positive rating as it slipped to $4.[15] With investors having suffered roundly in the stock market crash, few were open to buying shares in a struggling subprime lender. Nonetheless, our analysis was accurate, and the stock eventually rallied. In 2005, the company was acquired by Washington Mutual. Like Providian, Washington Mutual reacted to competitive pressure by underwriting risky loans. In 2008, as the loss rates on these loans became clear, Washington Mutual suffered a fatal run on the bank and was seized by bank regulators, wiping out its investors.

Chapter 3

The Balance Between Overconfidence
and Underconfidence, and the Special Risk
of Complex Modeling

The first principle is that you must not fool yourself—and you
are the easiest person to fool.

—Richard P. Feynman, *Cargo Cult Science*, 1974

One of the reasons for our success as a species has been our
ability to increase rapidly the complexity of our behavior.

—J. A. Tainter, 1992

Courage becomes the supreme virtue *after* adequate knowledge and a tested judgment are at hand.

—Benjamin Graham, *The Intelligent Investor*, 1949

Sometimes we reach accurate decisions in an intuitive flash; sometimes
our instincts are fatally flawed. Some answers emerge from intensive research
and sophisticated analysis; sometimes this approach fails, too. In recent decades social scientists have focused on overconfidence as a cause of many mistakes, blaming the phenomenon for excessive stock trading and market volatility, bad investment decisions by chief executive officers, costly delays in labor
negotiations, litigation, even wars.[1] In the investment markets, it is presumed
that investors who lost money when Black Swans struck must have been overconfident. To avoid such risks, investors might try to be less confident, refrain
from making decisions, and just stay in cash. This stance would leave them
immune to Black Swans, although they would earn no return. Trying to be
less confident would probably not help decision makers in other fields, either.

I think the social scientists miss the bigger picture: decision makers need to find the *right balance* between overconfidence and "underconfidence."

This chapter aims to help you find that balance as quickly and efficiently as possible. It starts with the story of a recommendation that was accurate but underconfident. Then we will see how confidence translates into options trades, how feeling confident can be an inaccurate signal for decisions, and how confidence emerges in real-world settings. The chapter includes a checklist to help readers train their sense of confidence to better signal the expected accuracy of a decision.

There is a special kind of overconfidence that can develop from the use of "sophisticated" or complex analysis—a dangerous trap in our increasingly information-intensive world. Two stories illustrate the perils of overconfident modeling. One involves my research into Countrywide, formerly the nation's leading mortgage company. The second describes how subprime losses ended up an order of magnitude more severe than mortgage analysts had projected, despite powerful computer models and plentiful data. This mistake was a major contributor to the Black Swan that swept through the mortgage and housing markets, so it is worth understanding what went wrong.

But first let us look at an example of underconfidence.

Underconfident but Accurate: The Trials of CIT

In late December 2007, my associate, Andy Bernard, and I attended a breakfast for about a dozen sell-side analysts hosted by the senior management of CIT Group at its Fifth Avenue headquarters. CIT was a commercial finance company, making a variety of commercial loans to middle-market businesses. Since it was not a bank, CIT did not gather deposits but rather funded itself by raising debt in the capital markets. The executives presented a slide deck reviewing the company's prospects, and one slide showed the schedule of upcoming debt maturities. CIT was planning to refinance some $10 billion in maturing bonds during 2008 with a combination of new unsecured and asset-backed debt.

This comment caught my attention. In late 2007, the capital markets were struggling with poor liquidity. I did not know that within months virtually all debt markets would be frozen, or that major financial institutions would

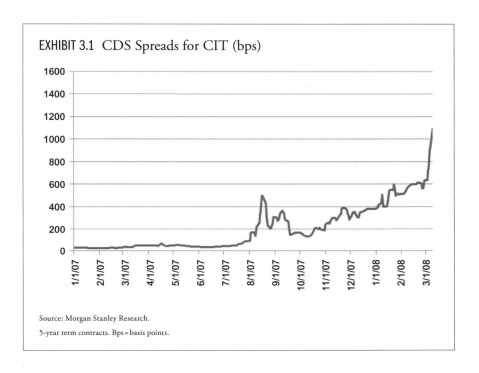

EXHIBIT 3.1 CDS Spreads for CIT (bps)

Source: Morgan Stanley Research.
5-year term contracts. Bps = basis points.

be dropping like flies. But I did know that debt traders thought liquidity was deteriorating. Further, I recalled that CIT had had trouble with wide spreads on its unsecured debt in past periods. However, since Andy and I were busy with other companies, I did not spend much time thinking about CIT or its looming debt maturities until a few weeks later, when I noticed that the credit default swaps (CDS) for CIT's unsecured debt were widening significantly, a sign that the markets were becoming uncomfortable with CIT's risk profile (Exhibit 3.1). (A CDS is a derivative contract whose values moves in relation to a company's bonds; the CDS pays off if a company defaults.) If spreads remained wide, issuing new unsecured debt was going to be costly, and perhaps infeasible. Yet the stock had not moved since the December breakfast.

If CIT could not issue new bonds to pay off those that were maturing, it would have to pony up a lot of cash. Could it scrape enough cash together? We were not sure, but no good could come of the situation. On February 22, 2008, Andy and I issued a recommendation for investors to sell short the stock, which we expressed by establishing a short position in our team's model portfolio:

> We are establishing a short position in CIT because of its precarious funding situation and negative credit outlook for 2008. CIT has a high level of exposure to commercial & industrial, as well as commercial real estate loans, which are just beginning to deteriorate. Additionally, CIT faces $10 bn in maturing unsecured debt in 2008, yet its credit default spreads have widened to the point that issuance of new unsecured debt is not likely feasible.[2]

To be honest, I did not feel particularly confident about this call; rather, I was a little nervous. The basis seemed logical, but the *quantity* of analysis and information was not overwhelming. We had not had a chance to talk with management or other sources. We had not modeled what would happen to CIT if it could not refinance its maturities. We did not publish an in-depth report with tables of supporting data.

Yet, there were several factors in favor of this recommendation. Having covered CIT for several years, I had expert knowledge about the company, giving me an intuitive grasp of the critical issues, foremost of which was liquidity. Second, we had information from the company on its debt maturities. Third, we had a view from debt traders. Fourth, we had a simple thesis, which would be tested soon enough when the company's bonds matured. Finally, with the stock trading cheaply but not at a distressed valuation, we made a judgment that there was room for it to fall further. This judgment was based on an assessment of how investors were thinking about and trading financial services stocks—part of the process of calibrating with the market.

As an aside, academics may continue to debate the question of market efficiency, but as a practitioner, I do not understand how there could be enough computational power for the market to discount all information instantaneously (a theme we will return to in Chapter 4). In this case, widening debt spreads had not yet caught the attention of equity investors. But soon enough they did: within a few weeks, CIT's stock price dropped from $25 to $12 (Exhibit 3.2).

Looking back, this was an unremarkable recommendation, one of countless short bets against financial services stocks when the entire industry was

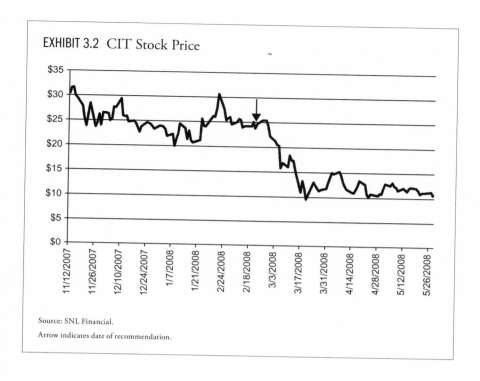

EXHIBIT 3.2 CIT Stock Price

Source: SNL Financial.

Arrow indicates date of recommendation.

melting down. What makes this call noteworthy was its *efficiency*, the positive return from a limited expenditure of resources (time, effort, budget). It showcases how understanding a single critical issue (in this case, liquidity) can be more important than the sense of emotional confidence gained from acquiring and analyzing volumes of information.

Confidence in the Markets

Finding the right balance between overconfidence and underconfidence is a form of calibrating one's intuitive thought processes with real-world probabilities. Such calibration is important for all decision makers, and this is seen clearly in the options markets, where profits and losses depend, in part, on drawing accurate confidence intervals around stock prices.

One reason that social scientists argue people are overconfident is that there is a long history of experiments in which test subjects overestimate the accuracy of their answers. For example, people may be asked to guess the answers to a series of trivia-type questions, such as Wal-Mart's revenues in 2008, the length of the Nile River, or the number of endangered species in South America. The subjects must not only provide their best guess, but also estimate a 90% confidence interval around the true answer. Typically, these confidence intervals cover only 40% of the correct answers, indicating that test subjects significantly overestimate the accuracy of their guesses. This is another way of saying that their assessment of probabilities is not properly calibrated with the real world.[3]

This is an odd finding, because presumably the human species would not have survived if our sense of confidence was dramatically miscalibrated. If our ancestors had been overconfident, they might have perished picking fights with saber-toothed cats. If they had been underconfident, they might have starved, too fearful of predators to venture from their caves in search of food.

There are also reasons to question the researchers' methodology. For one, in experiments people may *talk* with greater confidence than they *act* with in real-life situations. Additionally, it may also be easier (and more interesting) for social scientists to study overconfident decisions than to analyze missed opportunities that result from lack of confidence.

The options markets provide a real-world setting where we can watch traders placing bets on confidence intervals, just like the subjects in the scientists' experiments, but with higher stakes. A confidence interval in the options market is constructed by simultaneously selling a call option with a strike price above the current stock price and a put option with a strike price below the current stock price. (This is called a "short strangle," and the payoff is illustrated in Exhibit 3.3). If the trader estimates the correct confidence interval, and the stock remains within the range of the strike prices, she will pocket the premiums from selling the options without having to pay anything out at expiration. However, should the stock end up outside one of the strike prices at expiration, then the trader will have to pay the option holder. If traders were as overconfident as the subjects in the experiments, then we would observe an ongoing flow of wealth from option sellers to option buyers. Once the wealth of the option sellers had been exhausted, trading would come to a halt. This does not appear to have happened.[4]

The short strangle shown in Exhibit 3.3 consists of selling a put option struck at $10 for a premium of $2 (there is no payout on the put option un-

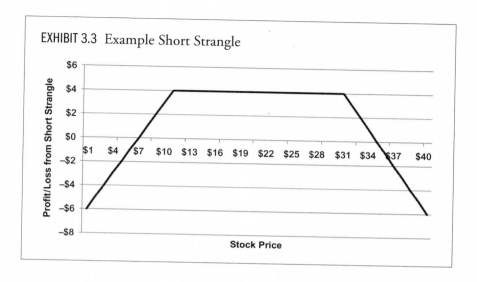

EXHIBIT 3.3 Example Short Strangle

less the stock price drops below $10) and selling a call option struck at $30 for a premium of $2 (there is no payout on the call option unless the stock closes above $30). As long as the stock stays within a "confidence interval" of $10 to 30, the strangle seller keeps $4 in premiums with no payout.

Incidentally, traders not only appear to understand the normal day-to-day confidence interval around stock prices, but also appear to recognize the risk of extreme volatility that could lead to outcomes well outside the normal distribution. We can tell this from the so-called volatility smile, which refers to the fact that out-of-the-money options (especially to the downside) trade at higher implied volatilities than do options struck near the current stock price.

Nonetheless, even if the option markets as a whole do not seem overconfident, there could still be plenty of overconfident traders. Presumably they get weeded out over time, as excessively bold bets wipe out their capital. Underconfident traders are also likely to be unsuccessful, because in failing to snatch legitimate opportunities, their trading likely produces low returns. For the individual analyst or investor who wants to continue competing, it is imperative to calibrate one's confidence with the probabilities of the real world. And that is likely to be an ongoing effort, because in a world of Black Swans, probabilities may suddenly shift.

Emotional Confidence: An Imperfect Signal

To persevere in the markets (and avoid being weeded out), one needs an accurate sense of confidence. What is this sense? No one really knows, although some researchers believe that the human sense of confidence evolved as a switch or signal, triggered by subconscious calculations, meant to stop endless rumination and encourage decision making. No doubt, confidence is most often a reliable signal, but it sometimes seems to misfire.

In fact, there are interesting examples where a sense of confidence has become completely separated from reality. Neuroscientist Robert Burton has studied the *feeling of knowing*—that is, the sense of confidence, certainty, or clarity that arises when we think we understand what is going on. Interestingly, Dr. Burton has found a number of examples in which an intense feeling of knowing is demonstrably invalid. For example, he cites studies in which people remain highly confident in their memories, even when confronted with evidence that their recollections are factually incorrect. He tells of near-death experiences in which people report that they believed with complete certainty that they had died (they had not). Burton also points to examples of powerful feelings of knowledge or clarity in people taking PCP (angel dust). And people in delusional states may express intense conviction in the truth of fantastic visions. These include people suffering from certain kinds of strokes, as well as schizophrenics.[5] In fact, magical thinking of one sort or another is widespread: people appear to believe with great conviction in extrasensory perception (41%, according to a 2005 Gallup poll), haunted houses (37%), possession by the devil (42%), telepathy (31%), extraterrestrial aliens having visited the earth (24%), and clairvoyance (26%).[6] One hopes that these kinds of examples are not germane to high-stakes decision making in the markets and other fields. But they do make the point that confidence is not always a reliable signal.

A feeling of confidence is often triggered by intuitive recognition—the sense of "aha" that arises when we recognize an important pattern in the data. In Chapter 4, we will discuss the importance of intuition in overcoming information overload and zeroing in on critical issues. However, there is a difference between recognizing an issue and making a decision. As a researcher in the field of decision making, Gary Klein has found that for decision makers in high-stakes situations—like pilots, nurses, or firefighters—intuition plays a critical role. But in complicated situations with large numbers of factors, he warns, "You cannot rely on overall intu-itions about what to do," and he puts the stock market in this category.[7] The reason is that intuition tends to find the best match to a single pattern, rather than weighing the implications of multiple patterns, a process that requires conscious, deliberative reasoning.

The confidence that arises from conscious and deliberative reasoning is not perfectly reliable, either. Researchers have found that people's sense of confidence increases with the quantity of available information, even if the accuracy of decisions does not improve. For example, in studies people have expressed heightened confidence in betting on horse races after being given more information about the horses and riders, or in identifying guilty sus-pects after watching more hours of videotaped interrogation. In another study, clinical psychologists grew more confident in their diagnoses when given additional background about the patients. However, in each of these studies, the accuracy of decisions did *not* improve with additional informa-tion.[8] Either the new information had no predictive value, or if it did, the subjects had no predictive skill. Perhaps the confidence signaled growing fa-miliarity with the situation and thus greater ease in digesting new data. Nonetheless, for decision-making *accuracy* (as opposed to facility), additional information inspired a kind of false confidence.

Conversely, in some situations, a surprisingly small amount of informa-tion can allow people to draw remarkably accurate conclusions. If people do not make decisions in these circumstances, then we would argue that they are underconfident. In *Blink*, Malcolm Gladwell describes a study in which people were asked to watch videotapes of doctor-patient interactions and predict which doctors were likely to be sued for malpractice. Surprisingly, the predictions were spot on, despite limited information on the videotapes. In fact, the predictions were good even when the tapes were limited to 40 seconds in duration and the soundtrack was distorted so that the doctor's comments could not be understood. Listeners were able to make accurate predictions just from the doctors' tone of voice. (Apparently, doctors with authoritarian styles are more likely to be sued than those with friendly styles.[9])

Many other factors influence our sense of confidence. For example, re-searchers have found that people tend to become overconfident after com-pleting complex or difficult tasks, whereas they may feel underconfident after taking on simple or easy tasks.[10]

Investors and other decision makers operate with varying amounts of information—sometimes too much (overload), sometimes not enough (uncertainty). Thus an important and necessary goal is getting the feeling of confidence properly calibrated with the accuracy of the analysis rather than with the quantity of information at hand.

Confidence and Competition

Like most fields, investing is a competitive business. Confidence must therefore be defined not only in relation to the *absolute* accuracy of the analysis, but also in terms of the accuracy *relative* to other investors, who are presumably working on the same or similar problems.[11] Since resources are limited, the analyst's goal is to produce as much accuracy as possible with the minimum resources, without wasting money or time. Time matters because the opportunity to act vanishes once the rest of the market catches on to the investment thesis.

Here is a hypothetical example of how confidence develops over time. Imagine we can track an analyst's sense of confidence as she works through a problem and compare this to the expected accuracy of her work. I have used the two charts below to illustrate how scenarios of overconfidence and underconfidence might evolve.

Exhibit 3.4 illustrates a scenario characterized by overconfidence. Imagine an analyst starting a new project—with little confidence at first, but as she spends time reading disclosures, scanning published research and industry trade journals, listening to a recording of the most recent conference call, she starts to feel comfortable with the situation. But although confidence is rising, it is not clear that accuracy has improved by any material degree. After all, plenty of other investors have already digested disclosures, research, and news. She has no clear advantage and at this point runs the risk of becoming overconfident, just like those who grew more confident betting on a race when given additional information on horses and jockeys. This is point A in the chart.

If the analyst persists in researching the company, she may start to develop a legitimate edge. Perhaps she has interviewed the company's customers or suppliers, or built a detailed model to forecast its earnings. Perhaps by focusing most of her time on this one company, she starts to pick up on new trends

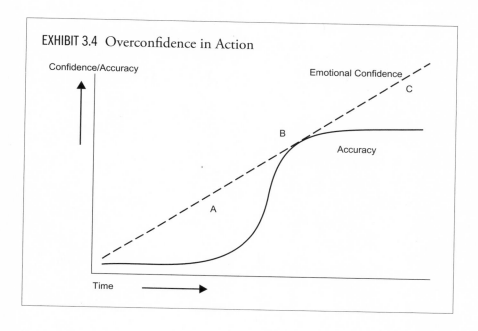

EXHIBIT 3.4 Overconfidence in Action

before others, who may be spreading their time over many other situations. At point B, the accuracy of her judgments suddenly rises as information and modeling come together to produce a testable and differentiated thesis. Point B would be the ideal point to make an investment decision, because accuracy is at its maximum level as a function of time (and other resources).

If the analyst continues to gather and analyze information, the accuracy of her work may increase further. But there could be diminishing returns. If the analyst has interviewed 30 customers, then the next 10 may not change the picture much. Relative accuracy might also plateau (or even decline) as competitors figure out many of the same issues. As they trade, the stock's price may come to discount what had been a proprietary insight but what is rapidly becoming the consensus view. This is labeled point C.

Now we are in a dangerous spot. As the analyst continues to analyze the company, her confidence may keep rising, a function of increasing quantities of information. Perhaps by now she views herself as the world's leading expert on the company or industry in question. Her confidence might also mount if her initial recommendations prove successful. Psychologists working with traders find that some individuals' confidence levels are overly affected by the successes of their recent trades.[12]

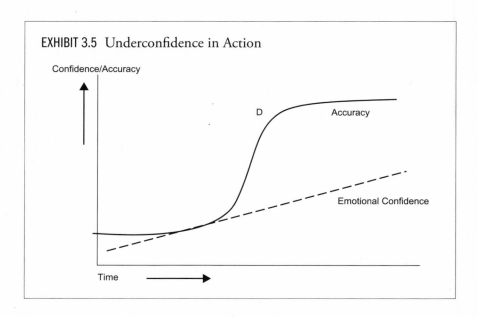

EXHIBIT 3.5 Underconfidence in Action

Exhibit 3.5 shows a different situation. Here, an analyst stumbles upon some combination of information and analysis and quickly recognizes one or more decisive factors in the situation, producing a sudden increase in accuracy (point D). With little time spent acquiring or analyzing information, he may not feel highly confident. Nonetheless, he may be in a position to make an accurate bet. He resembles the subjects who could make good judgments about which doctors would be sued just from watching 40 seconds of video with garbled sound. This would also be a fair description of the CIT call. If you do not make a forceful recommendation, the opportunity may pass.

What Goes Into Accurate Decisions?

To recognize the point of optimum accuracy, analysts need to understand the elements of their work that contribute to accuracy. The emotional sense of confidence may or may not be a good guide. To help spot where accuracy (as opposed to confidence) has risen to a competitive level, I have prepared the checklist in Exhibit 3.6, which summarizes a number of ideas in this book. Give yourself a point for each question you can answer with a "yes": the higher the score, the higher the expected accuracy of the decision.

EXHIBIT 3.6 A Checklist for More Accurate Decision Making

Hypotheses

Can you identify the critical issues on which the investment will depend?

Can you explain how the market or other investors are thinking about these critical issues?

Have you developed a thesis about something the market has missed?

Can you point to catalysts that will shed light on your thesis?

Will these catalysts become evident in the short term?

Probabilities

Have you considered different scenarios for each of the critical issues?

Have you assigned subjective probabilities to these scenarios?

Have you considered the possibility of asymmetric outcomes?

Have you compared your judgment of risk to the volatility in the stock or its options?

Information

Do you have expert knowledge of the company or industry?

Do you have information that helps you make a judgment on the critical issues?

Is this information proprietary (not widely held)?

Analysis

Do you have a statistically valid model as part of your forecast?

Is the model specified on the critical issues?

Have you considered variables outside the model that could affect the results?

Do you understand the causative relationships among critical issues?

Have you looked for signs of changing correlation among critical issues?

Have you considered whether the causative relationships might produce extreme outcomes?

Intuition

Before acting on an intuitive recognition, have you thought through the possibility that other variables might influence the results?

(continued)

EXHIBIT 3.6 (*continued*)

Cognitive Dissonance
Are you comfortable making a decision without worrying about self-identity, career prospects, institutional issues, and the like?

Judgment
Do you know something about the information and opinions of your competitors?

Remember, the goal is not to maximize the confidence for every decision—in a competitive situation, that would require unrealistic resource or time commitments. Instead, by documenting the elements of confidence, then going back after the outcome of the decision is clear, the checklist can serve as the foundation for a "learning cycle," where analysts and decision makers continually reassess which elements produce the best results. People learn from their mistakes naturally, but the learning cycle may improve if decisions are documented and reviewed. Even better is working in teams, when studying decisions allows analysts to learn from their peers' successes and mistakes in addition to their own.

Blinded by the Light: The Risk of Complex Modeling

The balance between overconfidence and underconfidence has no doubt perplexed humans since the dawn of time. What is different today is the explosion in information technology. Computer power allows us to solve tough problems, but they also produce an exponential increase in information, which can leave decision makers paralyzed. Models can help analyze all this information, but their byproduct may be a special (and dangerous) kind of overconfidence.

Model-related overconfidence derives from two sources. First, researchers have found that people's intuition tends to latch onto a single salient variable, rather than weighing all possible variables in a given situation. To describe this tendency, Daniel Kahneman and Amos Tversky coined the term *representativeness heuristic*. Modelers who suffer from this problem focus on a small set of intuitively plausible variables, potentially ignoring other critical issues. Second, as noted above, people's confidence tends to increase as they gather more information, even if the accuracy of their decisions does not. Running complex models produces lots of information, making it all too easy to feel comfortable and in control.

Latching onto a single variable and then growing increasingly confident as you model it can be dangerous. Consider shining a flashlight on a nighttime walk: anything in the cone of light is highly visible, but everything else disappears into inky darkness. There is a natural tendency to focus on modeling (the cone of light) because it produces specific and precise answers. Other information may appear in the form of anecdotes, impressions, and rumors, which are harder to weigh. Yet focusing on the cone of light could be a problem if a Black Swan is lurking in the shadows.

Fischer Black thought that much of current economic theory suffered from this kind of problem. He believed that economists focus on simple models whose solutions they already understand, and then test those models using data whose chief attraction is its ready availability.[13]

Other researchers hypothesize that investors put too much weight on "private information" (what they see in the cone of light) and are slow to react to public information (everything else out there in the dark). The researchers use this theory to explain certain quirks in the stock market. Short-term momentum in stock prices, for example, may reflect investors overconfidently bidding up prices for stocks when their private information is reinforced by public data.[14]

Similar questions confront analysts in other disciplines. For example, intelligence analysts have historically put more weight on classified human and signal intelligence than on open-source information (free or low-cost data available over the Internet, in the media, or from academic and industry conferences). This preference for classified information sources may have something to do with the cultural predominance of the Central Intelligence Agency's operations directorate. But some experts argue that in the age of the Internet, more emphasis should be placed on open-source information, which today provides an enormous amount of useful data.[15] Continuing to focus on classified data is like staring into the cone of light.

The Representativeness Heuristic

People use shortcuts all the time. Searching for patterns is hard work, and the strong sense of "aha" in an intuitive recognition immediately boosts confidence and encourages decisions. In simple terms, the representativeness heuristic occurs when we base predictions on a single important variable while neglecting others. Kahneman and Tversky first described this shortcoming more than 30 years ago, but in my experience, their ideas remains opaque to many practitioners.

In an early study, Kahneman and Tversky asked subjects to guess what field of graduate study a hypothetical fellow named Tom W. was enrolled in:

> Tom W. is of high intelligence, although lacking in true creativity. He has a need for order and clarity. . . . His writing is rather dull and mechanical, occasionally enlivened by somewhat corny puns and by flashes of imagination of the sci-fi type. . . . He seems to have little feel and little sympathy for other people and does not enjoy interacting with others.[16]

Most people guess that Tom is studying computer science, as they have a strong mental image of computer engineers being "nerdy" types, similar to the description. In a nutshell, Tom W. seems *representative* of the stereotypical computer science grad student. The subconscious mind latches onto this pattern and signals the match with an "aha!" However, confidence in this answer is misplaced because computer scientists make up only a small fraction of the graduate population—a relevant pattern that the subconscious mind often fails to take into account.

The probability tree in Exhibit 3.7 illustrates this problem. It assumes that 30% of computer scientists are nerdy, a ratio three times higher than the rest of the graduate student population. However, computer scientists make up only 10% of the population. Taking account of both patterns, the math shows that only 3% (or 30%×10%) of the graduate school population would consist of *nerdy computer scientists,* as opposed to 9% of the population (10%×90%) who would be *nerdy but not computer scientists.* Thus the odds of Tom W. being a computer engineer are only 1 in 4, or 3% divided by 12%, which represents the total population of nerdy students (3%+9%).

When complex analytics are involved, the representativeness heuristic can be especially hazardous. Ill-considered judgments result from the confluence

EXHIBIT 3.7 Tom W. and the Representativeness Heuristic

Probability that a computer engineer is nerdy: 30%
Probability that other graduate students are nerdy: 10%
Relative proportion of computer engineers: 10%
Relative proportion of other graduate students: 90%

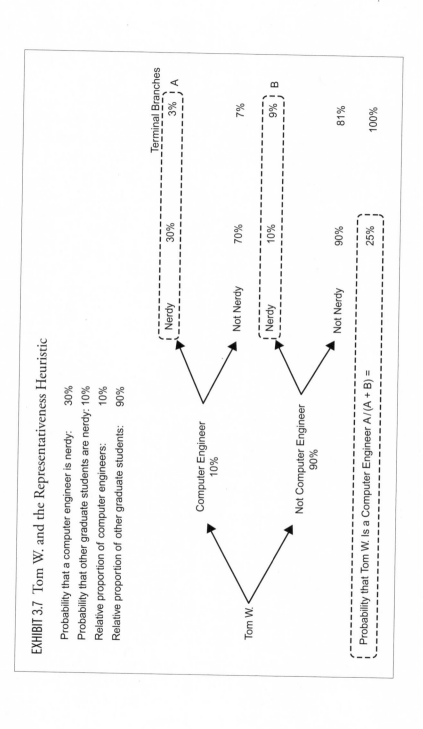

of two factors: intuitive confidence from pattern recognition and conscious confidence from information and modeling. Imagine a second probability tree that estimates the odds that a mortgage company with a relatively strong balance sheet will emerge from a housing slump as a competitive winner. Winners likely have stronger balance sheets than their weaker peers. But what happens if the slump is so severe as to claim victims from among the strongest operators? In this situation, careful analysis of a mortgage company's balance sheet could set up the analyst for the wrong decision.

Model-Related Overconfidence and an Ill-Fated Call on Countrywide

In May of 2006, I upgraded Countrywide, the nation's largest mortgage lender, from equal-weight to overweight at a price of $42 per share. My thesis hinged on the company's risk profile, as I thought investors did not appreciate improvements in the company's balance sheet. Countrywide, I argued, was not as risky as people thought:

> Execution skills in production, operating scale in servicing, the statistical validity of the so-called "macro hedge," and the substantial capital held by the bank—these factors add up to an enterprise risk profile that is considerably less volatile than that implied by debt spreads or option premiums. And they imply a sizeable competitive advantage over rivals that does not appear to be discounted in the stock price, which we view as 33% undervalued.[17]

We now know how this story ended: as the housing market slumped and then crashed, Countrywide found itself struggling with liquidity and credit problems, as well as a bad reputation in the media. In December 2007, under financial distress, Countrywide sold itself to Bank of America for $5 per share. If the 95% stock price decline over six months qualifies as a Black Swan, this one managed to get the better of me. The encounter demonstrated the danger of excessive reliance on seemingly sophisticated models during a period of turbulence—just the sort of risk the representativeness heuristic poses to unwary decision makers.

Founded in the 1960s by Dave Loeb and Angelo Mozilo, Countrywide had struggled and evolved through countless cycles as an independent operator, even as most of its competitors were absorbed by large commercial banks. Within the mortgage industry, Countrywide was regarded as an extraordinary company, held in high regard by competitors, partners, and consultants. It had invested in proprietary technology to streamline its servicing and origination businesses. Many of its senior managers had backgrounds in public accounting. The culture was disciplined and analytic, emphasizing careful number crunching before making decisions.

Respect from the markets, however, was a long time coming. Suspicious of how sensitive the mortgage market was to changes in interest rates, investors steered clear of Countrywide, especially after earnings fell short of management guidance in 1999 and 2000, a period when the Federal Reserve raised interest rates and the mortgage market temporarily cooled. The stock languished around book value, and I recall great difficulty in arranging meetings between management and investors.

Then Countrywide's moment in the sun arrived. In 2001, the Federal Reserve cut interest rates in a bid to stave off a deep recession following the Internet and technology stock crash. Lower rates triggered a massive refinance boom, and thanks to its technology and risk management, Countrywide captured a large share of the huge origination market, its margins expanding with rising volumes. By 2003, investors were thronging analyst conferences at its California and Texas facilities. Countrywide had emerged as the industry's leading mortgage company, with number one market share (Exhibit 3.8). Management had finally earned a token of respect. The stock soared from a trough near $6 in 2000 to a peak of nearly $40 in early 2005; this was equivalent to an average annual growth rate of 43%, in itself a rare event (Exhibit 3.9).

Back in 2006, my investment hypothesis for Countrywide hinged on steps the company had taken to strengthen its balance sheet and risk management. To mitigate interest rate risk, Countrywide had carefully balanced its origination and servicing businesses. Origination involves the production of new loans, which is typically more profitable when interest rates fall, because volumes pick up as consumers rush to refinance and margins widen as well. Servicing consists of collecting interest payments from borrowers and remitting them to investors. Servicing generates steady fees, but when interest rates drop and borrowers refinance, the servicing portfolio is at risk of "running off" or shrinking if the company cannot originate enough new loans to replace those that have refinanced. Accounting rules require the loss of servicing fees from loan payoffs to be recorded as an immediate charge,

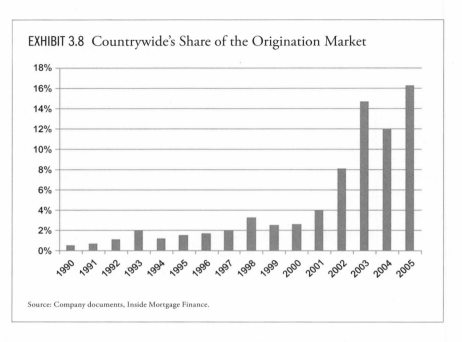

EXHIBIT 3.8 Countrywide's Share of the Origination Market

Source: Company documents, Inside Mortgage Finance.

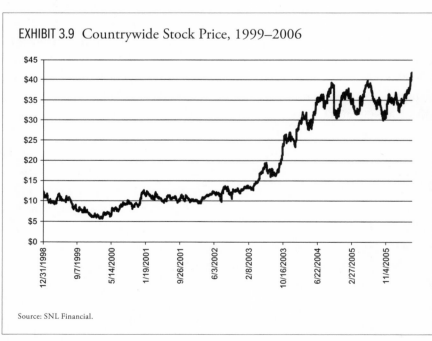

EXHIBIT 3.9 Countrywide Stock Price, 1999–2006

Source: SNL Financial.

which could imperil earnings or capital. By combining origination and servicing in the right proportions, a company can dampen the impact of shifting interest rates on profitability. Countrywide did a good job at this balancing act.

Additionally, Countrywide had acquired a small bank, giving it access to deposits and other forms of low-cost financing. Now Countrywide could more easily go head-to-head against rivals like JPMorgan, Bank of America, Wells Fargo, and Washington Mutual, which all enjoyed low-cost deposit funding. Countrywide held what appeared to be (at the time) high-quality prime mortgages in its bank. As the portfolio grew, the bank generated stable earnings. And the bank's capital base seemed more than adequate for the historical risk levels associated with prime mortgages.

Countrywide's executives seemed to recognize that strengthening the balance sheet was the key to the next stage of the firm's evolution. The rating agencies were grudgingly giving the firm higher marks for risk management, disclosure, and controls. A ratings upgrade was not out of the question.

Yet the implied volatility in Countrywide stock remained higher than that of other firms with heavy mortgage concentrations, suggesting that investors considered it risky (Exhibit 3.10). To me it seemed odd that implied volatility for Countrywide should be almost on top of that for New Century, a subprime specialist with a controversial reputation and a weak balance sheet. And why should Countrywide's implied volatility be so much higher than that of Washington Mutual, a large thrift notorious for operational problems?

To explore my risk-profile thesis, I set up a Monte Carlo simulation model that allowed me to examine the company's balance sheet in a wide range of interest rate and credit loss scenarios (we will explore these models in Chapter 8).

The conclusion of my analysis was that indeed, the options market was overestimating risk. Recognizing that investors were concerned about a slowdown in housing and deterioration in credit, I devised a strategy combining ownership of the stock together with a "short strangle"—the option transaction that effectively draws a confidence band around the stock, as already discussed. Specifically, I recommended buying the stock while simultaneously selling a put option struck at $35 and a call option struck at $47.50, allowing the investor to collect up-front premiums. If the stock shot up past $47.50, the call option would generate losses, offsetting gains from holding

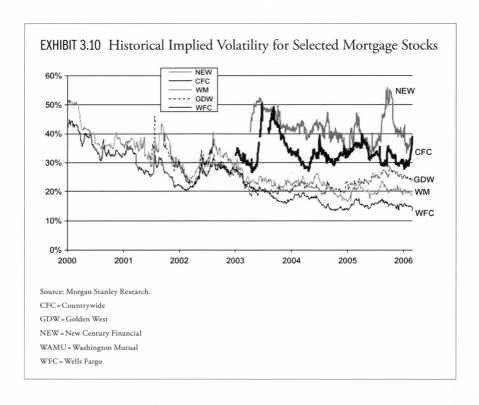

EXHIBIT 3.10 Historical Implied Volatility for Selected Mortgage Stocks

Source: Morgan Stanley Research.

CFC = Countrywide

GDW = Golden West

NEW = New Century Financial

WAMU = Washington Mutual

WFC = Wells Fargo

the stock, effectively capping any further upside. The bigger risk was the stock falling below $35, in which case the put would effectively double the losses associated with holding the shares, although the loss would be partly mitigated by the up-front premiums.

At first, this strategy worked nicely. Over the summer of 2006, the stock remained within the range of the option strike prices. An investor following the recommendation would have pocketed the premiums. Apparently, I was one of those option traders who accurately judged the proper confidence interval. I recommended the strategy again in early 2007. This time things did not work out so well.

By July 2007, subprime mortgage losses were rising so quickly that trading in the riskier tranches of the subprime securitization market came to a halt. This liquidity problem posed a critical decision for Countrywide's management. Subprime lending made up less than 10% of the company's total production. But subprime loans generated wide margins and, more important, kept Countrywide in good graces with home builders, realtors, and mortgage brokers, who were always looking for a loan for a marginal borrower. The company announced that it would continue making subprime loans; if market liquidity did not recover, it would hold the riskier tranches on its balance sheet instead of selling them, as had been its prior practice. But the market reacted unfavorably. The stock sold off, and the company's debt spreads widened. I argued with management that widening debt spreads indicated growing investor discomfort with risky assets. I told them they should cut back on production of subprime loans rather than try to hold these securities on balance sheet. Management was determined to defend its market share and blamed short-sellers for targeting its securities. They were correct, but the short-sellers had good reasons: the housing and capital markets were sliding into crisis, and Countrywide was not reacting quickly enough.

By late August 2007, trading had frozen in all subprime securities, even those rated AAA, and the market for other nontraditional mortgages had dried up, too. Now the company was stuck with an inventory of some $10 billion in these loans that could no longer be sold. Fanning the flames, an analyst downgraded the stock to "sell," predicting insolvency. This triggered a run on the bank: retail depositors started to withdraw funds. To marshal liquidity, Countrywide drew down its bank lines, which earned it an immediate downgrade from the rating agencies and closed off any further access to the debt market. To help stabilize the situation, the company secured a strategic investment from Bank of America. But this diluted existing shareholders. The stock plunged (Exhibit 3.11).

I had made the untimely decision to travel to Asia, and found myself on the phone throughout the night, trying to figure out what happened. My analysis had contemplated interest rate and credit risk, but I had not factored in liquidity risk. Once the company drew its bank lines, it was clear that my investment thesis was off target. I downgraded the stock at $21.[18]

To be sure, parts of my original thesis proved correct. Thanks to the bank, the company was able to obtain additional financing and rebuild its cash position. And one reason Bank of America acquired Countrywide was that it saw value in the company's origination and servicing franchise, just as I had. But the deteriorating credit quality of its portfolio; problems with regulators, the press, and customers; and, of course, frozen securitization markets dwarfed these positives. The buy recommendation had been poor, despite

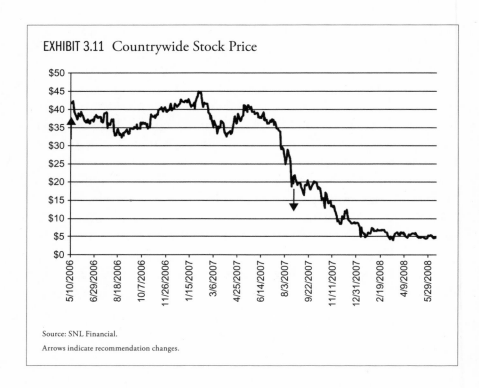

EXHIBIT 3.11 Countrywide Stock Price

Source: SNL Financial.

Arrows indicate recommendation changes.

sophisticated analysis—and perhaps because of it. That analysis caused me to overweight the variables I had studied and thus had confidence in. But variables outside of my cone of light proved decisive.

Reflecting on Countrywide's culture, I suspect that management, too, was blinded by its own flashlight. All my sources agreed these were the sharpest operators in the industry. Convinced by their own analytics, they, too, missed the bigger picture.

Overconfident Modeling and the Subprime Mortgage Collapse

Our second example of overconfident modeling concerns the mortgage industry's massive underestimation of subprime losses, despite detailed models, smart analysts, and quantities of data. Virtually all the major mortgage operators made this mistake. Not only did Countrywide underestimate credit risk, but so did Fannie Mae and Freddie Mac, thrifts and banks, private mortgage insurers, guarantors (including Ambac Financial Group,

MBIA Insurance, and American International Group), government regulators, rating agencies, and most of the major investment banks.

The 12-Standard-Deviation Surprise

The proximate cause of the 2007 securitization market collapse was a startling deterioration in the credit quality of subprime mortgages. To be sure, neither the housing slowdown nor rising mortgage losses came as a surprise— for several years the media had been speculating about the housing bubble and its pending deflation. Mortgage industry veterans knew that slower home price appreciation would lead to higher losses for subprime— and indeed all—mortgage loans, because struggling borrowers would have a harder time avoiding foreclosure.

As the housing market began to decelerate visibly in mid-2006, I tried to understand how modeling experts at the major mortgage companies were thinking about credit quality. I talked with credit risk experts at Countrywide, Fannie Mae, Freddie Mac, mortgage insurers, investment banks, rating agencies, and federal regulators. Thanks to booming home values in recent years, subprime losses had fallen as low as 0% to 2%. But no one expected this to last. My sense was that the experts expected subprime loss rates to revert to the historical average of around 5%, which would reflect defaults by something like 15 out of every 100 borrowers, with a loss of around 33% of the original loan balance on each default (5%=15%×33%).

Nor were the experts totally confident in a 5% loss rate. If the economy weakened, losses might move as high as 7%, or so they thought. On the basis of these conversations, I likened that 2 percentage point difference between 5% and 7% to roughly a one-standard-deviation shock.

By early 2007, newly originated mortgages were starting to go bad quickly. Investment banks that had securitized these mortgages started to "put back" to the originators the so-called early payment defaults—that is, loans that defaulted within their first 90 days. Subprime specialists like New Century bought back growing volumes of early payment defaults, until they ran out of cash and were forced into bankruptcy. Estimates for subprime losses rose from 5% to 7%. By early summer, a respected Asset Backed Securities analyst published a report predicting cumulative losses of 11%. This initially seemed alarmist. However, by the fall, even the rating agencies were assuming 12% to 14% in their calculations, and traders' opinions settled in the middle to upper teens. Toward the end of the year, the consensus view had shifted to the 20s, and by early 2008, it had settled in around 30% to 35%. Cumulative losses at these levels implied that something like two-thirds of the loans would eventually default, with the lenders suffering losses of at least 50%. By mid-2009, loss estimates for some vintages had risen to 40%.

If 2% was really a measure of a one-standard-deviation variance in losses, then from 2006 to 2008 expectations had changed by an improbably large 12 standard deviations. This surprise was the Black Swan at the heart of the economic crash, as subprime losses spiraled throughout the global financial system. How could the biggest companies with the best analysts, proprietary data, and models have been so wrong?

Part of the problem lay with the models used to predict subprime losses. These models had first appeared in the 1990s in connection with the development of consumer credit scores—themselves a statistical measure of consumers' debt obligations and payment histories. Combining the predictive value of credit scores with the historical record of mortgage defaults allowed for more consistent and accurate estimation of losses, at least compared to the intuitive judgment of human underwriters, who suffered from inconsistency and bias.

The loss estimation models incorporated large quantities of data about loan characteristics, such as the type of coupon (fixed-rate or floating) and the borrower's financial strength (as measured by credit score, debt-to-income ratios, and payment histories). They also factored in the purpose of the loan (refinance or purchase); the nature of the property (primary residence, investor property, or second home); and the loan-to-value ratio, among other factors. These data were available for large populations of loans

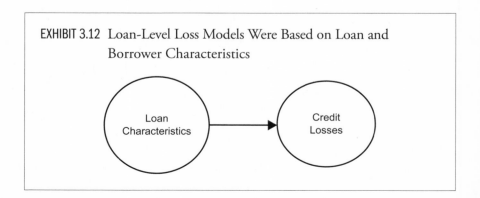

EXHIBIT 3.12 Loan-Level Loss Models Were Based on Loan and Borrower Characteristics

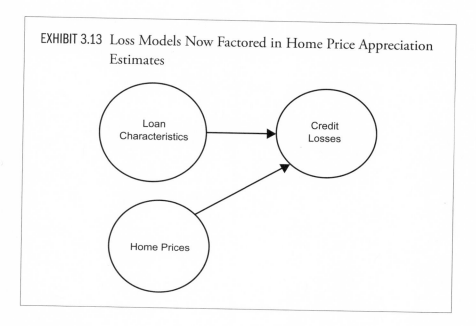

EXHIBIT 3.13 Loss Models Now Factored in Home Price Appreciation Estimates

dating back to the 1990s and sometimes earlier. Using these data, the models did a good job differentiating between relatively safer and riskier loans (Exhibit 3.12).

But credit risk modelers knew that weaker housing trends could throw a monkey wrench into these calculations. They began to factor in regional home price appreciation data into the loan loss models. By 2006, loss estimation models were commonly attached to Monte Carlo simulators, which generated thousands of random paths for home prices, interest rates, and employment conditions for different regions of the country so as to assess a portfolio's vulnerability to different economic scenarios (Exhibit 3.13). These paths were based on the last 20 years or so of regional economic history in the United States, including data from the California and New England housing busts of the 1990s as well as the Oil Patch shock of the late 1980s, when Texas real estate values collapsed. The rating agencies used these kinds of models to rate subprime mortgage-backed securities. Trading desks adopted them to better differentiate between bonds. Regulators used them to estimate how much capital banks should hold against their mortgage portfolios.

Unfortunately, data on loan characteristics and recent economic performance still missed the big picture. In the process of examining readily available data, the analysts and their firms lost sight of the underlying credit cycle.

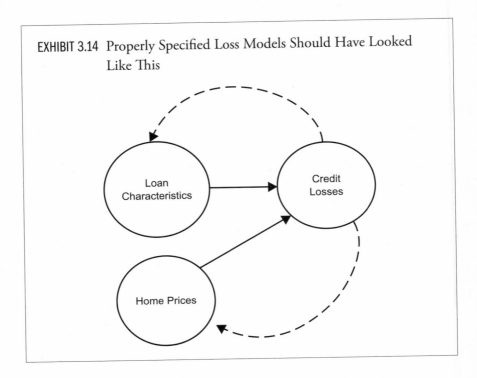

EXHIBIT 3.14 Properly Specified Loss Models Should Have Looked Like This

We saw in Chapter 1 how extreme volatility can erupt when the capital markets and fundamental world interact with each other, producing positive feedback effects. Credit cycles result when capital flows affect the value of the assets they are financing. We touched on this point in discussing the credit card loss cycle (Chapter 2). In the mortgage market, these feedback effects show up in two ways (Exhibit 3.14). First, as home prices rise, credit losses fall and reduced losses attract more capital, allowing more borrowers to buy homes, thus pushing up home prices further. Second, low loss rates encourage lenders to loosen underwriting standards, again allowing more borrowers into the market and pushing up prices. These feedback effects can lead to an acceleration in home prices—until the pool of new borrowers is exhausted or some other shock changes the equation, at which point the process swings into reverse. Models that focused on loan characteristics missed the underlying structure of the credit cycle.

How did this cycle develop in the United States? In 2000, the subprime market was small, and thanks to careful oversight by lenders, investment banks, and rating agencies, loan quality was reasonably good. The Federal

Reserve's decision to cut interest rates in 2001 lowered the cost of mortgage financing. As more people could afford to buy homes, rising demand pushed up the price of housing. Losses on subprime loans dropped. Improved credit performance attracted even more funding, because the spreads on mortgage securities seemed more than adequate compensation for the risk. New funding was facilitated by innovations in the securitization market, such as the growth of collateralized debt obligations and CDS. As spreads tightened, mortgage costs fell, increasing the number of borrowers who might qualify for mortgages, and their demand for new homes pushed up prices further.

This cycle continued until the Federal Reserve started to raise interest rates in 2005, increasing the cost of new loans and thus choking off the supply of marginal borrowers. To sustain volumes, lenders loosened underwriting standards. In some cases they layered together multiple risks in ways that they thought the rating agencies, investment banks, and investors would not notice; in other cases they turned a blind eye on sloppy underwriting. Weaker lenders adopted this behavior because their business models were not flexible enough to operate profitably at reduced volumes. Other lenders feared losing salespeople and market share if they did not offer aggressively underwritten mortgage products (this was part of the problem at Countrywide, too).

With home prices now slowing, the erosion in underwriting quality soon became apparent. By late 2006, new mortgages were going bad almost before the ink had dried on the loan documents. Efforts to tighten standards were too slow; not only was the 2006 vintage of poor quality, but the 2007 vintage turned out even worse. Investors pulled out of the market completely in late summer, shutting down the origination of new subprime loans (leaving Countrywide in the lurch). Even worse, the nontraditional mortgage market had become so large that its closing radically diminished the pool of new homebuyers, exacerbating the downturn in housing markets, triggering a capital markets crisis, and unleashing the worst global economic downturn in decades.

The properly specified model for subprime mortgage losses should have included variables for global liquidity, competitive pressure on lenders, and the risk of discontinuous shocks to home prices—and the circular logic between home prices and credit losses. Yet readily available data did not exist for these factors. Nor is there straightforward math to link them.

The good news is that this lesson has not been lost on the industry. For example, credit risk modelers from Moody's Economy.com now recommend that loan level models be used to separate safer from riskier loans, but not to forecast aggregate loss rates. Rather, they prefer to forecast losses with models based on aggregate vintage data (not loan level data), and keyed to the current macro outlook (not regional economic history). Loan level models can then be calibrated to the aggregate model's forecast, in a process they call "micro-macro calibration."[19] For such an admittedly imprecise exercise, frequent model updates and recalibration are crucial: the parallel to weather forecasting comes to mind.

To summarize, we have covered the limitations of emotional confidence as a guide to decision making, citing examples of both underconfidence and overconfidence and suggesting a team-based learning process to help analysts recognize the characteristics of accurate recommendations. Sophisticated models present a special case of overconfidence, but this does not mean that decision makers should throw away models and rely entirely on intuition—hardly a realistic choice when wrestling with complex problems in an information-intensive environment. We are going to spend more time on models in Chapters 7, 8, and 9, where we will discuss the importance of mapping out problems to minimize complexity, understanding causal variables, and using judgment to weigh model output against other factors—these steps will help mitigate the risk of overconfident modeling.

Part II

Information

Chapter 4

Fighting Information Overload with Strategy

The scarcity of information-handling ability is an essential feature for the understanding of both individual and organizational behavior.

—Kenneth J. Arrow, *The Limits of Organization*, 1974

Everyone knows what attention is. It is the taking possession by the mind, in clear and vivid form, of one out of what seem several simultaneously possible objects or trains of thought. Focalization, concentration of consciousness are its essence. It implies withdrawal from some things in order to deal effectively with others . . .

—William James, 1890

To be a successful decision-maker, we have to edit.

—Malcolm Gladwell, *Blink,* 2005

One reason we are surprised by episodes of extreme volatility is that the world contains more information than any person, team, or organization can process. Information overload is a fundamental reality of the modern world. This is evident in the markets, where processing huge volumes of data is a full-time job for legions of analysts, traders, and portfolio managers. Managing information is also a crucial skill for intelligence analysts, market researchers, corporate strategists, policymakers, and decision makers in many other fields. True, ever more powerful computers assist us in organizing and analyzing information. Unfortunately, any computational device, human or silicon, faces physical and mathematical limitations, so computers cannot solve the problem of information overload. Further, the same kinds of computers that help one set of decision makers analyze data are doubtlessly in use elsewhere creating new products and strategies—and hence more information. The result: we will never be able to process it all. And the areas we miss may well be breeding grounds for Black Swans.

This chapter highlights the difference between acquiring information under an active strategy and reacting passively to flows of new data. The active strategy focuses on critical issues and combines intuitive reactions to new information with conscious decisions about how to allocate limited processing resources. It also requires decision makers to accept the impossibility of processing all information and to recognize the need to take risk in devoting resources to certain issues and not others. The story of how a medium-sized hedge fund successfully anticipated the subprime mortgage crisis of 2007, whereas a large mutual fund did not, illustrates the consequences of following different information strategies during a volatile environment. And the story of investors in an initial public offering (IPO) who were dazzled by management shows the cost of missing the critical issue.

Winning and Losing Billions in the U.S. Subprime Crisis

In late 2006, the first signs of the long-awaited slowdown in U.S. housing markets were just starting to materialize, although few expected the crisis that would erupt the following summer. A financial services analyst I knew at a successful but relatively small hedge fund sensed the risk that a housing slowdown might pose for mortgage credit quality. This fellow grabbed his "staff" (a single junior analyst) and decided to study the ABX, an index based on a pool of securities backed by subprime mortgages. Because of growing concerns about subprime lending, the ABX had become a hot topic among investors.

In a securitization transaction, lenders transfer a pool of newly originated mortgages to what is called a special-purpose entity, basically a shell corporation funded with just enough equity to keep it off the lender's balance sheet. This entity in turn issues a variety of securities whose interest payments to investors are funded with the cash flow from the mortgage pools.

Thanks to the housing market boom and low loss rates on subprime mortgages, capital-market investors had become increasingly comfortable with these securities, and by late 2006, thousands of them were in circulation. The ABX was an index based on securities from roughly 20 of the largest issuers, a mix of investment banks and mortgage lenders. It provided a convenient way for investors to express a view on the entire market without having to spend time on the nuances of individual securities.

Since the ABX was not itself an actual security, trading it required entering into a derivatives contract, the payoff of which would be determined by future losses in the bonds underlying the index (another version of the credit default swap we saw in Chapter 2). An investor who foresaw serious credit problems could "purchase protection against the ABX." This transaction entailed making periodic payments over the life of the bonds in the ABX, in exchange for a payoff equal to any loss of principal or interest the bonds might suffer. The opposite trade, "selling protection on the ABX," would provide an investor with a stream of periodic cash receipts, but he or she would be on the hook for the losses.

The most important question for anyone trading the ABX in 2006 was how high losses would go. Let me provide some perspective: the highest losses on record for subprime mortgages stemmed from the 1999 vintage; these were estimated at around 7%. Recently, thanks to the housing boom and lower interest rates, losses had fallen to 0–2%, as discussed in Chapter 3. Now that the housing market was slowing down, losses were sure to return to more normal levels. Estimating this level involved judgments about the economy, the housing market, and underwriting quality. The place to start grappling with these questions was the performance of recently originated mortgages—that is, the rate at which new borrowers were falling behind on their payments. This is what our hedge fund analyst decided to do.

But it was no small task. Tracking credit quality required accessing databases of loan level characteristics and analyzing the trends. The industry standard source, First American's LoanPerformance servicing database, contained information on some 24 million prime, alt-A, and subprime loans dating back to 1997, with as many as 100 risk characteristic fields for each newly originated loan and almost 20 fields of performance statistics for each month the loan was outstanding. This totaled to more than 200 gigabytes of information—a lot of data for an analyst to wade through, even with the help of a junior colleague.

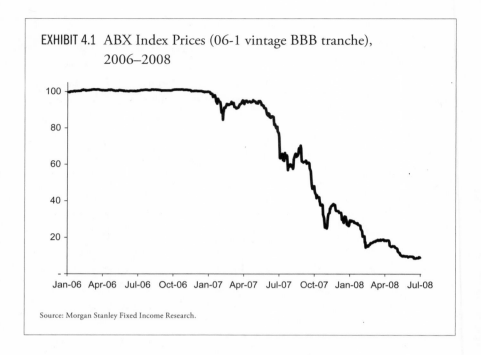

EXHIBIT 4.1 ABX Index Prices (06-1 vintage BBB tranche), 2006–2008

Source: Morgan Stanley Fixed Income Research.

Nonetheless, our two-man team locked itself in a room for several months until they got a feel for the broad trends emerging from the data. Having witnessed consumer credit cycles in Asian markets in the late 1990s, the hedge fund analyst understood the risk of aggressive underwriting. He thought he recognized a dangerous pattern in the U.S. data. Armed with intuition and supporting data, the analyst recommended that his fund buy protection against lower-rated tranches of the ABX index.

By early 2007, subprime borrowers were defaulting at a rapid pace. The underwriting was much worse than investors had realized. As it became clear that losses would surprise to the upside, prices on the lower-rated tranches of the ABX index fell from near 100 to around 50 (Exhibit 4.1). The hedge fund cleared $1 billion in profits on this trade. The analyst then recommended shorting stocks of mortgage lenders, regional banks, and other financial services firms, reasoning that subprime losses would weaken their balance sheets. This strategy produced additional profits for the fund.

Let us contrast this success story with the fate of a large mutual fund company with well over $100 billion in assets in equity and fixed-income funds and a dedicated research staff covering a wide swath of global industries.

I was familiar with this firm and knew some of its analysts and portfolio managers. The fund's analysts maintained earnings forecasts, intrinsic value models, and recommendations for large numbers of stocks. They reported to different portfolio managers and worked to keep them updated on important holdings as well as the analysts' recommendations. Staying on top of 30 to 40 companies is a full-time job. No one had time to undertake a big project like figuring out the ABX. Nor would it have made sense, under this organizational structure, for equity analysts to tangle with what was essentially a fixed-income product.

As the outlook for housing and mortgage markets darkened in the early part of 2007, financial services stocks began to sell off. And they sold off quickly, before the analysts had a clear sense about how to change the assumptions in their earnings forecasts and valuation models. Looking at the target prices generated by the analysts' valuation models, the portfolio managers saw significant upside. Also, using conventional valuation metrics, like price-to-earnings or price-to-book ratios, financial stocks looked suddenly quite cheap, appealing to those managers running portfolios with value styles. The stocks continued to sell off. But a premise of value investing is that one needs "mettle" to buy stocks when they are out of favor.[1] So the managers kept buying. From their peak in early 2007 through mid-2008, financials sold off by over 30% (Exhibit 4.2), seriously hurting the mutual funds' performance and leading to asset outflows, morale issues, turnover in senior management, and a restructuring that involved combining several funds and letting a number of managers go.

The hedge fund I described was not the only one that made huge profits betting against mortgages. And many value-oriented managers lost money on financial stocks. The point is not to promote midsized hedge funds over large mutual funds. Rather, the difference between these firms lay in how they were organized to acquire, process, and analyze information. The hedge fund pursued an active strategy: the analyst focused the vast majority of his resources on mortgage credit quality, a topic he had identified intuitively as a critical issue. In contrast, the mutual fund did not appear to highlight mortgage credit quality as a priority, or if it did, it took no steps to reallocate its resources to focus on it. Instead, it continued to operate under the status quo.

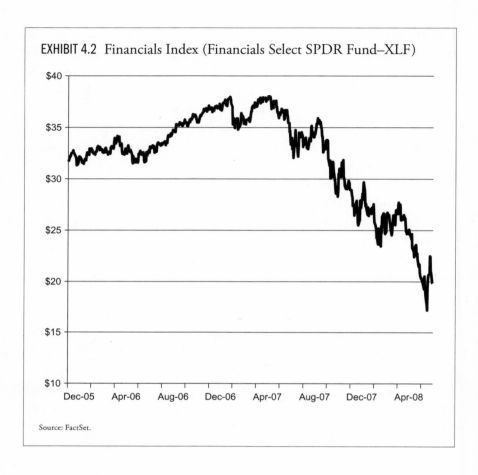

EXHIBIT 4.2   Financials Index (Financials Select SPDR Fund–XLF)

Source: FactSet.

Information Overload in the Markets

One of the reasons the mutual fund did not shift resources, I suspect, was that its management thought its staff of analysts gave it control over the information its fund managers needed to make decisions. But no such thing is possible. The quantity of information relevant to stock prices is, in practice, unlimited. That is why a strategic approach is necessary, involving conscious decisions about what kinds of information to focus on and what kinds to ignore.

To state the obvious, the world contains a great deal of information. Consider the physical world: according to one estimate, the subatomic organization of a one-kilogram rock is equivalent to 10^{27} bits of information, too much for the combined memory of all the computers in the world to store.[2] In practice, the quantity of information associated with even a single stock is so great that no individual or team could stay on top it all. As an example, see the summary of the data released by and about Freddie Mac during a single day, August 6, 2008, when company released its 2008 second-quarter earnings.

To put this information into context, one would have needed to understand something about Freddie Mac. There was no shortage of information about the company: a news search for articles on Freddie Mac over the preceding 3 months would have yielded 3,259 articles, and Googling Freddie Mac would have produced approximately 4.6 million listings. Of course, during the summer of 2008 Freddie Mac was a controversial stock. A screen on a stock in a sleepy sector would have generated a shorter list of news stories. For example, on the day when an aircraft leasing company called AerCap Holdings reported second-quarter 2008 earnings, only 5 news items surfaced on the tape. However, a news search on the industry classification

---

Freddie Mac's 2008 Second-Quarter Earnings, August 6, 2008

◆ The company issued a press release summarizing its financial results at 6:00 AM, accompanied by a set of 51 slides, with tables of information on loan credit quality and performance, updates on controls, and other important financial variables, many of which were new disclosures.

◆ At the same time, the company released its 10-Q, a 181-page document filed with the Securities and Exchange Commission.

◆ From 6:02 to 9:31 AM, Dow Jones News published 35 headlines on Freddie Mac, mostly single sentences or phrases relating key points from the earnings release, as well as a small number of short articles (2 or 3 paragraphs each) on such things as investor reactions to the news and an interview with the chief financial officer (CFO). I counted 128 articles published by the Bloomberg News Service, including media reports in different languages.

◆ At 9:40 AM, Moody's issued a press release stating that it was continuing to review the ratings of Freddie Mac's preferred stock and its bank financial strength rating, although second-quarter 2008 losses were "within its expectations." The press release was posted to the tape, and the news services published headlines summarizing the main points. Later on, Fitch downgraded Freddie's preferred stock rating.

- ◆ Freddie's management hosted a conference call which ran from 10:02 AM Eastern Standard Time to 11:23 AM. Company management spoke for the first 40 minutes, then took questions for 40 minutes from analysts and investors. A transcript of the call was available a few hours later, permitting a quicker review of what was discussed, but obviously missing the information included in the tone of voice.
- ◆ Sell-side analysts publish reports on company results, sometimes immediately, sometimes after a day or two. I noticed that reports on Freddie's results were released by Merrill Lynch at 10:29 AM and by Friedman Billings at 10:46 AM.

"aircraft leasing" would have generated 1,066 articles in the preceding 3 months, and a broader search under "airlines" (the company's end-market) would have yielded 62,081 articles.

In practice, investment companies confront these volumes of information by investing in expert knowledge; that is, by hiring analysts, retaining consultants, or subscribing to research services. People who understand industries and companies can cut through the noise and identify what is important. For this reason, expert knowledge is a necessary component of the active information strategy, although it is not by itself sufficient to overcome overload.

Amplification of Information by the Media and Other Traders

Whatever their quantity, data about a company do not constitute the entire information set relevant to the company's stock price. Information about how other people regard the data is also important. Media reports mix factual information with suppositions, inferences, opinions, and sometimes errors. Journalists may try to find explanations for recent price action, even if the price movements are essentially random. In this way, they may be injecting meaningless "noise" into the market.[3] But even so, the message could have a real impact. The media shape public opinion,[4] and since traders read media reports, even scurrilous commentary can become relevant to market prices. For this reason, investors ignore the media at their peril.

In addition to monitoring the media, an investor must understand how other investors or traders respond to information. Collective opinion forms in part through imitation (rational or otherwise, as discussed in Chapter 1). Decision makers who are insensitive to the risk of abrupt "phase shifts" in consensus opinion may be caught unprepared by episodes of extreme volatility.

Talking with analysts, traders, and investors; listening to their questions on conference calls; or watching how stocks, options, and bonds react to new information can give some sense of the consensus view. But even with unlimited time, it would be impossible to understand collective opinion fully. To do so would require understanding not just the opinions of other market participants but also how those participants regarded the opinions of others, and so forth in an infinitely recursive loop. Keynes makes this point in his famous reference to the beauty contests once popular in the newspapers:

> Professional investment may be likened to those newspaper competitions in which the competitors have to pick out the six prettiest faces from a hundred photographs, the prize being awarded to the competitor whose choice most nearly corresponds to the average preferences of the competitors as a whole; so that each competitor has to pick, not those faces which he himself finds prettiest, but those which he thinks likeliest to catch the fancy of the other competitors, all of whom are looking at the problem from the same point of view. It is not a case of choosing those which, to the best of one's judgment, are really the prettiest, nor even those which average opinion genuinely thinks the prettiest. We have reached the third degree where we devote our intelligences to anticipating what average opinion expects the average opinion to be. And there are some, I believe, who practise the fourth, fifth and higher degrees.[5]

As an aside, we have here another reason why the market cannot be perfectly efficient: to fully discount all information about stocks, the market (which consists of traders) would need to understand all information about the market (which includes the opinions of traders). No system possesses complete self-knowledge. The inability of the market to fully understand itself is one of the reasons that credit cycles, such as the one we have just experienced, end up so severe: it takes time for lenders to recognize that the underwriting has been loosened too far, and during this period, they originate a lot of bad loans. The limits of self-consciousness, for individuals as well as groups, is one of the reasons why I believe that society will never banish the Black Swan, a theme that we will return to in Chapter 9.

Although information overload cannot be solved, making decisions does not require mastering all information, but rather reducing it to a smaller set of relevant data. The way we do this is through computation.

The Nature and Limits of Computation

In an effort to handle growing quantities of information, Wall Street has invested enormous sums in computer technology. The hedge fund analyst in our case study used statistical models to wade through a large database of mortgage performance. Thanks to ongoing innovations in information technology, computer processing power continues to advance, for example, in models used to project subprime credit losses (Chapter 3) as well as more complex scenario analysis and Monte Carlo simulations (Chapters 7 and 8) and algorithmic investing (Chapter 9), where computer programs buy and sell stocks without human intervention.

Like expert knowledge, computational power is helpful, important, and necessary. But no matter how powerful computers become, they remain subject to physical and mathematical constraints, just like any computational device, including human brains. To make the best possible decisions during periods of extreme volatility, we need to understand the inherent limitations of our processing tools.

Physical Limits of Computation

One reason that computation cannot solve all of our information processing needs is that computation consumes energy. We sometimes draw a line between mental processes and the physical world. In this worldview, computation seems like an abstract process, just as we tend to think of consciousness or imagination as more spiritual than material. But computation is a physical process that consumes energy and is subject to the laws of physics.

Computation transforms a relatively disordered set of inputs into a more orderly set of outputs. To take a simple example, imagine calculating the average of 10 numbers on a hand calculator: The output is a single number, a much smaller quantity of information than the numbers you punched in, but it is more ordered, giving you a single statistic that describes the set of input numbers. Information theorists describe computation as a means of reducing *entropy*, a term that can be thought of loosely as a measure of randomness. So far, so good: this is how computation helps us compress large volumes of information into something more meaningful.

However, computation is also a mechanical process subject to the second law of thermodynamics, which requires that entropy continually increase. To offset the reduction in entropy associated with producing a more ordered set of information, the computational device must consume energy and then expel heat, a highly disordered form of energy. Scientists have studied such properties as the maximum theoretical computational power and the maximum speed of computing devices as a function of available energy.[6] The bottom line: while brains and computers can process a great deal of information, they cannot answer all the questions relevant to stocks, markets, or other important issues, because they do not have an unlimited energy supply.

Mathematical Limits of Computation—The "Halting Problem"

Energy is not the only limit. No matter how powerful computers may become, there are mathematical limits to the ability of any processing device to generate useful results.

In the 1930s, the code breaker and computer scientist Alan Turing discovered what has come to be called the "halting problem." Think of an algorithm as any systematic procedure employed by a computing device to solve a problem—in other words, a kind of mindless, turn-the-crank routine or program.[7] In the early 20th century, there was great excitement in the scientific community about the potential for algorithmic processes to solve the outstanding problems of mathematics. To understand the power and limits of algorithmic processing, Turing developed a theoretical version of a general-purpose computer, which has come to be called a Universal Turing Machine. As he worked through the mathematical implications of this theoretical construct, Turing did not reach an optimistic conclusion. Rather, he proved that while some algorithms will produce the right answer, others will go on calculating forever without producing any results. Further, one cannot necessarily tell in advance whether an algorithmic process will halt, making it difficult to know which problems are computable and which are not. This finding has come to be called the "halting problem."[8] Put simply, it means that some problems are not solvable.

Computer designers go to great lengths to avoid the "halting problem" in the software they sell. But we have all encountered the problem when on occasion our personal computer "freezes" or "hangs." You can find the problem in other areas. For example, projecting financial statements in a spreadsheet program typically involves circular logic to get the balance sheet and income statement to reconcile. Microsoft Excel gives the user the option to specify the maximum number of iterations after which the calculation function stops. Without that option, spreadsheets with circular logic would not stop calculating.

The "halting problem" applies to any algorithmic process. Imagine that a portfolio manager asks an analyst to predict the implications of a housing slowdown on mortgage credit quality. If the analyst tried to calculate the answer by applying the theorems of classic macroeconomics (in essence, following an algorithm), he might not come to an answer, because of the complexity and circularity of the relationships that tie home prices, credit losses, and liquidity together. If not told to stop, the analyst might continue trying to solve the problem indefinitely (or until losing interest and finding a different job). The portfolio manager cannot know in advance if the "human algorithm" will halt.[9]

Even algorithms that reliably produce answers may take too long to run. Complexity theory, a branch of computational theory, teaches that for certain algorithms, the time needed to compute the results increases exponentially with the number of inputs. For example, to solve a game of chess by running out all the possible moves from start to finish would require something like 10^{120} computations. A computer as large as the universe and operating since the beginning of time would not be able to fully solve a game of chess in this way. The problem is considered "intractable," as are many classes of problems in mathematics, not to mention the real world.[10]

Too much information, and not enough time, energy, or computational power, leaves us with information overload. There is no escape, because it is just one way we experience entropy, and as we know from the laws of thermodynamics, entropy must continuously increase. In practical terms, more or faster computers will not deliver us from information overload, because other people will use them, too, so the collective result will be ever more information about the world.

So what should one do? The idea behind information strategy is to allocate our limited computational power as judiciously as possible.

Information Strategy

The elements of an information strategy include zeroing in on critical issues, reacting intuitively to new developments, and making thoughtful decisions about allocating limited resources. I have summarized some of these steps in Exhibit 4.3.

The dean of corporate strategy, Michael Porter, reminds us that strategy means deciding both what to do and what not to do. Managers have become caught up in the goal of operational effectiveness, Porter observes, and have lost sight of the need to make trade-offs. An organization that tries to maximize its proficiency in every activity ends up with an indistinct strategy, a vague positioning, and a "me-too" set of skills. "The essence of strategy," Porter writes, "is choosing what *not* to do."[11]

In our case, strategy means emphasizing certain types of information and downplaying others. Trying to stay on top of everything would probably leave you with a set of positions that looked very much like the market. Your thinking might be well calibrated, but you would have no resources left to achieve discrimination—a situation in which superior performance would remain elusive.

What kinds of information warrant strategic focus? The answer is information relevant to the "critical issues" or "critical uncertainties," a concept I have borrowed from the discipline of scenario planning.[12] A critical issue is a causal variable with two characteristics. First, its outcome will have a significant impact on the value of a security (or some other question). Second, its

---

EXHIBIT 4.3 Steps to Developing an Information Strategy

- Set aside time to think about emerging issues.
- Pay attention to intuitive reactions to new developments.
- Make a list of critical issues and discuss them with staff or peers.
- Reserve flexibility to reallocate resources (time, staff, budget) to critical issues; an organization that cannot do this quickly is not well positioned to anticipate or react to Black Swans.
- Accept the risk of leaving some bases uncovered.
- Cultivate, develop, or acquire expert knowledge.

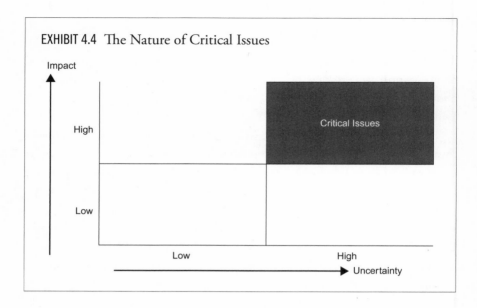

EXHIBIT 4.4 The Nature of Critical Issues

outcome is highly uncertain, spanning a wide range of possible values. Exhibit 4.4 illustrates these two properties. Getting a handle on critical issues will help decompose a problem into its most important causative elements. Other variables are not worth the focus, as they contribute mostly noise.[13]

In the hedge fund story, mortgage credit risk qualified as a critical issue. It turned out to have enormous implications for the price of the ABX and financial services stocks. And the range of possible outcomes was large (in fact, larger than most realized). In Chapter 2, the critical issues for Providian included the economy, the credit cycle, the stability of Providian's business model, and competitive pressure. In Chapter 3, credit quality and liquidity risk were critical issues for both CIT Group and Countrywide.

In a normal environment, humans naturally focus on critical issues, as do other animals.[14] However, when information becomes overwhelming, focus gets tougher. Madeleine Van Hecke, a psychologist who has studied blind spots in human behavior, argues that people have trouble stopping and thinking, a problem she attributes to the information overload of modern society. "We fail to think," she writes, "because we are snowed under by the sheer amount of new information we are trying to take in."[15]

Similarly, decision-making expert Gary Klein warns that the proliferation of information technologies (and hence of ever growing piles of data) can become paralyzing:

Information technologies have a very strong tendency to reduce users to passive recipients of data, particularly users who are not intimately familiar with the way hardware and software is designed, which makes them reluctant to try to work around problems or strike out on their own. With the emergence of information technology, we may be creating a new breed of decision-makers who become mentally blind in that they will have lost their ability to look, to search.[16]

One of the purposes of coming up with an information strategy is to get decision makers to stop and think. Then, they can make conscious decisions about how to allocate their resources, rather than responding passively to the flow of new information. In our case study, the hedge fund analyst allocated limited resources (his time and his junior colleague's) to searching for information relevant to mortgage credit. This strategy was not riskless, because while he was so engaged, he must have ignored a great deal of information about other topics relevant to financial services stocks. In contrast, his counterparts at the mutual fund continued to operate under their standard sector-based research model with no apparent effort to focus on mortgage credit risk. In this case, the payoff to the right allocation decision was sizable.

In the military context, information overload is referred to as the "fog of war." Overwhelmed by the stimulus of combat, commanders lose the ability to make decisions. The key to moving forward is focusing on the critical issues unique to the battlefield. Consider the thoughts of Delta Force operator Paul Howe during a 1992 firefight in Mogadishu, as recounted in *Black Hawk Down*:

> Howe felt [his team of operators] were the perfect soldiers for this situation. They'd learned to filter out the confusion, put up a mental curtain. The only information that came fully through was the most critical at that moment. Howe could ignore the pop of a rifle or the snap of a nearby round. It was usually just somebody shooting airballs. It would take chips flying from a wall near him to make him react.[17]

The Role of Intuition in Identifying Critical Issues

Sometimes critical issues are obvious. But often they pertain to emerging issues that are not yet well understood. In these cases, identifying them may be more art than science. Look at fully quantitative investing, a field one might associate with scientific precision, not gut-level feel. Au contraire, explains David Shaw of DE Shaw:

> One thing I think is often misunderstood, not just about our type of business [quantitative investing] but about the nature of science in general, is that the hardest part, the part that really distinguishes a world-class scientist from a knowledgeable laboratory technician, is that *right-brain, creative part.* . . . Although it might seem surprising, that sort of [creative] thinking actually is very important to us in the first phase of our work. That really is what makes it possible for us to generate hypotheses, to come up with ideas to test. It's definitely a *non-mechanical process.* It requires people who've developed a *gut-level feel* for the market models we've built up over the years. . . .[18] (emphasis added)

The "right-brain, creative part" Shaw refers to is human intuition. For now, intuition is our best tool for recognizing critical issues, because it is substantially more powerful than modern computers, thanks to the brain's 100 trillion intraneural connections, massive parallel processing capabilities, and ability to search large volumes of expert knowledge and retrieve information in fractions of a second.[19] Computers may one day become powerful enough to identify critical issues, but for now they do not have as many connections as the human brain and they lack even the most rudimentary form of conceptual reasoning.

Shaw's comments are similar to what Gary Klein has observed in studies of how nurses, pilots, and firefighters act in stressful, high-stakes situations. These decision makers do not follow the textbook approach, drawing up lists of alternatives and choosing the optimal course of action based on some weighting system. Instead, they intuitively pick up critical cues recognized through expert knowledge. The cues then prompt the choice of action.[20]

Military history also demonstrates the importance of intuition. Napoleon was noted for his "coup d'oeil," the ability to size up the battlefield at a single glance and decide how to deploy his forces.[21]

Obstacles to Information Strategy

Coming up with an information strategy may seem straightforward. In practice, people run into many kinds of obstacles:

Where Effective Strategies Break Down

- Using "brute force" in search of data
- Relying on biased sources
- "Data mining" at the expense of conceptual thinking
- Giving in to communication overload
- Succumbing to bureaucratic inertia
- Failing to tap expert knowledge
- Failing to allocate limited resources thoughtfully

Trying to Follow a "Brute-Force" Approach

Without a strategy, information gathering devolves to a brute-force approach, a systematic and exhaustive process to collect all relevant information. Since it is not physically possible to collect all information, brute force becomes a trial-and-error process, like wandering randomly through a maze, and is thus unlikely to produce valuable insights, except by accident.[22] Of course, without expert knowledge, there may be no alternative.

Data Mining

The speed and memory capacity of computers may seem to help with brute-force information gathering and analysis. While they cannot reason conceptually or intuitively recognize critical issues, computers can identify correlations in numerical data. But since their operations are limited to finite data sets, the resulting output misses variables that lie outside those sets.[23] Decision makers who rely on data mining to economize on human analysis may overlook Black Swans whose force did not influence past data.

Relying on Low-Cost or Biased Information Sources

Sometimes we start out searching randomly, but are soon attracted to low-cost, easy, familiar, or friendly information sources. There is nothing wrong with low-cost information, except that its purveyors may have a commercial interest in providing it to you, which is why it costs little. For example, the media may emphasize new and exciting information to interest you in reading their stories and being exposed to their advertisers. Broker-dealers may issue buy and sell recommendations in an effort to encourage investors to trade more frequently, producing more commissions. Tiring of financial statement analysis, a new analyst may find it easier to listen to friendly peers. But these friends have an interest in "talking their books" to encourage other investors to bid up stocks they already own. Competitive intelligence expert Ben Gilad warns chief executive officers (CEOs) against relying on small circles of trusted advisers for competitive information gathering. These advisers typically include investment bankers, consultants, and attorneys, all with commercial agendas to pursue. As the CEO and these advisers travel in the same circles, dine in the same restaurants, and read the same periodicals, the CEO's information sources start to overlap, and the "walls may close in" around her vision.[24]

Communication Overload

In a large firm, analysts may be so burdened by duties to keep portfolio managers and other colleagues up-to-date that they lack the time to research emerging issues. No doubt, collaboration provides important benefits: for example, a division of labor across products or industries makes it easier for analysts to focus on emerging issues within their sectors. But collaboration is also costly, because even a quick e-mail or a shout across the trading floor is time consuming, and communicating within large organizations often involves detailed reports, attendance at meetings, and other bureaucratic time sinks.

The larger the firm, the more colleagues each person will have, and thus more time must be spent in communicating. The burden of peer-to-peer communication increases geometrically when markets become volatile, because fast-changing situations require more frequent updates. I suspect that part of the problem at the mutual fund in our case study was a high ratio of portfolio managers per analyst. This high ratio required analysts not only to spend time with multiple decision makers, but also to stay on top of too many stocks of interest to different managers. In a similar vein, analysts working in the Central Intelligence Agency have been known to complain that they spend so much time on current reporting that they cannot focus on long-term forecasting or analysis.[25] We could call this "communication overload." It is typical of the bureaucratic complications that engulf large organizations. The implication for investment firms—and possibly other organizations with a focus on forecasting and decision making—is that the optimal size might be relatively small.

Bureaucratic Inertia

Another problem with large organizations is the inertia that builds up when management turnover leads to an institutional loss of memory. In stable environments, it may be sensible for new managers to continue the policies of their predecessors, even if they no longer have access to the information that motivated past decisions. But inertia can hamstring an organization when the environment becomes more volatile.[26] In formulating an information strategy, decision makers ought to be looking not to past practices but instead at critical issues in the current environment, and reorganizing as necessary.

Lack of Expert Knowledge

Intuition works by matching patterns in the current environment to patterns in our memory. For technical issues, this requires expert knowledge. Those who had not followed credit cycles in emerging markets in the 1990s would have had a hard time recognizing the warning signs in the U.S. subprime mortgage market. Similarly, people who did not understand the quality of loans on the balance sheets of financial services firms, or their leverage, would not have easily predicted their vulnerability to a credit cycle. As such, cultivation of expert knowledge, either by hiring experienced analysts or subscribing to the services of research firms, should be a priority for decision makers who have the budget to do so.

Limited Resources

Finally, taking time to think about critical issues detracts from other productive activities. In competitive businesses, with all resources focused on current production, stopping to think may be an unaffordable luxury. Recall how much time the hedge fund analyst in our case study put into studying mortgage credit quality. Obviously, individual investors—or professional traders with a limited staff—would have trouble devoting so much time to a single issue while simultaneously managing a diversified portfolio.

Everyone's resources are limited. For this reason, making strategic decisions about information entails risk—the risk of searching in the wrong area and being surprised.[27] If nothing else, investors and other decision makers should make these determinations consciously, rather than being passively swept along in the massive flows of information that characterize the markets and the modern world.

Information and Strategy: Advance America

We will close this chapter with a second story illustrating the importance of information strategy. In the summer of 2006, I was asked to conduct due diligence on a company called Advance America, which was planning an IPO. My role as a research analyst was to give my firm's equity commitment committee my views on valuation, earnings, and risk factors.

Advance America was a "payday lender," making small-denomination, short-term loans to borrowers in a cash pinch. These loans averaged $300, lasted a couple of weeks, were secured by a postdated check, and carried fees equivalent to an annual percentage rate of 700% to 800%. This high interest rate jogged my memory of other high-priced lending businesses that got in trouble with consumer activists and regulators (Providian being just one example among many). After a little thought, I identified regulatory risk as a critical issue and made the strategic decision to allocate substantial time to researching it. My resources were not extensive, but fortunately I had a college intern named Yared Alula on my team that summer. I asked him to search the Internet for references to payday lending, then pick up the phone and talk to any regulator, attorney, or community activist who would take his call. Yared discovered significant concerns: many likened the business to a legal form of "loan sharking," especially for consumers who did not promptly pay off the loans and thus got trapped by the high interest payments in a deepening cycle of indebtedness.

Another issue that caught my attention was the relationship between payday lenders and banks. About a dozen states had passed laws severely curtailing payday lending or banning it outright. But if a payday lender operated as the agent of an out-of-state bank, it could get around those laws. The reason is that under federal regulations, banks are subject only to the laws of the states in which they are domiciled.

In searching for information on the Internet, we happened on the agenda for a payday lending conference, which included a speaker from the Federal Deposit Insurance Corporation (FDIC), one of the main regulators for banks. I called him, explained my purpose, and asked how regulators viewed the banks' involvement in this business. He refused to say anything but repeat information contained in the FDIC's previous public statements. His tone struck me as icy. As we continued to research the subject, we found that one of the FDIC's directors had broken ranks with his peers, publicly condemning banks' involvement in payday lending—a sign of growing controversy.

Another clue came when we checked in with the company's auditors. During our conversation, the audit partner mentioned that the company's arrangements with banks seemed risky from a business perspective, although the accounting was completely proper.

Finally, we spent some time with our lawyers reviewing pending lawsuits against the company. The magnitude of possible damages did not seem problematic, but we noticed that the lawsuits were seeking to characterize the firm's bank relationships as illegal.

Regulatory risk was not the only critical issue. The company had generated fast revenue growth and strong margins, and we needed to consider whether it could continue producing profits at these levels. We spent time going through U.S. census data to understand the population of households that fit the demographic profile for payday lending customers. Then we compared this information to the number of payday branches in each state, to form a rough judgment about the extent to which the market might have become saturated. The importance of the bank model suddenly became clear, because the 30-odd states that allowed payday lending looked increasingly competitive. Much of the remaining growth opportunity seemed concentrated in those states that had legal barriers to payday lending, which could only be surmounted by operating as the agent of a bank.

As the IPO approached, we did other standard due diligence, such as visiting the company's headquarters, interviewing management, and analyzing the financial statements. We requested follow-up information ranging from human resources policies to management reports, but we focused our available time on the two key issues we had identified as being critical—namely regulatory risk and revenue growth.

It soon became apparent that management had made a positive impression on investors during the IPO road show—not surprisingly, since it was a competent, articulate, and professional team that could point to an excellent track record. The CEO had worked in Washington, DC, and had an extensive set of political contacts. The chief operating officer had a background with one of the largest public consumer finance companies. The chief financial officer had a strong command of the numbers. Investors told me they really liked this management team as opposed to other operators who seemed more "entrepreneurial," to put it politely.

With strong demand, the IPO price was raised from $13 to $15 per share. After the pricing, the shares continued to appreciate, peaking at almost $24. I initiated coverage with an underweight rating. While giving credit to the company's scale, efficiency, and revenue growth, I argued that the payday industry was entering a more mature stage of development, forcing even the best-run operators to seek out growth in states with hostile political environments, which they accomplished by crafting partnerships with out-of-state banks. I warned that

> Payday operators may be vulnerable to regulatory and legal risk when they partner with banks to avoid unfavorable laws in certain states (the so-called "agent-bank" model). As disclosed at length in the IPO prospectus, some states have banned the agent-bank model, an attorney general may be investigating it, putative class action lawsuits are attacking it, and senior bank regulators have spoken out against the practice. For Advance America, the agent-bank model accounted for almost 30% of revenues in the first nine months of 2004. In setting our price target, we discount the company's agent-bank revenues by 50%, reflecting our subjective assessment of regulatory, litigation, and legislative risk. The market may be less concerned.[28]

A few weeks later, bank regulators announced a new set of rules governing relationships between banks and payday operators that made it uneconomic to continue the partnership model. Advance America's shares collapsed from the low $20s to around $12 per share. An immediate 50% correction qualifies as a single-company Black Swan, an example of extreme volatility playing out against a backdrop of calm markets (Exhibit 4.5).

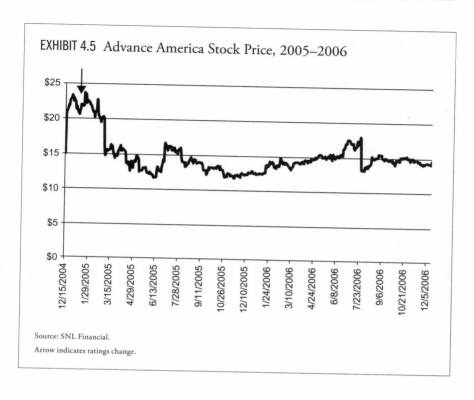

EXHIBIT 4.5 Advance America Stock Price, 2005–2006

Source: SNL Financial.

Arrow indicates ratings change.

Why did the stock drop so far? After all, the regulatory risks were disclosed in the prospectus. What had happened was that investors had followed a different strategy from mine: rather than searching for information on critical issues, they opted to rely on an "easy" information source, namely the management meetings arranged during the roadshow, for which they did not even need to leave their offices. As a result, the collective view on the stock was "fragile" (Chapter 1); investors' understanding of the company did not accurately reflect the critical issues. In Chapter 6, we will explore how to obtain useful information from management interviews.

Chapter 5

Making Decisions in Real Time
*How to React to New Information Without
Falling Victim to Cognitive Dissonance*

Their judgment was based more on wishful thinking than on
a sound calculation of probabilities; for the usual thing among
men is that when they want something they will, without any
reflection, leave that to hope, while they will employ the full
force of reason in rejecting what they find unpalatable.

—Thucydides, *History of the Peloponnesian War*,
(c. 460 B.C.–c. 395 B.C.)

Such ill-founded judgments were accepted without debate by
the Kennedy administration, as they had been by its Demo-
cratic and Republican predecessors. We failed to analyze our
assumptions critically, then or later.

—Robert S. McNamara,
In Retrospect: The Tragedy and Lessons of Vietnam, 1995

We are like sailors who must rebuild their ship on the open
sea, never able to dismantle it in drydock and to reconstruct it
there out of the best materials.

—Otto Neurath[1]

I will look at any additional evidence to confirm the opinion
to which I have already come.

—Lord Molson, British politician (1903–1991)

The textbook approach presumes decision makers have all the time in the world to assemble and weigh information, but in the real world, things happen on the fly. From 2000 through late 2005, Fannie Mae's stock fell by about 30%, a result of political pressure, slowing growth, and accounting problems. At least there was time to analyze the issues. In October 2007, Fannie's stock fell 30% in a single day. As discussed in the previous chapter, the speed of computation is limited by physical and mathematical constraints. Extreme volatility—when great change is compressed into short time periods—does not loosen those constraints. In a world with Black Swans, reacting quickly and accurately to new information is a critical survival skill.

Further complicating the decision maker's job are certain human quirks that affect how we react to new information. Terms such as *cognitive dissonance, change blindness*, and the *boiling frog syndrome* refer to the trouble people sometimes have changing their minds until the evidence is overwhelming—at which point it may be too late to take action. This kind of behavior vexes decision makers in many other fields besides investing. For example, the possibility that close-minded thinking may blind analysts to signs of impending attack is a major concern in the intelligence community.

This chapter has two goals. The first is to help the reader recognize cognitive dissonance and so avoid it. The second is to explain the *diagnostic power* of new information, the key to reacting properly. Two stories illustrate how to react effectively to new information—and how not to. One involves the commercial finance company CIT, and the other the credit card issuer Discover Financial Services.

How Not to React in Real Time: The Spin-Off of CIT

We last encountered CIT in Chapter 4, when I recommended shorting the stock in 2008 in anticipation of a funding crisis (which, unfortunately, by late 2009 was to force the company into bankruptcy). But this was not the first time CIT had run into funding problems.

In late 1999, CIT had just announced the acquisition of a large Canadian finance company called Newcourt. The transaction was billed as an opportunity to gain scale and enter new markets. Controversial from the start, it became more so when, even before the deal closed, Newcourt's quarterly earnings fell short of company guidance, a sign that neither it nor CIT had a handle on the situation. CIT renegotiated the acquisition price, but investors questioned its due diligence, strategy, and negotiating skills. Confidence in CIT weakened. At the same time, the macro backdrop was turning gloomy as the technology stock boom was coming to an end and the economy began slipping into recession. CIT's debt spreads began to widen, jeopardizing its ability to raise cost-effective financing, without which it could not remain competitive.

In March 2001, CIT surprised the markets by announcing that it would sell itself to Tyco, the industrial conglomerate run by the colorful Dennis Kozlowski, for $35 per share or 1.5 times book value. The idea behind the deal was that Tyco's various industrial businesses would benefit from an in-house financing capacity, much as General Electric was thought to gain advantage from its GE Capital subsidiary. However, there was a small problem. GE Capital enjoyed the low borrowing costs of its AAA-rated parent, which allowed it to earn high returns even in mature businesses. Tyco did not have a AAA rating; in fact, its funding costs were even higher than CIT's.[2] The transaction did nothing to address uncompetitive funding costs, the root cause of CIT's deteriorating market position. It was instead the desperate union of two troubled firms, and not much good was to come of it.

Once CIT joined the Tyco fold, it proceeded to recognize sizable charge-offs from poor-quality loans taken on in the Newcourt acquisition, as well as its own collection of problem assets. These charges were costly to Tyco and contributed to the collapse of its stock price and the removal of its management team, including Kozlowski, who was later convicted of misappropriating $400 million of company assets. Tyco's new management team decided it had had enough of CIT and opted to spin it off at the first available opportunity, in the summer of 2002.

My colleague Athina Meehan and I initiated coverage with an underweight rating on July 5, 2002, shortly after the issuance of shares in the spin-off. We warned investors that

> regaining investor confidence in the economic profit potential of CIT will take time and effort. On the heels of mediocre credit performance over the last three years and the early disastrous association with Tyco, CIT's debt is now trading at indicative spreads in excess of 260 bps. Without much lower funding costs, the company will not be able to compete against the likes of

Bank of America, GE Capital, Wells Fargo, and Citigroup, in our view, as well as the thousands of local and regional banks that fund themselves with deposits. To issue debt at narrower spreads, CIT will have to win back the confidence of fixed-income investors. However, without low-cost funding, CIT may have difficulty demonstrating the growth and profitability necessary to rebuild investor confidence. It's a Catch-22 situation, which management will work hard to overcome, but which presents enough of a challenge for us to hold out for a lower valuation on the stock.[3]

Several risk factors concerned us. First, we knew CIT had taken significant credit-related charges while it was part of Tyco, but given the speed with which Tyco had disgorged CIT, we could not rule out the possibility of more credit problems, perhaps serious ones. If so, the capital markets might refuse to refinance the company's debt, raising the possibility of a liquidity crisis. Conversely, it was also possible that CIT's debt spreads might improve, the company might regain a stronger market position, and eventually some firm (this time, one with *lower* financing costs) might acquire it at a premium price.

We summarized these possibilities in a probability tree and assigned values to the various terminal branches (Exhibit 5.1). The weighted-average value across the branches came to $23 per share, which coincidentally was where the underwriters priced the new shares. Since our rating system was defined on a relative basis, and thinking that other stocks in our coverage universe offered legitimate upside potential, we opted for the underweight rating.

In the next few months, the stock sold off as investors worried about the credit, funding, and liquidity risks, just as we had warned. By October, the stock had traded below $15, and it dropped near this level again in early 2003. In our probability tree, $15 would have corresponded to a scenario where additional credit problems were a virtual certainty.

What was my reaction? When it got down to $15, I thought about upgrading the stock, as I had no new information to indicate that credit or funding problems had deepened. I had been studying the company's aircraft portfolio, which I thought might warrant an impairment charge, given the poor health of the airline industry. I was discussing the company with a client and wondering aloud about the stock's valuation when he interrupted: "I sure wouldn't buy any stock with exposure to the aircraft industry—did you hear what happened at Heathrow?"

EXHIBIT 5.1 Probability Tree for CIT

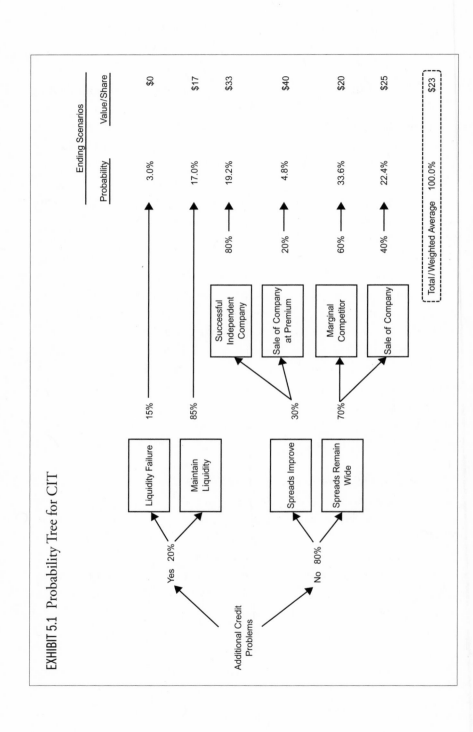

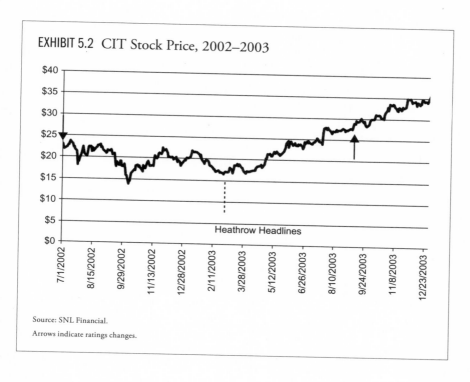

EXHIBIT 5.2 CIT Stock Price, 2002–2003

Source: SNL Financial.

Arrows indicate ratings changes.

I had not, but a quick news search revealed that there had been a scare that weekend over the possibility of a terrorist attack involving surface-to-air missiles (SAMs), presumably targeting one of the hundreds of passenger aircraft transiting the airport on a daily basis. What such an attack would have meant for the airline industry and hence CIT (given its portfolio) was hard to fathom, but it would not have been positive. With such risks floating about, I felt comfortable keeping CIT as an underweight, especially given my concern about the company's credit and funding issues. I put the stock out of my mind and focused on other things.

As time rolled on, CIT's credit profile began to improve, but I stayed focused on the aircraft portfolio. By September 2003, the economy had begun to look a little less dismal and worries about credit and liquidity risk at CIT were starting to fade. By then it was too late to reap any remaining benefit of the underweight call: I finally upgraded the stock to equal-weight at $27.55.[4] (See Exhibit 5.2.) What might have been a 30% gain on the underweight recommendation at $23 (had I upgraded at $16) ended up instead as a 20% loss. Where did I go wrong?

New Information and Cognitive Dissonance

CIT is an example of an inaccurate reaction to new information. We will return in a moment for a full diagnosis. But first let us review some research on cognitive dissonance, which in my experience is a frequent contributor to real-time mistakes. In a nutshell, cognitive dissonance arises when we cannot resolve complex problems and opt instead to ignore conflicting data; the result is that we become blind to changing circumstances.

The Computational Roots of Cognitive Dissonance

When new information conflicts with our preexisting hypotheses, we have a problem that needs to be resolved. *Cognitive dissonance* refers to the state of tension that occurs when a person holds two ideas, beliefs, attitudes, or opinions that are psychologically inconsistent.[5] This conflict manifests itself as a state of mental tension or dissonance, the intensity of which is visible in magnetic resonance imaging studies of the brain.[6] The theory was developed in 1957 by Leon Festinger, who observed in a series of experiments that people would change their attitudes to make them more consistent with actions they had just taken. In popular usage, cognitive dissonance refers to the tendency to ignore information that conflicts with preexisting views, to rationalize certain behaviors to make them seem more consistent with self-image, or to change attitudes to make them consistent with actions already taken. In some cases, it is the equivalent of telling ourselves "little white lies," but in other cases it no doubt contributes to logical errors like the "confirmation trap," where people deliberately search for data to confirm existing views rather than challenge them.[7]

There is no avoiding dissonance, a natural part of decision making. After all, any decision entails the risk of being wrong. Generating an investment hypothesis inevitably exposes the investor to dissonance because, as discussed in Chapter 1, the thesis must be different from the "null hypothesis" that the market's current view is correct. To picture the dissonance, imagine you are arguing with an avid bull about why his investment thesis is wrong.

Unfortunately, the brain does not have unlimited resources to resolve dissonant situations. Some of our hypotheses, like self-image or other deeply held beliefs, are too complicated to rethink on the fly. Indeed, many of life's questions are "intractable," unsolvable in any realistic amount of time (Chapter 4). Faced with these conundrums, the brain appears to make a cost-benefit decision, and sometimes it take the easy way out, ignoring, rationalizing, or changing an attitude instead of trying to resolve the dissonance between a hypothesis and conflicting data. Presumably over millions of years of evolution, our brains have gotten efficient at making these kinds of computational trade-offs. But sometimes the choices are suboptimal—and this may be especially the case during periods of extreme volatility, when the quantity of conflicting data escalates, creating an enormous computational load.

Sticking with invalid hypotheses in the face of contradictory evidence (a classic manifestation of cognitive dissonance) has been blamed for bad decisions in science, politics, international relations, police work and prosecution, and interpersonal relationships, just to mention a few examples.[8] It is also a concern in the intelligence community, where close-minded thinking can lead analysts to ignore new information. Cognitive dissonance has been blamed for failures to react to signs of impending invasion, such as the surprise Egyptian attack in the 1973 Yom Kippur War.[9] Some psychology researchers believe that people are naturally slow to change their opinions. These researchers estimate as a rough approximation that it takes two to five new observations to produce the change in thinking that ought to occur with a single new data point. They conjecture that people have trouble calculating the diagnostic implications of multiple pieces of data because of the computational complexity of the task.[10]

Sources of Cognitive Dissonance

A first step in avoiding cognitive dissonance is to recognize some of its sources.

SELF-IMAGE. In some cases, cognitive dissonance arises when a person's self-image is threatened. A young analyst whose recommendation loses money may insist that his view is correct and that the market is wrong. If the stock reacts adversely to new information, he may argue that the news has been excessively discounted in the stock price. This counterproductive stance reflects the analyst's effort to preserve his positive self-image, which might be based on the assumption that he is shrewder than other investors. This dissonance strikes deep, because self-doubt about his ability to generate successful investment ideas will raise questions about compensation, career, and liveli-hood. Most of us rethink career decisions from time to time, but it is usually not a quick and easy task. The brain's decision to put off the processing bur-den is understandable. But the computationally easy way out—refusing to recognize a mistake—can distort the decision-making process. Researchers have found evidence that mutual fund managers hold on to losers longer than winners and that they resist selling losers on bad news. One explana-tion is that cognitive dissonance is clouding their decisions.[11]

LIMITED CHOICES. The internal protocols of investment firms may intensify cog-nitive dissonance. Some firms emphasize long-term, high-conviction recom-mendations and accordingly discourage frequent changes of opinion. This attitude is understandable, since decision makers would have a harder time keeping track of the quality of analysts' ideas if they were constantly chang-ing. In such an environment, however, if new information conflicts with an existing recommendation, the analyst faces a conundrum: change the recom-mendation, in which case he will be criticized for lack of conviction, or live with the dissonance. In the latter case, there is a subconscious temptation to mitigate the dissonance by "proving" that the preexisting views are correct, for example, by searching for new information to support the view or by ig-noring the conflicting data. Experts point to a similar behavior in intelligence organizations like the Central Intelligence Agency: once an analyst commits to a position in writing and superiors sign off on it, the organization has a vested interest in maintaining that assessment, lest it be criticized for chang-ing its views.[12]

Change Blindness, or the Boiling Frog Syndrome

Cognitive dissonance may manifest itself in a phenomenon known as *change blindness*. According to behavioral researchers, change blindness is a situa-tion where people fail to notice change because it takes place slowly and in-crementally. It is also called the "boiling frog syndrome," referring to the folk wisdom that if you throw a frog in boiling water it will jump out, but if you put it into cold water that is gradually heated, the frog will never notice the change. Most of the studies in this area focus on difficulties in perceiving change visually, but researchers think there is a parallel to decision making.[13]

Change Blindness and Political and Regulatory Risk at Fannie Mae

From 1999 through 2004, I was recommending Fannie Mae's stock under the thesis that competitive advantages stemming from its charter (low borrowing costs, high leverage, duopolistic market position) would produce better-than-expected earnings growth. I certainly understood that political and regulatory pressure constituted a risk. But during that period, each new data point seemed, on its own, too small to shake my positive thesis on the stock. I was faced with a binary choice of defending the recommendation or giving up on the call, which led me to incorrectly dismiss conflicting data (Exhibit 5.3).

◆ In an October 2000 deal with Rep. Richard Baker, a longtime critic, the government-sponsored enterprises (GSEs) agreed to publish new financial disclosures; I thought these would mitigate political risk.

EXHIBIT 5.3 Fannie Mae Stock Price, 1998–2005

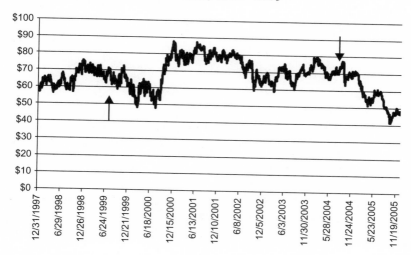

Source: SNL Financial.

Arrows indicate ratings changes.

(continued)

- In May 2001, the Congressional Budget Office updated its estimate of subsidies absorbed by the GSEs; I argued that these subsidies were modest compared to other housing programs.
- In December 2002, a new Treasury Secretary (John Snow) was appointed; I thought he would be more supportive of the GSEs.
- In April 2003, Federal Reserve Chairman Alan Greenspan wrote a letter to Representative Baker discussing the systemic risk posed by the GSEs; I argued that the negative reaction in the stock prices was overblown.
- In June 2003, the Department of Justice launched an investigation into the accounting practices of sibling GSE Freddie Mac; I thought the pressure on Fannie's stock was excessive.
- In September 2004, I downplayed a special report by Fannie Mae's regulator that was critical of the company's accounting.

In late September 2004, as the accounting crisis started to affect Fannie's debt spreads, I finally downgraded the stock. If each data point had incrementally weakened my conviction, I might have arrived at the right answer sooner.

In my case, I recall that in the period between 2000 and 2005, the political controversy surrounding Fannie Mae and Freddie Mac reached the boiling point. But each event along the way seemed containable. By the time I finally reacted to the rising temperature it was almost too late (see the sidebar above). Similarly, intelligence experts have sometimes found that a new analyst assigned to a certain topic for the first time comes up with accurate insights overlooked by experienced colleagues who worked on the same problem for years.[14] (That is the sort of comeuppance that analysts in any profession would like to avoid.)

Change blindness happens when we filter out the implications of new information rather than assigning them even partial weight in our thinking. Imagine we subscribe to a certain hypothesis with a high degree of conviction. New information comes along, one data point at a time. For each datum, we subject the strongly held hypothesis to a test with a binary outcome: either keep the hypothesis or reject it. If each increment is too weak on its own to warrant rejecting the hypothesis, we maintain our confidence at

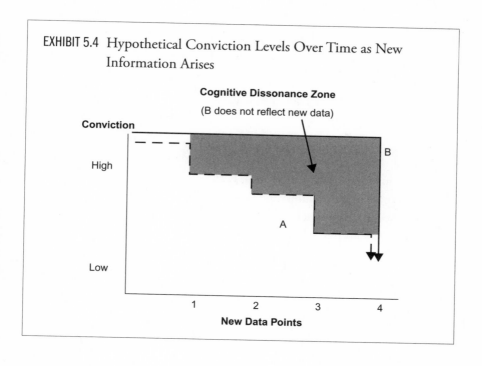

EXHIBIT 5.4 Hypothetical Conviction Levels Over Time as New Information Arises

the 100% level—until finally some data point emerges that tips the scales and we realize suddenly that our thesis is wrong (Exhibit 5.4, line B). The more accurate approach would have been to incrementally adjust our confidence level for each data point (line A).

To follow line A, it helps to have

- A work environment where colleagues tolerate shadings of opinion rather than demanding "high-conviction" opinions.
- Freedom (as much as possible) from issues of self-identity or self-image, which may prevent you from processing the implications of new data points. Put simply, you want to focus on what the data means for the analytic question, and avoid the cognitive load entailed in rethinking your self-image and other deeply rooted beliefs.
- A sense of the critical issues implicit in the question, so you can adjust the appropriate probabilities based on the new information.
- A grasp of the diagnostic power of new information, so that you know how much weight to put on it and thus to what extent you need to change your view of the probabilities.

- A recognition that some new issues require additional research or analysis before you can make any realistic assessment of the outlook.

Stubbornness and Wishy-Washiness: Finding the Right Balance

Cognitive dissonance often manifests itself as excessive stubbornness, but it's just as easy to make the opposite mistake. Stubbornness is risky, especially during periods of extreme volatility. However, for all those who stick with a thesis too long, there may be others making the opposite mistake, namely dropping it too soon. These kinds of people are continually weighing the odds, rather than coming to a conclusion. They are indecisive, "wishy-washy," caught up in "analysis paralysis," unable to "stick to their guns," prone to "jumping at shadows." So we really ought to look at cognitive dissonance as we do the issue of confidence, by seeking the right balance. For example, in the story about CIT, I stuck with a hypothesis for too long, also part of the problem with my Countrywide recommendation (Chapter 3). Conversely, I should have stayed negative on Fannie Mae (Chapter 1) for a longer time.

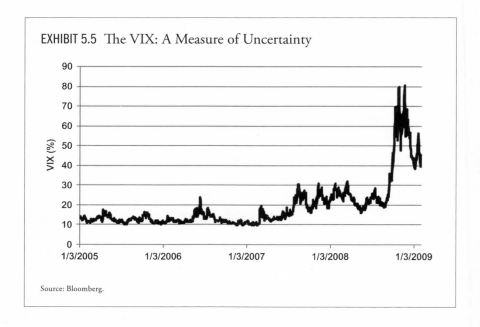

EXHIBIT 5.5   The VIX: A Measure of Uncertainty

Source: Bloomberg.

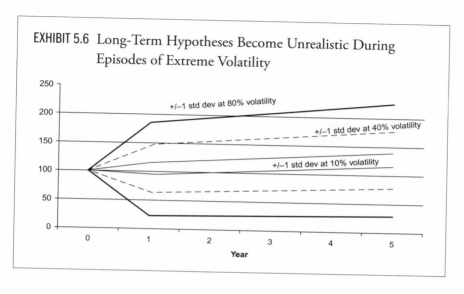

EXHIBIT 5.6 Long-Term Hypotheses Become Unrealistic During Episodes of Extreme Volatility

Finding this balance is complicated by volatility. An appropriate level of persistence in a normal environment becomes dangerous when things are changing rapidly. Exhibit 5.5 shows the Chicago Board Options Volatility Index (VIX), a measure of volatility implied by options on the S&P 500. From 2005 through mid-2007, the index ranged between 10% and 20%. In late 2008, in the aftermath of the Lehman failure, the VIX spiked to 80%, the highest reading in its 20-year history. Exhibit 5.6 shows what happens to a simple forecast of an arbitrary quantity under a one-standard-deviation shock at various levels of volatility. In the base case, the forecast ends year 5 at 127 units. In the 10% volatility scenario, a one-standard-deviation shock knocks the terminal value up to 140, a modest increase. When volatility is 40%, the 1-standard deviation shock pushes the terminal value to 176. Assuming 80% volatility, the terminal value shoots to 225. This wide divergence illustrates the reality that in volatile environments, long-term hypotheses are swamped by uncertainty. Investors should be less confident about their hypotheses, quicker to drop them when conflicting data arise.

Conversely, when volatility settles down, it makes sense to stick with hypotheses longer. By early 2009, the VIX had settled back to around 40%, a level consistent with ordinary recessions. At these levels of volatility, longer-term forecasts become more realistic.

Traditional Approaches to Real-Time Decision Making

To deal with volatility and dissonance, market participants typically adopt one of two strategies. Some seek to develop the emotional fortitude to withstand dissonance. As already noted, long-term value investors believe you need "mettle" to buy out-of-favor stocks.[15] When stocks move against them, value investors dig in their heels, reason that the market has it wrong, and add to their positions. This strategy embraces dissonance. In contrast to long-term investors, short-term traders typically follow a *stop-loss* rule, which requires a position to be closed when the price goes a specified amount in the wrong direction—regardless of whatever confidence the trader feels in the position. This strategy recognizes the danger of cognitive dissonance.

These strategies sound logical, but their effectiveness depends on market conditions (Exhibit 5.7). In an extreme environment, long-term investors will capture enormous gains if the bets are right or enormous losses if they stick with losing positions—in which case, no doubt, they will be accused of falling victim to cognitive dissonance. In extreme environments, traders will be protected by the stop-loss rule, which forces them into cash; however, in missing the opportunity to profit from the big move, they may be criticized for lack of confidence.

EXHIBIT 5.7 The Performance of Traditional Risk Strategies in the Face of Volatility

	High Conviction	Low Conviction
Normal Volatility	Small Losses or Small Gains	Big Losses or Big Gains
Extreme Volatility	Big Losses or Big Gains	Small Losses or Small Gains

In a world where volatility shifts back and forth unpredictably between "normal" and "extreme" levels, neither strategy will consistently mitigate risk. The bigger problem is that neither strategy encourages the decision maker to adjust her sense of confidence to changes in the environment. And neither helps analysts decide how to react to new information.

A Strategy for Real-Time Updating

Reacting to new information requires that fundamental researchers understand its *diagnostic power*—that is, the degree to which new information helps narrow the range of possible scenarios. The greater the diagnostic power associated with new information, the more weight analysts should give it in changing their assessment of the probabilities.

Most people are familiar with the concept of diagnostic power in the context of medical tests. A test's diagnostic power can be thought of as the ratio between true positives and false positives. Scientists can accurately assess the diagnostic power of medical tests because they have large quantities of data gathered in controlled conditions. In the highly fluid situations that investors and other decision makers commonly face, such precision is not possible. To assess diagnostic power in these circumstances may require thinking through counterfactual scenarios, or imagining alternate branches of a probability tree that are consistent with the new information.

Sometimes the diagnostic power of new information is obvious. For example, in the Providian case study (Chapter 2), it was pretty clear that the company was in trouble when the board of directors fired the CEO. This rarely happens when companies are doing well. Similarly, drawing down bank lines was a damning signal that Countrywide was fighting a life-or-death battle for liquidity: rating agencies regard such decisions as acts of desperation and immediately downgrade the company's ratings (as they did with Countrywide), thus shutting off further access to the debt markets.

It sounds simple enough. But recognizing diagnostic power is not entirely intuitive because it requires thinking through multiple scenarios, whereas our intuition tends to latch on to the most representative pattern (recall the representativeness heuristic from Chapter 3). Right or wrong, the consensus among researchers is that humans are not innately skillful in updating their hypotheses for new information.[16]

Reviewing the Second-Quarter 2001 Surprise at Providian

To illustrate the idea of real-time updating, let us return to the Providian story at the point where I was starting to worry about the sustainability of Providian's business model in the wake of its run-in with the Office of the Comptroller of the Currency. As part of the settlement, regulators ordered the company to cease deceptive marketing practices. It complied by instituting new controls, improving disclosures, writing more careful scripts for its telemarketers, and hiring a well-regarded chief compliance officer. Some investors worried these changes might hamper growth, but so far there was no evidence. I had initially assessed a 50% probability of problems with the business model, as illustrated in the probability tree in Exhibit 5.8.

When the company reported second-quarter 2001 results, I noticed the rapid amortization of the balance sheet account, "deferred revenues," which, as explained in Chapter 2, implied a sharp falloff in cash revenues. How should this new information have changed my view of the odds?

To answer this question requires assessing the new information's diagnostic power. Was the amortization a reliable indicator of business model problems, or might it have been a kind of false positive, explainable by some other cause? This is the kind of question for which there is no database. To answer it, I had to imagine different scenarios that might have produced the signal, such as an undisclosed change in accounting policies, or revenues from new products hitting the books over a longer time period.

On the basis of this line of reasoning, I estimated a 70% probability of observing the deferred revenue amortization signal in scenarios where the business model was actually under pressure. (In this case, the signal would be a valid indicator of problems.) At the same time, I thought that even if the business model were actually fine, there could be a 20% probability of observing the amortization (this would be a false positive). These estimates are located on the second node of the probability tree in Exhibit 5.8, under the heading "Conditional Probabilities."

To be sure, these are all subjective estimates. Nonetheless, the probability tree lets us calculate a *revised probability* for business model pressure consistent with these estimates. We calculate this revised probability by dividing the terminal probability for the "true" indicator branch (35%) by the sum of all terminal branches where deferred revenue amortization is observed (45% = 35% + 10%). The revised probability is 78%, a sharp increase from

EXHIBIT 5.8 Estimating the Diagnostic Power of New Information at Providian

	Initial Probability		Conditional Probabilities	Terminal Probabilities	
Business Model Pressure					
Yes	50%	Deferred Revenue Amortization — Yes	70%	35%	a
		No	30%	15%	
No	50%	Deferred Revenue Amortization — Yes	20%	10%	b
		No	80%	40%	
		Revised Probability = a/(a + b) =		78%	

the prior estimate of 50%. My alarm on reviewing these results (I was recommending the stock) should be understandable.

The Misjudgment with CIT

The problem was that I did not react properly to the SAM scare. If I had more carefully thought through the diagnostic power of this new information, my valuation estimate of $23 for CIT stock would not have materially changed. With hindsight, I should have upgraded CIT at $15.

How should I have thought through the situation? The key to the stock's valuation in the teens was the risk of a fatal liquidity crisis, which would have left the stock worthless (refer again to Exhibit 5.1). And the proximate cause of liquidity failure, according to the probability tree, was the risk of "additional credit problems." Without this factor, liquidity failure would have seemed as remote for CIT as for any finance company in reasonable health, at least during a period when the capital markets were functioning normally.

Before the SAM scare, I had estimated the probability of "additional credit problems" at 20%. How should that estimate have changed once I became aware of the SAM scare?

My response should have been to think through the probability that an actual attack would occur. Here I should have come to the conclusion that the scare was likely a false positive. After all, given the worldwide preoccupation with terrorism that followed in the wake of the 9/11 attacks, there had been plenty of scares, but relatively few attacks, at least in Western countries. Further, there had never been a confirmed SAM attack against a civilian airliner, thanks to the technical complexity involved in firing a SAM and the concentration of security forces in and around major airports.

This line of reasoning shows up in the probability tree in Exhibit 5.9 as a relatively modest probability that the scare was an accurate indicator of an impending attack (55%), as opposed to the probability of the scare being a false positive (45%). The math suggests that, if I started with, say, a 10% probability of a SAM attack occurring, then after observing the scare, the probability should have increased only marginally, to 12%. The SAM scare was not a strong enough indicator to warrant staying with the underweight rating, once the stock had dropped into the teens.

EXHIBIT 5.9 Initial and Revised Probabilities of a SAM Attack

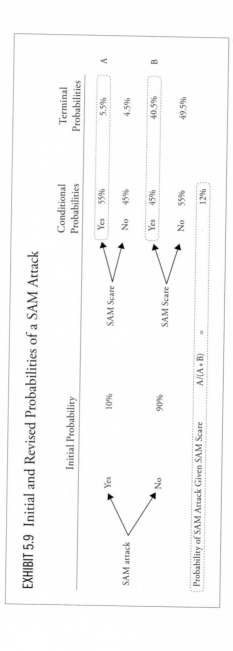

Practical Techniques for Real-Time Decision Making

Focusing on the diagnostic power of new information, rather than resisting information that conflicts with deeply held beliefs, should help improve decision-making accuracy. Here are some techniques:

• Sometimes cognitive dissonance is so intense that the astute investor realizes he has lost objectivity and can no longer make an unbiased decision. This might be a good time to involve colleagues or review the position with a committee.

• While conscious dissonance can be stressful, the risk of bad decisions may be greater when the sensation is subconscious. To counter this risk, analysts should pay attention to feelings of surprise when a particular new fact does not fit their prior understanding. Rather than ignoring the new data—which would represent cognitive dissonance operating at the barely conscious level—they could highlight the sense of the novelty and use it as an excuse to dig deeper into the situation.[17]

• Another thought is to budget your exposure to dissonant situations. Experiencing dissonance is taxing: there is only so much stress that most of us can handle. If an investor is facing three situations characterized by significant dissonance, perhaps she should close one and concentrate on the remaining two. One of the benefits of the stop-loss rule is that it prevents dissonant situations from draining one's mental resources (Exhibit 5.10 provides a series of questions for helping to identify when it is time to close out a position).

• It is also helpful to identify indicators for future scenarios; these are sometimes known as signposts, milestones, or tripwires.[18] An indicator is a form of catalyst that helps you recognize which branch of the probability tree you are on. It gives an early warning for certain scenarios so you can take appropriate action. Indicators can also shake one's complacency with objective evidence that challenges personal views or hopes.

• One way to avoid dissonance is to recognize the limits of our abilities and not try to go beyond them. In many cases, when new information breaks, the right answer may be to close a position rather than to try to defend a thesis. Monitoring information takes time and effort, and models need to be updated, recalibrated, and sometimes rebuilt. In some cases, new information will require thinking through new scenarios. Analysts may not be able to make timely, thoughtful decisions on these issues until they have a chance to study them.

EXHIBIT 5.10 The "Sell Decision"—Reasons for Closing a Position

Answering "yes" to these questions suggests it may be time to close a position rather than defend your thesis:

◆ Has the stock price moved toward your valuation target?
◆ Has the stock price moved away from your valuation target for reasons you have trouble understanding?
◆ Have the catalysts you identified to test the thesis come and passed?
◆ Does new information require studying a new set of critical issues?
◆ Have new developments made it necessary to rebuild your forecast models?
◆ Do you need to consider adding new branches to a probability tree?
◆ Are you feeling anger or irritation, or are you dismissing other investors as irrational?
◆ Is the investment decision getting entangled with considerations of self-identity, career prospects, or institutional pressures?
◆ Has volatility increased, possibly swamping the value of your information or analysis?

• Finally, decision makers should be cognizant of volatility indicators, such as the VIX. During periods when such indicators register at heightened levels, pay sharp attention to near-term catalysts and be ready to drop hypotheses quickly when conflicting data arise. When volatility settles down, it makes sense to be a little more stubborn with hypotheses and to look out over the longer term.

Accurate Updating: Discover Financial Services

We will end this chapter with Discover Financial Services, a credit card and payment company spun off from Morgan Stanley in 2007, and a story that illustrates some of the principals of accurate updating. As measured by the volume of purchases on its cards, Discover was the fourth largest credit card company that year, behind Visa, MasterCard, and American Express. But it was a distant fourth, with U.S. market share of only 5% and virtually no presence overseas. Like American Express, Discover issued credit cards under its own brand, held credit card loans on its balance sheet, collected a mix of interest income and fees, and used its own proprietary network to authorize and settle transactions, rather than relying on Visa or MasterCard. Started by Sears, Roebuck and Co. in the 1980s, Discover was spun off as part of Dean Witter & Co. in the early 1990s. Dean Witter merged with Morgan Stanley in 1996. Eventually, Morgan Stanley management concluded there was little synergy between an investment bank and a credit card company.

In researching Discover, I considered a range of scenarios (Exhibit 5.11). In the most positive ones, Discover's network could have interested large banks, like Bank of America or JP Morgan, which might have wanted a proprietary card network to reduce their reliance on Visa and MasterCard and keep network-related fee revenues for themselves. These banks could bring significant volumes of their own cardholders to the Discover network, boosting its value by adding to its scale. They could have paid a hefty premium for the company, in the $30s or perhaps even north of $40 per share. Chapter 7 relates the astonishing performance of MasterCard's stock price; after its 2006 initial public offering, investors were intrigued by any company with a payments business.

Another alternative for Discover would have been throwing in the towel on its own network, which was arguably subscale, and switching to Visa, or MasterCard. In this case, Discover would operate much like the banks, issuing cards under its own brand that would work on the Visa or MasterCard networks. The cost savings I envisioned might also justify a value in the $40s.

Less favorable scenarios reflected the credit risk in the company's credit card receivables. It had been six years since the disaster at Providian, and the credit card industry was yet again enjoying a period of suspiciously low credit losses, leading skeptics to worry about a turn in the cycle for the worse. If credit turned out to be a problem, I could imagine Discover's stock trading down to book value ($14 per share), a level financial stocks often hit when investors lost confidence.

At the spin-off, the stock flirted briefly with prices in the low $30s. The MasterCard crowd sniffed but did not bite. By the time I was ready to publish a report in mid-August, the stock had sunk to $22. By probability-weighting various scenarios, I could argue for a price target in the $30s,

EXHIBIT 5.11 Probability Tree for Discover Financial Services

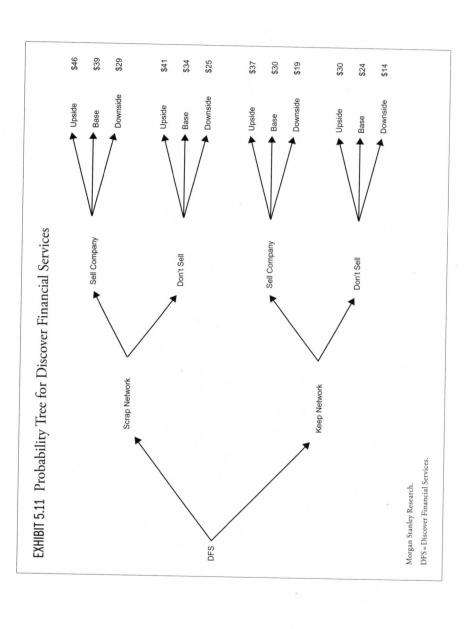

Morgan Stanley Research.

DFS = Discover Financial Services.

which would have offered significant upside. But I hesitated. Much of the upside depended on radical strategic actions, such as scrapping the network or selling the company. I did not expect the managers to undertake such radical moves in the short term; more likely, the board of directors would give them a chance to show what kind of growth they could generate under the status quo. I could not think of near-term catalysts that would test my thesis about the strategic alternatives. Sticking with the hypothesis-testing discipline from Chapter 1, I opted to initiate coverage with an equal-weight rating (Exhibit 5.12).[19] I was also mindful that clouds were starting to gather on the macroeconomic horizon.

By September, the asset-backed markets for subprime and alt-A mortgages had shut down—the unexpected failure of the securitization markets that caught Countrywide by surprise (Chapter 3). The implications of such a large withdrawal of liquidity for the U.S. economy were unsettling. My colleague Betsy Graseck, who was covering the large-cap bank stocks, thought that the withdrawal of liquidity would plunge the country into a consumer recession. She reasoned that weaker borrowers would have trouble continuing to use

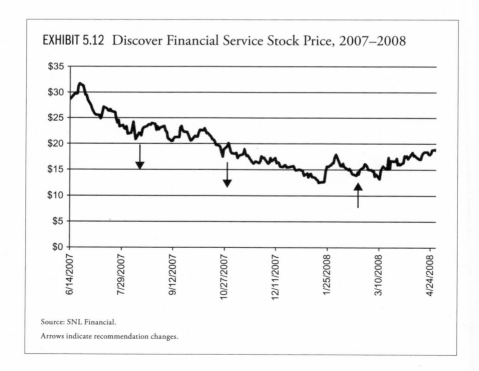

EXHIBIT 5.12   Discover Financial Service Stock Price, 2007–2008

Source: SNL Financial.

Arrows indicate recommendation changes.

nontraditional mortgage loans to pay off credit cards and other debts, as had become common in recent years. Betsy also predicted that banks would be hit with severe losses, forcing them to reduce all forms of consumer credit, including credit cards, auto loans, and prime mortgages. This was a different credit cycle from what I witnessed in 2000, when capital market liquidity and the health of the banking system were not causative variables. But Betsy's logic made sense, and certain indicators in the environment supported her call. Personal bankruptcy filings were beginning to rise again. I concluded that credit card loss rates were going to rise faster than investors realized. The downside branch of Discover's probability tree now seemed increasingly likely. With the stock at $20, I downgraded it to underweight.[20]

By early January 2008, bankruptcy filings were rising briskly and credit card issuers were reporting higher delinquency and charge-off rates. Discover stock bottomed at just over $12. At this point, a new factor came into play. The Federal Reserve was aggressively lowering interest rates. We had thought the Fed would cut rates to 3.25%, but now 2.00% seemed more likely (eventually it would cut to 0%). A few clients called to ask about the implications for credit card issuers' margins. Some of them had heard Discover management talk at a recent conference about having structured the company's balance sheet to benefit from lower interest rates. I quickly pulled up the link to the presentation. Then I studied the company's 10-Q filings and arranged a follow-up call with the company's chief financial officer. In this case, I did not pick up on any diagnostic clues in the company filings or the manager's comments. So I took time to rebuild my forecast model to reflect an assumption of reduced borrowing costs. I upgraded the stock to overweight at just over $14 per share.[21] The catalyst to test my thesis would be higher-than-expected earnings in 2008, with expanded margins more than offsetting elevated credit costs.

When Discover reported first-quarter 2008 earnings, it did indeed beat the consensus estimate, thanks to the company's borrowing strategy and the Fed's aggressive rate cuts. By May, the stock topped out at almost $19 per share. Later on, as the recession intensified, it sank back below $10 (by this time, I was no longer following the stock).

These recommendations demonstrated the discipline of identifying catalysts to test hypotheses (and avoiding decisions without near-term catalysts), recognizing diagnostic power for new information (bankruptcies), and taking the time to rebuild models and consider new scenarios as the situation changed. I would not claim to have anticipated a Black Swan; however, had I started the sequence by recommending Discover, it would have looked as though I was on the wrong side of a Black Swan, as I would have suffered a loss of 45% by the time the stock troughed at $12 per share. During periods of extreme volatility, reacting quickly and accurately to new information, rather than digging in your heels, is a critical survival skill.

Chapter 6

Mitigating Information Asymmetry

If you ask the right questions, you will always find out more than the next guy.

—Michael Price[1]

Judge of a man by his questions, rather than his answers.

—Voltaire (1694–1778)

Visitors were our eyes, and had to be welcomed. My business was to see everyone with news, and let him talk himself out to me, afterwards arranging and combining the truth of these tales into a complete picture in my mind. Complete because it gave me certainty of judgment: but it was not conscious or logical, for my informants were so many that they informed me to distraction, and my single mind bent under all its claims.

—T. E. Lawrence, *Revolt in the Desert*, 1919

Facts are better than dreams.

—Winston S. Churchill, *The Gathering Storm*, 1948

Who ends up on the wrong side of a Black Swan? It may be those analysts who do not react properly to new information but instead dig in their heels and stick with their prior views, as discussed in the last chapter. Or it may be an investor who focuses on the wrong variables, failing to allocate resources to the critical issues (Chapter 4). But even decision makers who sidestep these traps may fail because they do not get their hands on the relevant information. The Black Swan's victims include those who were simply uninformed.

Investors who tire of relying on the media and other low-cost information set out in search of proprietary sources. Access to management teams ranks high on many wish lists, because rarely does anyone have more information about a business than the people running it. However, trying to acquire information from management teams can be difficult or even counterproductive. The challenge lies in *information asymmetry*. The vast amount of information that managers have about their businesses lets them shape investors' perceptions by selectively revealing information that may not be broadly representative. This problem has irked even the most successful investors. For example, while a member of the board of directors of Salomon Brothers, Warren Buffett discovered that he had been taken in by a form of "information rationing": the management team withheld from its directors some of the most important facts about the Treasury auction scandal that nearly scuttled the firm.[2] And information asymmetry is not a challenge just for investors. Any decision maker who relies on managers, agents, analysts, or experts is likely to encounter the problem.

This chapter presents two strategies for mitigating information asymmetry. The first involves monitoring a company's message for signs of cognitive dissonance. The second concerns how to design interview questions to elicit information with diagnostic power.

Information Asymmetry Between Managers and Investors

In economic theory, *asymmetric information* is a term used when one party has more or superior information than another. The better informed have stronger leverage in negotiations.[3] Being on the wrong side of asymmetry is like playing poker with an open hand while your opponent keeps his cards close to the vest. A wealth of proprietary information gives management teams an advantage in communicating with investors. They can fashion compelling arguments, speak with authority, and refute challenges decisively. To promote their own interests, they may reveal some information and keep other data hidden. Managers often tout their company's successes and downplay disappointments, trying to encourage listeners to extrapolate from the high points to the company's aggregate prospects. In this way, managers are setting up the "representativeness" trap discussed in Chapter 3, encouraging investors to latch on to a single bullish variable.

Of course, it would be surprising if managers did not present their businesses in the best light. Those who inspire confidence and boost the stock price may produce benefits in employee morale, hiring, negotiating with partners, raising capital, and making acquisitions (Chapter 1). Sometimes managers emphasize the negative in order to lower investor expectations. In either case, they use their information advantage to advance their own interests. Of course, selective disclosure of information can amount to fraud. But there is a large gray area where managers can put a positive spin on things without violating the law.

Like all analysts, I have seen countless examples of selective disclosure. In one analyst presentation, American Express described its success with credit cards in certain overseas markets, such as Mexico, and Australia. But the slides had no information on countries—for example, Italy and the United Kingdom—where the company's card programs were unsuccessful or their market share marginal. The success stories were not representative of the company's overall international business. In other presentations, it touted the high returns from recruiting banks to issue cobranded American Express cards. While the returns were indeed high, they were not representative of the company's aggregate profitability. American Express's management team is hardly unique in trying to get investors excited about the best parts of its business; most managements act like this.

Another example of selective disclosure involves the credit card issuer Capital One. For many years its credit card portfolio generated wide margins because a large proportion of its customers were subprime borrowers who paid high fees. But the company steadfastly refused to disclose the size or loss rate of the subprime portfolio. Estimating sensitivity to an economic slowdown is very difficult without those facts: although subprime credit cards may perform well in a strong economy, in a recession the loss rates might go through the roof (recall Providian's experience from Chapter 2).

Capital One ducked investor questions about subprime loans for several years. But it could not dodge its regulators, who became concerned about a host of business practices, including credit risk. In 2002, regulators forced the company to sign a so-called memorandum of understanding (MOU) in which it agreed to limit its growth until it addressed the regulators' concerns.

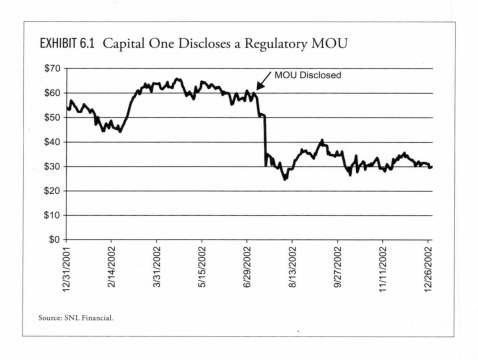

EXHIBIT 6.1   Capital One Discloses a Regulatory MOU

Source: SNL Financial.

When the MOU was disclosed, the stock dropped by 50% (Exhibit 6.1). Since the company had never fully leveled with investors about the nature of its risky portfolio, the regulators' action caught the markets by surprise, reflecting the fragility of consensus opinion when important information is withheld. Information asymmetry can contribute to Black Swan-like surprises.

Trying to Level the Playing Field

One way to fight asymmetry is for analysts to acquire more information, so as to level the playing field with the managers. This can be tough to do. Company managers have up-to-date information on business trends from their line reports, as well as staff who monitor political, regulatory, competitive, and economic developments (and keep track of analysts and investors, too).

In 2005, I surveyed financial aid officers at approximately 300 colleges and universities to learn about the competitive landscape for financial institutions operating in the student loan niche. JP Morgan had recently dissolved a student lending joint venture with the nation's leading student loan originator, Sallie Mae, over a disagreement on how to split the revenues, and I was especially interested in how this would affect Sallie Mae. Sallie was unquestionably the market leader, with the largest portfolio of student loans and a dominant share of new originations. But the joint venture was important, accounting for almost 40% of Sallie's new loans. In the survey, schools expressed a preference to shift their business to JP Morgan, because of concerns about Sallie's customer service. I concluded that the dissolution of the joint venture would cost Sallie a large block of business, thus dampening its growth prospects. My report stated:

> We recently conducted a survey of financial aid offices in order to learn about several trends in the student lending marketplace, with a special purpose of gathering information on the dissolution of the student lending venture between Sallie Mae and JPMorgan. The survey results leave us believing that Sallie will ultimately lose the majority of the volumes once sourced through JPMorgan. At the same time, the survey uncovers signs of increasing competition among lenders and the possibility of decelerating market growth.[4]

Sallie Mae strongly disagreed with my findings. On the next conference call, the chief executive officer (CEO) Tim Fitzpatrick emphasized the company's strong momentum:

> This new academic year was the first year that we've operated under what we would call our redefined relationships with [JP Morgan]. And in short we did just fine without them. In fact we prospered. The numbers tell the tale very well. We look at our internal brands that are demonstrating widespread success and acceptance on college campuses across the country. They continue to be our pace setters by growing more than 50% just in this quarter alone. No doubt they're our most valuable lending brand as we can originate through them without paying any premium and they certainly hit our balance sheet immediately.[5]

It seemed that the company, anticipating the loss of the joint venture, had put considerable effort into marketing its "internal brands," that is, the origination units that operated under the Sallie Mae name. Indeed, fast growth in the Sallie brands continued over the next few quarters. My long-term volume forecasts for Sallie now seemed too conservative, raising questions about the accuracy of my survey.

Within a few months, however, it became apparent that part of the reason for fast growth was a decision by Sallie to cut prices: the company started waiving the origination fees usually paid by students. Competitors told me that under this new pricing scheme, traditional student lending was no longer profitable but rather had become a loss leader, positioning lenders to compete for other products, like "private student loans," that were riskier. Thanks to the price cuts, Sallie was gaining market share, but its revenues came under pressure, and this led to disappointing earnings.

The CEO's message about volume growth was accurate, but it was not representative of the company's prospects. The survey had accurately uncovered Sallie's competitive vulnerability. But even with the survey data, it was still difficult to make sense of what was going on, at least until the effect of the price cuts became clear.

Recognizing Cognitive Dissonance in Companies

Analysts follow many strategies to overcome asymmetry. For example, they compare information across companies. Arguments about competitive advantage may sound convincing at some firms and ring hollow at others. Analysts also make a point to monitor managers' "tone" and body language. One can be skeptical about the representativeness of management communications but still recognize that they affect stock prices. One of the most important strategies, in my opinion, is recognizing signs of cognitive dissonance affecting management, as these may be indicators of impending change.

Cognitive dissonance affects executives and organizations, just as it does analysts and investors. After all, everyone faces the same challenge of evaluating conflicting data with limited computational resources. Corporate strategy guides executive decisions, employee actions, and investor expectations. When fast-breaking information conflicts with the strategy, the managers must decide whether to dismiss the data and stay the course or rethink the strategy. These decisions may be difficult or even intractable, meaning there is no way to figure out a "right" answer in a limited amount of time. Conflicting data may trigger emotions in the managers like irritation, surprise, or overconfidence, just as they do in investors. These emotional indicators may provide the discerning analyst with important clues. Ben Gilad, the corporate intelligence specialist, makes this point when he observes that "answers in response to analysts' questions, especially questions that irk the executives, are invaluable as they reveal true thought patterns rather than window-dressing communication."[6] Gilad uses the term *industry dissonance* to describe the divergence between corporate strategy and reality that often precedes corporate disaster:

> A surprising number of powerful executives at the top of leading corporations are captive to a special class of internal convictions that relate to the future direction of the industry in which they compete. When these convictions and "visions" are out of tune with the evolving market, they obscure the ability of otherwise smart and knowledgeable executives to adjust their strategies accordingly. . . . Executives who are trapped in their obsolete assumptions often refuse to believe the intelligence flowing from their own people, who deal with the markets, the customers, the suppliers, and the competitors on a daily basis.[7]

Countrywide's managers exhibited this kind of dissonance over the summer of 2007. If they had pulled the plug on originating risky loans a few weeks earlier, the company might have survived. But they were not prepared to switch strategies so quickly. After all, they had put much thought into their strategy, which they revised every five years in a careful process that included bringing in outside experts to help them research industry and competitive trends. Under the most recent plan, they anticipated the mortgage industry consolidating into a small number of large operators, and they put a premium on defending their hard-won position as industry leader. As they confronted what was to be a life-or-death decision, the managers revealed their cognitive dissonance by lashing out at short-sellers.

Countrywide is not the only industry leader to have stumbled. In a six-year study of the causes of major corporate failures, Dartmouth professor Sydney Finkelstein found that firms that dominated their markets had special trouble reacting to new challenges. The problem with a successful company, according to Finkelstein, is that being number one becomes part of its self-image. Managers start to dismiss information that contradicts this self-image, creating an inaccurate picture of reality and setting the stage for strategic mistakes.[8]

When Dissonance Is Rational

For large organizations, strategic dissonance may be unavoidable, no matter how rational the managers. In Chapter 5, I emphasized the importance of reacting incrementally to new data rather than waiting for the evidence to become overwhelming. Individuals may adjust their hypotheses quickly. But it is difficult and costly for organizations to change strategies: it may require not only restructuring the organization but also gaining buy-in from employees, investors, customers, and other constituencies. For this reason, it may be entirely rational for managers to hold off on a new strategy until the cost of sticking with the status quo clearly outweighs the cost of change. During this period, managers might not care to acknowledge that they are weighing multiple directions. After all, uncertainty might hurt employee morale or weaken the company's competitive standing.

Clues to Dissonance at Wachovia

During episodes of strategic dissonance, corporate managers may indulge in "little white lies," just like individuals trying to rationalize their decisions. Consider Wachovia Bancorp, one of the nation's largest banks until it was acquired by Wells Fargo on the brink of failure in 2008. Wachovia's problems started with the 2006 acquisition of Golden West, an Oakland-based savings and loan whose portfolio contained option adjustable-rate mortgages (ARMs), the residential mortgages with flexible payment terms that became infamous for attracting unqualified and speculative buyers. Golden West had a reputation for conservative underwriting. But even its careful managers were to be surprised by the force of the housing slump. Further, once Wachovia closed the deal, its executives pressed for faster loan growth and encouraged more aggressive underwriting. As delinquency rates on these mortgages escalated, it became clear that Wachovia was in trouble. The board of directors fired Ken Thompson, the CEO who had negotiated the acquisition, and brought in a new CEO, Bob Steel, a former Goldman Sachs partner and undersecretary of the treasury.

On his first conference call with investors, Steel articulated a strategy of husbanding capital. He had decided to cut the dividend and trim costs, rather than issue new equity, which would have diluted existing investors. This stance came out under pointed questioning by Mike Mayo, a well-known bank analyst:

(Q—Michael Mayo): Bob, you're new as CEO, you have had a record in government and many years at Goldman Sachs. You have nothing to defend. What's your view about Wachovia needing to raise additional capital?

(A—Robert Steel): I think that we've taken what we believe are some really clear and instantly measurable steps, which were hard decisions: to reduce the dividend, point one. Point two, we've outlined a series of projects and plans that are in process already that we believe will give us a substantial improvement in our capital ratios. We have other levers should those not be enough, but I think you can hopefully hear the determination to work through this situation and, to the very best of our ability, be thinking about what's best for our shareholders as we work through this.

(Q—Michael Mayo): So do I read that to say you're not raising additional capital anytime soon?

(A—Robert Steel): We're raising lots of capital by reducing the dividend, managing our expenses, and running our businesses better, and that's the plan for now.

(Q—Michael Mayo): What about through a common stock issuance?

(A—Robert Steel): That's not on the plan. We recognize the different costs of capital, and as I tried to describe we have lots of options for what we can do, and while I can't tell you what will unfold, I can tell you that for now, that our plans are to improve our capital position by the ways in which we have outlined in this presentation.[9]

Steel must have genuinely believed in this strategy, because he had bought stock in Wachovia upon his appointment as CEO. Given the short time he had to take charge and set a new course for the struggling bank, there was no way he could have come up with a perfect strategy that was consistent with all information, especially in such a volatile environment. Once the direction was set, it was time to execute, not fret over potentially conflicting data, nor succumb to "analysis paralysis."

The conflicting data surfaced in the form of "little white lies," which were, unfortunately for the company, readily apparent to knowledgeable observers.

The deck of slides accompanying the conference call included extensive information on Wachovia's portfolio of option ARMs, including details on a new model to estimate cumulative loss rates. The model's estimate of a 12% loss rate was an enormous disconnect from prevailing opinion at the time. A respected securitization analyst named Laurie Goodman had recently published a research report observing that delinquencies on option ARMs were escalating even faster than those on subprime loans. Goodman estimated that losses for option ARMs might approach or surpass 30%. For those doing the math, the difference between 12% and 30% would have been enough to wipe out most of Wachovia's capital. Shortly thereafter, business customers began withdrawing billions of dollars in deposits, throwing Wachovia into a liquidity crisis that ended with its distress sale to Wells Fargo.

Clues to Dissonance at Freddie Mac

Sometimes cognitive dissonance within organizations becomes visible in SEC filings. Managers who want to reiterate the corporate strategy may run afoul of lawyers who worry about disclosure standards, and the resulting negotiations and compromise may be visible in awkward or contradictory sentences.

Take Freddie Mac's second-quarter 2008 disclosure about its deferred tax asset.[10] When asked about the deferred tax assets during its quarterly conference call, Freddie's chief financial officer, Anthony "Buddy" Piszel, had acknowledged, "We grant you that it is a large number relative to capital," but went on to argue, "At least at this point, we do not believe that the deferred tax assets should be seen as some kind of an impaired asset, nor should it be looked at from that standpoint from a regulator for determining capital."[11]

However, the unclear discussion in the company's second-quarter 2008 10-Q filing (see the Freddie Mac Second-Quarter 2008 sidebar) revealed symptoms of institutional cognitive dissonance. In one paragraph, the company argued that it would generate sufficient future income to utilize its tax deductions because it has assessed that "prevailing market trends and conditions in the U.S. housing market are not a continuing condition." In another, it acknowledged "difficulty in predicting potential unsettled circumstances," an admission that seems to undercut its confident outlook for the housing market. It admitted that it might need to take a write-down "if future events significantly differ from our current forecasts." That was the real issue: the decision lay with the auditors, who might lose confidence in

Freddie Mac Second-Quarter 2008 10-Q, Note 12: Income Taxes
(*emphasis added*)

At June 30, 2008, we had a net deferred tax asset of $18 billion, of which $11 billion related to the tax effect of losses in our available-for-sale securities portfolio. We believe that the realization of our net deferred tax asset is more likely than not. In making this determination, we considered all available evidence, both positive and negative. The positive evidence we considered primarily included our intent and ability to hold the available-for-sale securities until losses can be recovered, our history of taxable income, capital adequacy and the duration of statutory carryback and carryforward periods and forecasts of future profitability. The negative evidence we considered was the three-year cumulative book loss, including losses in AOCI and the *difficulty in predicting potential unsettled circumstances.* If future events significantly differ from our current forecasts, a valuation allowance may need to be established.

Prevailing market trends and conditions in the U.S. housing market have created difficulties for mortgage lending institutions and contributed to our experiencing cumulative pre-tax book losses over the most recent three-year period. Such cumulative losses generally make it difficult to conclude under FAS 109 that a valuation allowance is not needed. However, our strong earnings history and *our assessment that the prevailing market trends and conditions in the U.S. housing market are not a continuing condition* support the conclusion that a valuation allowance is not needed. Our strong earnings history on a pre-tax book income basis is also reflected in our historical federal income tax returns. In addition, we anticipate that we will be able to generate future taxable income from the following sources to realize our deferred tax assets: (1) reversals of existing taxable temporary differences; (2) taxable income exclusive of reversing temporary differences and carryforwards; (3) taxable income in prior carryback years; and (4) tax-planning strategies.

> ### A Strategy for Eliciting Information
> #### Overcoming Information Asymmetry in Interviews
>
> ◆ Confine the agenda to critical issues.
> ◆ Bring specific questions with diagnostic power.
> ◆ Ask "how" and "why," not "what."
> ◆ Pay attention to ducked questions and nonanswers.
> ◆ Avoid debating your own views.

the company's ability to generate future income sufficient to use the tax deductions if management's forecasts turned out to be incorrect, as indeed proved to be the case. After the government seized Freddie Mac later in the fall, the company recorded a sizable write-down to the deferred tax asset, wiping out most of its remaining capital.[12]

When analysts can gain an audience with managers, the proper structuring of questions may help overcome information asymmetry. But that requires preparation. Not only do managers enjoy an information advantage, but also securities laws prevent them from disclosing nonpublic information in private meetings, so analysts cannot ask direct questions about many pressing issues. By encouraging managers to stay "on script," the laws offer a handy excuse to duck inconvenient questions. Also, managers do not attain responsible positions unless they are confident, charismatic, and capable of inspiring confidence. During the Internet and technology boom of the late 1990s, some thought that personality and image had become more important in CEOs than business abilities, knowledge, and experience.[13] This sounds crazy, until you remember how stock prices and fundamentals may interact, as discussed in Chapter 1. Promotional skills are indeed important, and this makes interviewing CEOs something of a challenge. The art of interviewing is to maneuver the manager into a spot where she cannot credibly deliver a scripted answer and where even a nonanswer would have diagnostic power for critical issues. There are several elements to this approach.

CONTROL THE AGENDA. Part of the problem with asymmetric information is that the better-informed party will naturally set the agenda, steering the conversation to points that she would like to make. And these may or may not be representative of the company's overall situation. The analyst following an active information strategy will want to elicit information about critical issues. That means controlling the agenda, either by sending a list of agenda points to the company in advance or by politely interrupting and redirecting the flow of conversation.

ASK SPECIFIC QUESTIONS. Loosely phrased questions give the manager plenty of leeway in answering, which makes it likely she will steer the answer back to points she wants to make rather than reveal information about the critical issues you are interested in. "Tell me how you feel about credit quality" is a loose question. "Tell me what macroeconomic indicators you use to forecast defaults" is specific. The sidebar presents a brainteaser illustrating how the diagnostic power of an answer depends on the nature of the question.

AIM QUESTIONS AT THE "HOW" AND "WHY." Asking directly for managers' forecasts and opinions is rarely productive, because these questions produce scripted answers. Instead, try asking about the information managers rely on—and how they analyze it—in forming their judgments. After all, anyone who has an opinion ought to be able to explain the basis for it. For example, in the fall of 2007, I asked some executives at American Express *how* they came up with their earnings guidance. It became clear that the guidance was predicated on *current* macroeconomic trends, as they felt it inappropriate to speculate on *future* states of the economy. As the economy deteriorated, it became logical to expect the company to reduce its guidance, as indeed it did in the spring of 2008.

RECOGNIZE NONANSWERS. A properly formulated question should put an executive on the spot, not in a threatening way, but in the sense that a specific question deserves a precise answer. But that does not mean he will actually answer. A skillful dissembler may appear to answer the question, but if you listen closely, you will find he ducked the question or attempted to sway the analyst with vague expressions of confidence such as, "We feel really good about our business," or with positive body language, direct eye contact, or a forceful tone. If a senior executive does not have a good answer to a tough question, that can be an incredibly important clue—provided you recognize it.

BE WARY OF REVEALING YOUR OWN VIEWS. If the executive understands how the analyst is thinking about an issue, he may choose to reveal specific data to shape the analyst's thinking in ways consistent with the company's communication objectives. When asked a question, you should resist the compulsion to show off your knowledge unless you are ready for a head-to-head debate. For example, if asked, "What do you think about credit quality?" it might be dangerous to say, "I am concerned." Then the executive can lay out his arguments for why credit quality is under control and buttress them with proprietary data. The analyst is forced to sit and nod. This kind of one-sided discussion is unproductive. A safer answer might be, "I'm not totally sure, but I certainly hear a lot of investors talking about the topic. What do you think has got them focused on credit quality?" This could be an effective

---

The Paradox of the Three Prisoners

This brainteaser makes the point that the diagnostic power of an answer depends critically on how you ask a question. (It is adapted from a book on probabilistic reasoning by Judea Pearl, a researcher in artificial intelligence.[14])

Three prisoners—A, B, and C—have been tried for murder, and their verdicts will be revealed in the morning. One of them will be found guilty and hanged, whereas the others will be released. Their guard knows which of the prisoners is guilty. But the prisoners do not.

In the middle of the night, prisoner A calls the guard over and asks, "Please give this letter to one of the other prisoners to take home to my family in case I am executed. We both know that at least one of them will be released." The guard agrees.

An hour later, prisoner A calls the guard again and asks, "Can you tell me which of the other two prisoners you gave the letter to? The answer won't give me any clue to my own fate." The guard agrees and reveals that he gave the letter to prisoner B.

Upon hearing this answer, prisoner A becomes alarmed, reasoning that the guilty sentence now falls with equal likelihood on himself or prisoner C. Before asking the question, he had thought that his own probability of being executed was one-third. Now it seems to be 50%.

But in fact this is wrong. The probability of A's execution remains one-third, because the question has no diagnostic power with regard to A's fate: no matter which prisoner is the unlucky one, the guard can always give A's letter to one of the other two prisoners, so A really learns nothing new about himself. What changes in this story is the probability of C being executed, which rises from one-third to two-thirds, because the guard did not give him the letter.

Prisoner A could have learned more about his own fate had he asked the guard a different question, such as, "Will prisoner B be executed tomorrow?" If the guard said "Yes," then the probability of A suffering that fate would drop to zero, since only one prisoner will be executed. If the guard revealed that B would go free, then A would realize that his own odds of being executed were indeed now 50% (split equally between himself and C).

How you phrase a question may determine whether the answer provides information relevant to your particular set of critical issues—or to other variables.

---

counterquestion, because it forces the executive to choose between discussing specific credit quality indicators and giving a nonanswer, such as dismissing other investors as uninformed.

Some Examples

Most of the time, a properly formulated question elicits a small amount of incrementally useful data. Occasionally, it hits the mother lode.

Recall the Providian case study (Chapter 2). In the spring of 2001, I met with senior management at Providian's Market Street, San Francisco headquarters. In preparing for this interview, I reviewed critical issues in my analysis, including the question of whether the business model would still produce revenue growth following Providian's run-in with bank regulators. Obvious questions—such as "What is your guidance for revenue growth?"—were not going to work, likely eliciting nothing but scripted answers, referencing the company's most recent public comments and no doubt delivered in a confident tone. It would have been equally unproductive to ask, "How have revenues trended since the last quarter?" because under securities law, the managers could not disclose that information in a private meeting with me and my clients.

To get at revenue growth, it might be productive to explore *how* the company was responding to the new regulatory controls. One idea was to ask about new products. Perhaps the company's business model was fine and had merely fallen afoul of overzealous regulators because of technical violations. In this case, I would expect to hear that the company was designing a new set of products that were competitive, profitable, and in compliance with consumer protection standards. On the other hand, suppose Providian's business model had really depended on exploiting unsophisticated customers. In this case, with the company now operating under the close eye of regulators, new products were not going to help. The question I asked during the meeting went as follows: "Investors are concerned that regulators have mandated changes to your marketing practices that will constrain revenue growth. To offset these pressures, what kind of new credit card products is Providian introducing?"

The question was met with blank stares. The management team had not introduced new products and had no ready answer on this point. This was one of the rare occasions in my experience when managers did not brush aside a potentially dangerous question with a breezily confident nonanswer. The probability tree in Exhibit 6.2 demonstrates the diagnostic power associated with this answer. Walking into the meeting, I had assessed the risk of business model problems at 50%. Based on my subjective estimates for the odds of hearing about new products, my revised estimate after hearing the nonanswer rose to 78%.

Another example of an effective interviewing strategy involved American Express. Chapter 7 will recount the story in full; suffice it to say here that I was meeting with the executive in charge of the U.S. lending portfolio in order to get information on the critical issue of credit quality. I knew that direct questions about current trends would elicit nothing but scripted answers. Like many big companies, American Express's investor relations officials kept their executives on a tight leash and interrupted the conversation whenever an analyst asked questions about recent trends or forward-looking guidance.

Credit quality was a critical issue for American Express, not only because of general concerns about the environment in the fall of 2007, but also because the company's loan portfolio had grown much faster than its competitors' in recent years. I thought about how best to formulate a question. The one that ended up working the best: "Given that American Express has grown its credit card portfolio so much faster than the rest of the industry in

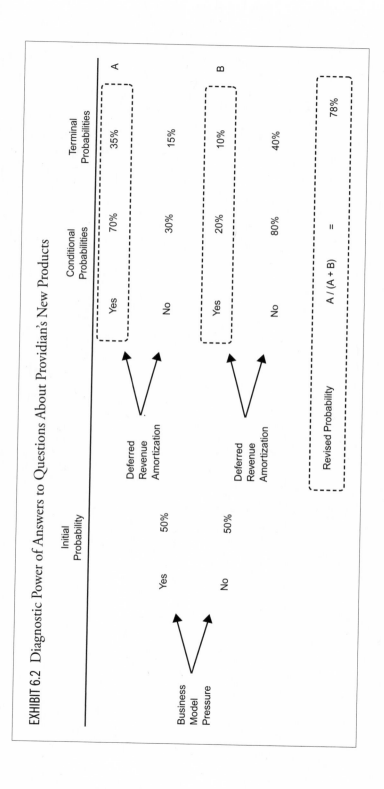

EXHIBIT 6.2 Diagnostic Power of Answers to Questions About Providian's New Products

recent years, can you explain which of the following factors produced that growth: marketing, underwriting, product features, or brand?"

If the answer was convincing, it would give me confidence in the company's portfolio. A nonanswer would lead me to suspect sloppy underwriting as the reason for fast growth. Truth be told, I worried that I had left myself open to a long-winded discussion of the power of the American Express brand, a fair argument but not new information. To my surprise, the executive paused, took a deep breath, and responded, "We keep asking ourselves that very question." Indeed, credit quality became a serious problem for the company, as we will see in Chapter 7.

A final example comes from my first interview with Sallie Mae, which took place at the company's Virginia headquarters in 2002, well before the survey already discussed in this chapter. One of the firm's senior executives entered the boardroom, exuberant about Sallie's growth prospects in the student lending marketplace. However, growth was not at the top of my agenda, so I interrupted him to ask the following question: "According to Sallie Mae's 10-K, 'A large percentage of our private credit student loans have not matured to a point at which predictable loan loss patterns have developed.' If you do not have predictable patterns to work with, how do you forecast loss rates?"

The executive shot back, "That's just legal boilerplate. It doesn't mean anything." This nonanswer had immense diagnostic significance, as it suggested that credit risk was a concern for the lawyers drafting the company's 10-K, but not for senior management. It would take several years for credit quality problems with the private student loan portfolio to become apparent. I will relate the conclusion of the Sallie Mae story in Chapter 9.

Part III

Analysis and Judgment

Chapter 7

Mapping from Simple Ideas to Complex Analysis

In that Empire, the Art of Cartography attained such Perfection that the map of a single Province occupied the entirety of a City, and the map of the Empire, the entirety of a Province. In time, those Unconscionable Maps no longer satisfied, and the Cartographers Guilds struck a Map of the Empire whose size was that of the Empire, and which coincided point for point with it. The following Generations, who were not so fond of the Study of Cartography as their Forebears had been, saw that that vast Map was Useless, and not without some Pitilessness was it, that they delivered it up to the Inclemencies of Sun and Winters. In the Deserts of the West, still today, there are Tattered Ruins of that Map, inhabited by Animals and Beggars; in all the Land there is no other Relic of the Disciplines of Geography.

— Jorge Luis Borges, *On Exactitude in Science*, 1946

In an increasingly complex world, some kind of modeling is a necessary part of decision making in almost any field. Sophisticated or simple, models can dramatically extend our forecasting capability. But modeling also introduces a new source of complexity into the decision-making process—namely, questions about the model's accuracy and reliability. In the worst case, modeling mistakes may leave decision makers vulnerable to Black Swan surprises by blinding them to the true range of possible outcomes, as we saw with subprime loss forecasting (Chapter 3).

After all, it is only with hindsight that Black Swans seem simple. And it is only after the fact that the people who zeroed in on the principal causative variable look like geniuses. Beforehand, decision makers must contend with a range of variables. Analysts must trace the impact of these variables through numerous scenarios to the economics of a company or industry, and then, for stock picking, through the rules of accounting to the financial statements, and finally to valuation. Most people find models necessary for these tasks.

The idea behind "mapping" is the linking of critical issues with a model's output, in a manner that maximizes accuracy and minimizes complexity.[1] Sounds simple, but in practice it is not always so. Those subprime loss models may have been sophisticated, but they were not built on the right critical variables. The opposite mistake is to identify the issues but fail to project the implications accurately. Finding the right balance between accuracy and complexity is one of the analyst's most important contributions to the decision-making process. This chapter will illustrate the practice of mapping in stories about MasterCard and American Express, high-profile competitors in the global payments industry whose stocks managed to produce surprising outcomes.

The IPO of MasterCard

Credit cards are one of the simplest and most popular of financial products. But credit card companies' business models are more complicated. The story of MasterCard's initial public offering (IPO) provides an example of a complex, high-stakes forecasting exercise with significant upside potential—and downside risk.

In the spring of 2006, MasterCard was weeks away from selling stock in an IPO. This was an interesting and controversial transaction: interesting because the company operated a high-margin network business model, controversial because litigation threatened the company's solvency. My research associate Andrew Chen and I set to work.

By way of background, MasterCard and Visa are the two dominant global payment networks, with American Express in third place and Discover Financial Services a distant fourth. These payment networks act as the backbone for the widespread use of debit and credit cards. When a cardholder pays with Visa or MasterCard, the merchant swipes the card on a terminal that transmits card number and purchase amount to the payment network, which then obtains approval from the cardholder's bank and sends the authorization back to the merchant, all in a matter of seconds. A few days later, the network routes the funds from the bank to the merchant to settle the transaction. For this service, Visa and MasterCard withhold a "merchant discount" of roughly 2% to 3% of the merchant's sales proceeds. Most of the discount goes to the bank whose customer used the card (this is called the "interchange"), but Visa and MasterCard keep a small sliver of the discount for themselves (on the order of 0.1% to 0.2% of sales), and they also charge the banks an annual assessment and various other fees. The banks issue the cards, provide customer service, extend loans, collect past-due balances, and process the merchants' accounts.

Visa and MasterCard stand in the center of this system, like toll takers on a bridge. Theirs is a so-called network business model that links two classes of customer: cardholders and merchants. If customers on both sides of a network become hooked on its services, the network may become extremely valuable.[2] Some investors thought of MasterCard as a distant cousin of Intel, Microsoft, or Google. As our discussion of Jensen's inequality (Chapter 2) concluded, a network business model may warrant a premium valuation because of the possibility of asymmetric upside potential.

But the litigation risk was troubling. Before its IPO, MasterCard was owned by its customers, the banks, as indeed Visa still was (it was to execute its own IPO a year later). The cozy relationship between networks and banks had endured for many years. To accommodate their owners, Visa and MasterCard hiked the interchange fee by a small amount each year, boosting bank profits. In time, retailers became restive at the rising fees, which were eating into their thin margins. Some began to threaten antitrust litigation, arguing that Visa, MasterCard, and the banks were acting in collusion to set merchant fees at illegal, uncompetitive levels. The card industry suffered a serious legal defeat at the hands of the Department of Justice, which convinced the courts that the card industry had set anticompetitive rules to exclude new entrants. Then Wal-Mart led a class action suit of retailers that forced Visa and MasterCard to back off on the fees they charged on *debit* cards. In 2004 I had stumbled across legal papers revealing that certain large retailers were threatening to extend the battle to *credit* card fees.[3]

Given the size of the payment industry and the potential for treble damages under antitrust law, a class action lawsuit could be massive. I estimated merchant fees in the United States alone at $20 billion or more per year. If damages were demonstrated over a multiyear period and then trebled, the sums would easily exceed $100 billion. Even before the IPO, some analysts were warning that litigation could bankrupt MasterCard, whose capital was only $1.3 billion.[4]

Recall the other side of Jensen's inequality: asymmetric downside risk might warrant a discount in MasterCard's valuation. Clearly, this was a complicated situation. Andrew and I studied the IPO prospectus, poured through industry journals, reached out to contacts in the payments business, and talked with investors about the pros and cons of the offering. This research uncovered several critical issues.

First was the question of revenue growth. Investors were enthusiastic about the long-term potential for electronic payments. Consumers had been gradually shifting from paying with paper money and checks to using plastic, that is, debit and credit cards. Yet with checks still accounting for 50% of transactions in the United States, there seemed to be much room to grow. In international markets, the outlook was even more interesting; credit and debit cards had only begun to penetrate fast-growing emerging markets like India and China. Furthermore, in the European Union, the second largest payment market after the United States, new regulations seemed likely to force many smaller processing firms out of the market. Already well entrenched in Europe, MasterCard and Visa seemed like shoo-ins to expand share.

Another critical issue was operating leverage, or the ratio of revenue growth to expense growth. Firms with relatively fixed costs enjoy positive operating leverage, meaning that rising revenues translate into wider margins. MasterCard's margins were similar to those of other processing companies. But given its scale, the low costs of routing additional transactions across its network, and limited competition, some investors thought Master-Card's margins should be much higher. Some of my clients considered the company's marketing expenses too high, and others thought compensation was excessive. If MasterCard could keep these costs under control while increasing revenues, it ought to generate widening margins and faster earnings growth. The transition from a private company (owned by the banks) to a public company (answerable to shareholders) would create powerful incentives for management to do so.

Competition was a critical issue, too. According to industry journals, MasterCard had lost market share in Europe, Asia, and the United States.

I wondered if MasterCard was outgunned by Visa and undifferentiated vis-à-vis American Express. A key source of uncertainty was whether the company could recoup some of its lost market share or whether it would fall further behind.

Another competitive challenge for MasterCard was the growing concentration among its customers, the banks. Of course, after the IPO, the banks would no longer control MasterCard. But they would still dominate the business of issuing cards. After years of consolidation in the banking industry, the top banks now accounted for a considerable share of MasterCard's business. Specifically, four of the largest—Citigroup, JP Morgan, Bank of America, and HSBC—made up 30% of MasterCard's revenues. The banks had pressured the company to share part of its network fees with them, and these "rebates" had increased from 16% of revenues in 2003 to 21% in 2005. This trend was not lost on investors, especially those who followed the banks. Whether the rebates would grow further, or stabilize, had significant implications for revenue growth.

The final issue was litigation risk, which hung over the company like a dark cloud. What were the odds of MasterCard losing or settling, and if so, how many billions might it have to pay?

To summarize, after our initial review, Andrew and I had identified 6 critical issues: payments growth, the European opportunity, operating leverage, market share, banks' bargaining leverage, and litigation. Of these variables, litigation posed potentially enormous downside risk, while the fixed-cost nature of the business model offered sizable upside potential. Unlike the situation with CIT (Chapter 3), the outlook for MasterCard did not appear to turn on a single issue. The question was, how could we properly weight and combine these variables to produce an accurate forecast?

The Trade-Off Between Accuracy and Complexity

In a complicated forecasting exercise, such as the MasterCard situation, the goal is to find the right balance between accuracy and complexity. Gary Klein, the researcher whose study of real-world decision making we referenced in Chapters 3 and 4, draws a distinction between intuitive pattern recognition and mental simulation. The first produces cues about how to react to a situation; the second is the process by which the decision maker imagines people, objects, or concepts, then transforms them to arrive at a hypothetical end state. Mental simulation is a more deliberate, conscious process than intuition. However, as with any computational exercise, the power of mental simulation is limited. Our short-term memory is finite. Mental calculations are imprecise. Situations that involve multiple interactions are complicated. From his fieldwork on high-pressure situations, Klein estimates that decision makers can typically handle no more than three variables and a handful of transformations in their mental simulations.[5] The goal of modeling is to extend the reach and accuracy of the decision maker's mental simulation without burdening her with excessive modeling complexity.

In building a forecast model, one hopes to improve accuracy by breaking down a difficult problem into more manageable chunks, a process referred to as decomposition.[6] Eventually, each part of the problem will require some kind of assumption on which to base the projections. Since assumptions are guesses about the future, each assumption in the model will be characterized by random error. With more assumptions, some of the random error should cancel out, in the same way that some of the volatility of individual securities cancels out in a diversified portfolio (Exhibit 7.1). Using a larger set of assumptions in a bigger model can be worth the time and effort if it leads to a more accurate forecast. MasterCard was a brand new stock, which investors did not yet fully understand. Andrew and I thought an accurate forecast would produce a big payoff, so we were willing to invest the time to build a detailed model.

However, there is a cost to adding assumptions: the escalating complexity of the model. As it grows larger, a model has a greater risk of calculation

EXHIBIT 7.1 Volatility of Model Forecast as a Function of Number of Assumptions

Number of Assumptions				
1	2	3	4	5
30%	21%	17%	15%	13%

Assumes that each assumption is characterized by a standard deviation (volatility) of 30% and that inputs are independent (uncorrelated).

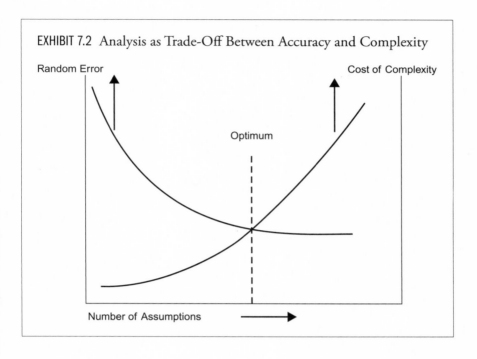

EXHIBIT 7.2 Analysis as Trade-Off Between Accuracy and Complexity

errors that could throw off the results. It also takes longer to build and check complex models, and they can be slow to update for changing information. If overconfidence or cognitive dissonance is distorting an analyst's views, a complicated model may leave more room for the analyst to bias the results by fine-tuning assumptions to get the answer he would like to see. Finally, as we add more variables to the model, possible interactions among them will increase at a geometric pace, leading to what computer scientists call "the combinatorial explosion"—a problem whose complexity renders its solution intractable.[7] Recall that a game of chess could not be fully solved by even an "ideal computer" that occupied the entire universe and that had been running since the beginning of time (Chapter 4). Real-world problems are more complicated than board games. In this light, model building can be likened to a balancing act: one should add more variables until, at the margin, the cost of complexity starts to outweigh the benefit of incremental accuracy (Exhibit 7.2). Finding this optimum point should be an imperative for the model builder and the decision maker.

EXHIBIT 7.3 MasterCard's Combinatorial Explosion

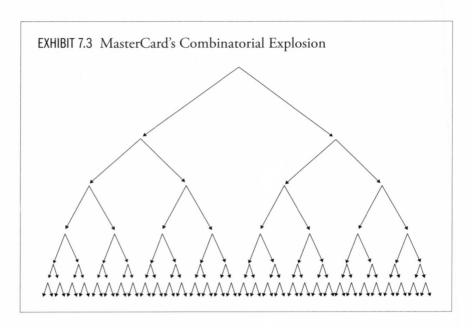

MasterCard: The Plot Thickens

With 6 critical issues, Andrew and I faced our own version of the combinatorial explosion. Recall the probability tree for Providian in Chapter 2, where 3 critical issues were associated with 2 branches each, leading to 8 terminal scenarios. That was manageable. But 6 critical issues for MasterCard would leave us with 64 scenarios, more than we cared to work with (Exhibit 7.3).

To simplify the MasterCard analysis, we collapsed 4 of the critical issues—payments growth, the European opportunity, bargaining power, and market share—into a single variable for revenue growth (Exhibit 7.4). This left us with 3 critical issues, for each of which we made a series of upside, base-case, and downside assumptions. We repackaged the resulting 9 terminal branches into 3 final scenarios, which served as the basis for our detailed earnings projection and valuation models. To summarize, we thought revenue growth could range from 9% in the worst case to 13% in the best case. The company would expand margins by somewhere between 0.5% and 0.9% per year. Finally, after hiring lawyers to help us understand the theory of damages and war-gaming various settlement options, we estimated MasterCard's exposure to litigation at somewhere between $500 million and $2.7 billion.

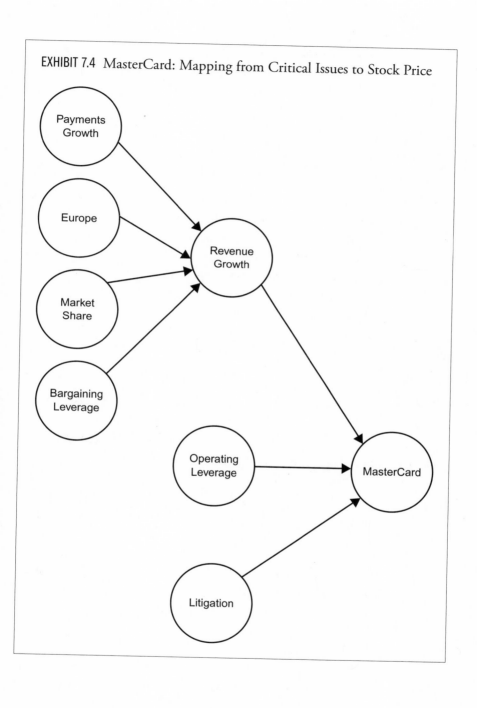

EXHIBIT 7.4 MasterCard: Mapping from Critical Issues to Stock Price

The result of all this work was a base-case price target of $56, an upside case target at $67, and a downside case target at $44. With MasterCard trading in the mid-$40s in May 2006, the odds seemed tilted to the upside, so I initiated coverage of the stock and recommended it with an overweight rating, arguing that the market was overestimating litigation risk.

The prospects for MasterCard as a new public company and the expected path of its stock price boil down to two primary questions, in our view. First, whether growth prospects in the global payments industry outweigh the mounting pressure on margins stemming from consolidation among major banks, which would have the payment networks operate as quasi-utilities. Second, whether the company's legal exposure will compromise the firm's financial and strategic flexibility, or wipe out its equity holders. Our analysis leads us to a guardedly optimistic view on both points.[8]

A few weeks later, MasterCard reported stronger-than-expected second-quarter earnings. The results for the third quarter, reported in October, also surprised to the upside. The stock rallied by 14% on the news. Concerns about litigation were starting to fade as investors focused on the company's earnings power. By November, the stock was trading in the mid-$80s, more than double its IPO price of $39. By this point, I had raised my 2008 earnings estimate from $2.96 per share to $4.46, reflecting stronger revenue growth and faster operating leverage than I had initially anticipated—in fact, the earnings trajectory had shot through my upside case. Updating our valuation model for the revised forecast generated a new target price of $88, equivalent to a generous-seeming 20× multiple on the new 2007 earnings per share (EPS) forecast.

With the stock at $85, there did not seem much point in continuing to recommend it. After all, market share losses and pricing pressure remained concerns. I downgraded the stock to equal-weight in late November at $85.[9] Six months later, the stock had doubled again to $180 (Exhibit 7.5).

Everything possible had gone right. Revenue growth accelerated into the high teens, well above my projections of 9% to 13%, not to mention the company's own guidance of 8% to 10%. MasterCard wooed some banks away from Visa, benefited from strong international travel, and implemented price hikes for some of its services. The company held the reins on marketing, with no appreciable impact on revenues. With high returns, fast earnings growth,

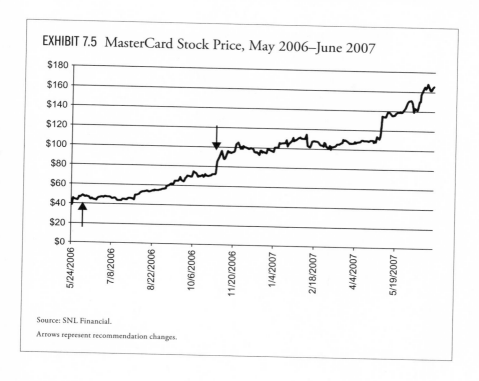

EXHIBIT 7.5 MasterCard Stock Price, May 2006–June 2007

Source: SNL Financial.

Arrows represent recommendation changes.

and no direct credit or interest rate risk, MasterCard became a Wall Street darling.

Investors referred to MasterCard as a Black Swan, and rightfully so. The stock had appreciated roughly 300% in a 12-month period. Yet MasterCard options had discounted implied volatility not much higher than 30%. On this basis, the stock's performance reflected something like a 5-standard-deviation surprise, the odds of which should have been fantastically remote.

Hindsight showed the errors in my ill-timed downgrade. I put too much weight on valuation and not enough on my earnings forecast, which was still ahead of the consensus, a possible positive catalyst. The complex modeling had succeeded in getting me into the right ballpark, but in trying to keep track of the six critical issues, I was slow to update my analysis—an example of the cost of complexity.

There was a second lesson in the MasterCard swan. Just as with Providian, it became clear that many of the critical issues were driven by a single underlying factor. The transition from a private entity controlled by customers to a public company answerable to shareholders appeared to catalyze a

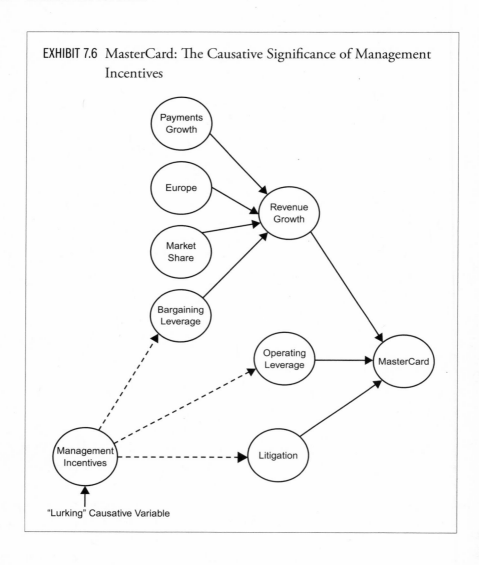

EXHIBIT 7.6 MasterCard: The Causative Significance of Management Incentives

major shift in management incentives—and thus in the company's performance (Exhibit 7.6). A hedge fund analyst made this point in scolding me for the premature downgrade. With a cynical tone, he accused MasterCard executives of deliberately giving lowball earnings guidance at the IPO so that they could get their stock options struck at a low price. "We often see this behavior in 'demutualization' situations," he added, "and sell-side research analysts usually fall for their ultraconservative guidance." I wanted to point out that I had not fallen for their guidance, but rather had come up with my own proprietary forecast, based on an analysis of 6 separate critical issues. However, another problem with complex modeling is that it can be difficult to explain (especially when it comes up short).

MasterCard and American Express

My colleagues and I took a second crack at MasterCard a year later, in the fall of 2007. Because of staffing issues on my team, I turned responsibility for MasterCard over to my colleague Charlie Murphy, who covered payment processing companies and other business services firms. Charlie and I thought it would be interesting to compare MasterCard with American Express, as both companies were high-profile players in the global payments industry, yet we sensed some confusion among investors about the differences between the firms. From late summer until early fall, we met once a week to talk about the payments industry and to brainstorm ideas for research and analysis. In due course, we identified three critical issues.

The first critical issue was pricing power. MasterCard had continued to deliver extremely strong results. I had overestimated the bargaining leverage of banks, which I had feared would press for ever-steeper rebates. The company's backbone had stiffened following the shift to a for-profit model answerable to public shareholders. As we took a fresh look at strategic positions in the industry (banks, payment networks, and retailers), it dawned on us that with Visa and MasterCard's IPOs, bargaining leverage might be shifting from the banks to the payment networks. The question now was not whether MasterCard would raise prices, but how quickly and how far. We reasoned that even a year after the IPO, MasterCard must be raising prices in a quiet and subtle manner, hoping not to create undue controversy.

How far this pricing shift might go we did not know. But there were reasons to think the bargaining leverage of payment networks was naturally strong. For one, these networks are protected by virtually insurmountable entry barriers: creating a new payment network would require years and billions of dollars to recruit consumers to use new cards and merchants to accept them—a classic problem of chicken and egg. No matter what they thought of MasterCard's pricing, banks and retailers were not likely to go out and start their own networks. Further, our calculations suggested that raising prices by a basis point or two would be barely perceptible to the banks, yet would add significantly to MasterCard's revenues.

Finally, we figured that once Visa completed its own IPO, its managers, too, would discover the virtue of rational pricing, helping to shield Master-Card from scrutiny. Charlie noticed in Visa's IPO filings that the company was already starting to raise prices. All these thoughts, taken together, led us to consider a much steeper path of revenue growth than in my prior forecasts.

Pricing power was a relevant concept at American Express, too. But the company's business model was different. MasterCard's revenues came mainly from banks. American Express's revenues came mainly from cardholders and merchants. Cardholders seemed happy to pay a premium for the prestige associated with the American Express brand: we had measured this propensity in a survey of affluent cardholders.[10] Merchants may not have been happy, but they did not want to alienate the well-heeled customers who used American Express cards. A premium customer base was the foundation of the American Express franchise, but unlike the situation with MasterCard, we did not see much opportunity to raise prices further. Our survey had suggested that even with its premium brand, American Express might lose customers to banks offering similar perks at lower prices. And raising prices on merchants did not seem prudent, given their growing litigiousness.

In one area, the American Express business model was much like Master-Card's. American Express had decided to open its network, and it recruited several banks to issue cards that ran on the American Express network. These cards generated network fees for American Express, but the business of marketing, customer service, and lending remained with the banks, which also pocketed the lion's share of revenues. Early participants included Citigroup and Bank of America. American Express senior management talked a great deal about this initiative, but they declined to disclose the profits. We thought the partnership business would contribute only modestly to earnings, because the network fees were much smaller than revenues from American Express cards.

The second critical issue was operating leverage. Since MasterCard's costs were relatively fixed, it could profit from wider margins as revenues grew. American Express executives appreciated the operating leverage associated with a payment-network business model. To their credit, they had built the company's franchise around high-spending cardholders, a strategy they referred to as "spend-centric." And margins had widened in recent years. Notwithstanding the strategic focus on *spending*, however, much of American Express's growth in recent years derived from *lending*, specifically through its rapidly growing portfolio of credit card receivables. But most of the costs in this segment were variable, namely the credit losses that resulted when borrowers fell behind on their payments—this was not a business characterized by natural operating leverage. Furthermore, no one thought American Express should cut its marketing budget. Finally, American Express had long been public, and its managers were already focused on cutting costs. They had picked the low-hanging fruit.

Finally, American Express and MasterCard had different exposures to the economy. MasterCard did not market directly to consumers or hold credit card loans on its balance sheet (that was the business of its bank customers). So rising credit losses were not going to affect profits directly. In contrast, American Express's rapidly growing credit card portfolio exposed the company to the risk of higher charge-offs. We reasoned that this portfolio would perform poorly in 2008.

Mapping Causal Relationships

Having identified these critical issues, Charlie and I were in position to map out the linkages from critical issues to earnings and valuation. Exhibit 7.7 shows how I mapped out these relationships for American Express. Before we get into the details, notice that the causal relationships between the critical issues and the output variable flow in different ways, as illustrated generically in Exhibit 7.8.

In some cases, there is a direct one-to-one relationship. For example, the critical issue of "operating leverage" (the ability to increase revenues faster than expenses) maps directly to the forecast for fixed costs. Whether American Express enjoyed a greater or lesser degree of operating leverage, one would need simply to adjust the level of fixed costs flowing through the income statement, without worrying about other variables. One-to-one relationships fit in nicely with the rules of formal logic, where the mapping can be expressed using if-then statements: if American Express enjoys operating leverage, then fixed costs will remain low. One-to-one relationships can also

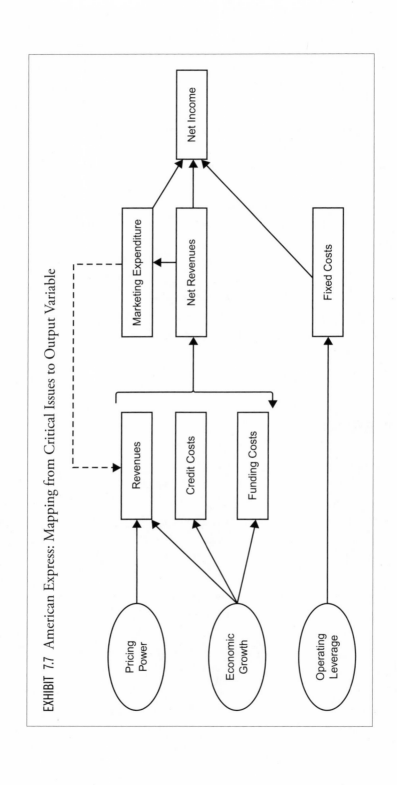

EXHIBIT 7.7 American Express: Mapping from Critical Issues to Output Variable

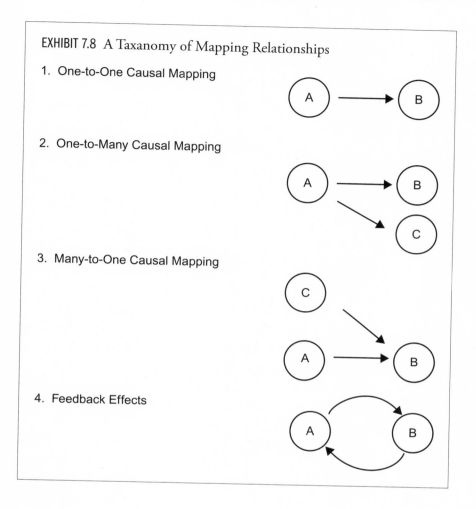

EXHIBIT 7.8 A Taxanomy of Mapping Relationships

1. One-to-One Causal Mapping

2. One-to-Many Causal Mapping

3. Many-to-One Causal Mapping

4. Feedback Effects

be translated into simple linear functions: the more (less) operating leverage American Express enjoys, the lower (higher) its fixed costs will be. One-to-one relationships are easy to sketch out in probability trees or code into spreadsheets or computer programs; thus, this kind of logic tends to dominate high-powered modeling, such as Monte Carlo simulation models, which we will discuss in Chapter 8. But real-world causal relationships are often more nuanced.

The term *one-to-many* describes a mapping relationship in which a single critical issue affects a range of output variables. For example, the macroeconomic environment has implications for several elements of American

Express's business model, including revenue growth (as corporate and consumer credit card spending fluctuates with the economy), credit losses (due to unemployment), and funding costs (affected by the level of interest rates and the spreads on American Express bonds). One-to-many variables may be quite powerful. But recall that our intuition tends to latch on to the single best pattern, sometimes missing other relationships. If we miss the full range of impacts from a critical issue, we may seriously underestimate volatility.

"Many-to-one relationships" reflect the influence of several factors on the output variable and can be especially tricky to model. Consider revenue growth at American Express. Revenues depend on economic growth, pricing, and the marketing budget. In theory, with enough data, a multiple regression model could produce coefficients for each variable, combining their weights in a single equation to predict revenues. In practice, however, the data may not exist, the relationships may not be precise, and the coefficients may change over time. For example, in 2003 American Express changed the disclosure for marketing expense, frustrating the effort to measure the long-term relationship with revenues. In these situations, the best one can do may be to hazard a rough judgment. Better this than a precise calculation that misses important causative drivers.

Finally, notice the positive feedback loop from net revenues to marketing expenditures and back to revenues. American Express's executives had established an earnings target of low to middle teens growth. When earnings seemed likely to come in above target, management would increase the marketing budget, an expense that prevented net income from exceeding the upper band of the guidance. Higher marketing spending, in turn, would help generate faster revenue growth in future periods as additional advertising, mailings, and brand campaigns produced new customers—in effect, creating a virtuous circle of improving results. In previous research, I had noticed a long-term trend of margin expansion in American Express's card business. Margins had widened from a low of 12% in 1993 to 19% in 2005, as the company had benefited from improved operating leverage and declining interest rates.[11] Expanding margins had, in turn, fueled additional marketing. When the Federal Reserve cut interest rates in 2001 to stave off recession, the company's borrowing costs plunged, and its managers plowed this windfall into the marketing budget, which grew at a 20% rate for several years, helping the company gain market share from Visa and MasterCard.

But in 2007, the outlook was for higher credit costs, which stood to crimp the company's margins. Certainly, the company could absorb these costs by trimming its marketing budget. But this would slow revenue growth, potentially changing the virtuous circle experienced over the last few years into a vicious one. As the reader will recall from Chapter 1, positive feedback effects can produce episodes of extreme volatility, so the relationship between marketing and revenue growth seemed important to understand.

American Express and MasterCard: The Outcome

After completing our analysis and coming to our respective decisions, Charlie and I packaged our recommendations together: I downgraded American Express to underweight, and he took over coverage for MasterCard and upgraded it to overweight. Our argument was simple: "Having compared the two firms, we see MasterCard as highly leveraged to a one-time shift in pricing power from banks to payment networks, while American Express seems more exposed to the US economy and consumer credit."[12]

In this exercise, we managed to find the right balance between accuracy and complexity. After we published the recommendation, MasterCard's stock continued to rally (Exhibit 7.9). In perusing a trade journal, Charlie discovered that MasterCard was quietly raising its fees for international payments and accurately predicted that the earnings would top consensus estimates.[13] Higher fees supported the pricing power hypothesis. After breaching $300, MasterCard's stock settled in around $250 by midsummer.

American Express's credit card receivables soon began to show signs of stress. It became apparent that the company had lent too freely in hot housing markets like California and Florida, where consumers in trouble with their mortgages were falling behind on their credit cards as well. As housing markets weakened and consumer confidence plummeted, credit issues spread throughout the company's portfolio. Even its long-standing affluent customers fell behind. In early 2008, I noticed its funding costs were widening ominously, in an echo of the plight of CIT a year earlier. It was hard to imagine American Express suffering the same kind of liquidity crisis as CIT, and indeed I never forecast any such outcome. But higher funding costs stood to cut into margins, adding to the cyclical pressure on earnings.[14] By spring

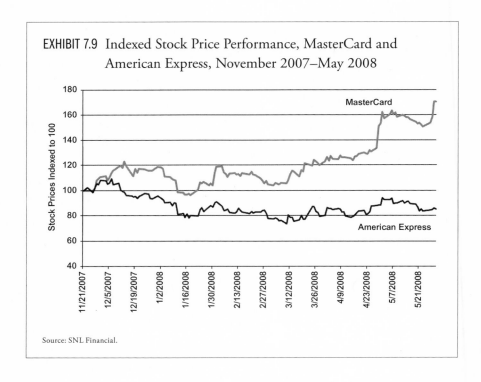

EXHIBIT 7.9 Indexed Stock Price Performance, MasterCard and American Express, November 2007–May 2008

Source: SNL Financial.

2008, American Express had sold off from the high $50s to the high $30s. I had to suppress a touch of schadenfreude in learning the same hedge fund analyst who had chided me for missing MasterCard was caught by surprise in the American Express sell-off.

As the full force of global recession hit, MasterCard's stock sold off, ending back around $150 per share as consumers and corporate cardholders pulled back on spending. But the company's payments-oriented business model continued to operate successfully, and the stock stabilized at a level still much higher than its IPO. The merchants' lawsuit languished, and the company settled other litigation.

In contrast, American Express shares continued to drift lower, reaching the low $20s by early 2009. The company was cutting marketing expense, which declined year over year by 35% in the fourth quarter. At this point, the company's revenues were holding up better than those of other card issuers. It was still too early to tell whether reductions in marketing would injure its franchise, leading to a reversal of the market share gains of the last few years.

Reflecting on American Express's results, it is clear to me that the company's management understood the power of a payments-oriented business model and did everything it could to push the company in that direction. For example, the company jettisoned weak businesses, spinning off American Express Financial Advisors (which consisted of insurance, asset management, and a network of financial advisors) and selling some of its underperforming international operations. Recruiting banks to issue cobranded cards on the American Express network remained a focus for senior executives. And it continued to target high spenders as the core of its "spend-centric" franchise.

But to transform the company into a network business like MasterCard or Visa was not in its power. To do so would have required capturing a much larger share of the spending volumes controlled by banks, and banks had little incentive to partner with a company that was also a competitor, especially one with as strong a brand as American Express. The company could gain no leverage over its marketing and credit costs. And in hindsight, the managers made a mistake similar to Countrywide's: they placed too much reliance on seemingly sophisticated underwriting models, without recognizing that booming home prices and easy mortgage credit were also influencing the loss rates on credit cards.

Chapter 8

The Power and Pitfalls of Monte Carlo Modeling

In the early 1970s, we generated thousands of possible futures. We had to use a computer to sort through them. It was silly.

—Peter Schwartz, *The Art of the Long View*, 1991

Entia non sunt multiplicanda praeter necessitatem *(entities should not be multiplied beyond necessity).*

—William of Ockham (c. 1285–1347)

All correct reasoning is a grand system of tautologies, but only God can make direct use of that fact. The rest of us must painstakingly and fallibly tease out the consequences of our assumptions.

—Herbert A. Simon, *The Sciences of the Artificial*, 1996

In a world of information and complexity, high-powered computer models have become essential tools for many decision makers. Among the most versatile of these, the Monte Carlo model generates probability trees with thousands or millions of branches—however many it takes to resolve problems too complex or uncertain to be worked out by hand. The model's accuracy sometimes seems eerie. A mainstay of science, engineering, and quantitative finance, the model finds uses in other areas, even locating sunken treasure.

However, if not used properly, Monte Carlo models can be hazardous to your health. Their results are unreliable if you do not accurately estimate the correlation between variables. These estimates require a sound grasp of underlying causative relationships. To those who miss this point, the models may produce an illusion of precision, even though they are built upon the imprecision of random outcomes. Misuse of Monte Carlo models has contributed to some of the biggest Black Swan events of recent years, including the 1998 failure of Long-Term Capital Management (LTCM) and, just a few years later, the collapse of the multi-hundred billion dollar correlation trading market.

This chapter includes stories about American Express and Fannie Mae, showcasing the use of Monte Carlo models to produce accurate forecasts in complicated situations. However, the chapter's main theme is the importance of understanding causation. We will see how in the end, Monte Carlo modeling could not save Fannie, as the models failed to anticipate not only the full extent of the housing crisis but also the shift in the company's special charter, from source of strength to fatal liability.

Introduction to Monte Carlo Models

In Monte Carlo models, the analyst specifies the assumptions as random variables rather than point estimates. For example, instead of assuming that, say, a mortgage company's subprime loans will produce losses of 5%, the analyst might specify that losses will equal 5% or 30% with equal probability, or vary uniformly across that range, or follow a bell-shaped distribution (off-the-shelf software packages provide much flexibility in how you specify variables). The Monte Carlo model then generates large numbers of scenarios using different values for the random variable, allowing the analyst to observe a range of possible outcomes. These scenarios can be thought of as constituting a giant probability tree, with thousands or millions of branches, however many it takes to untangle an intricate problem. In the last chapter, it became clear that with just a handful of critical issues, the resulting probability trees for MasterCard and American Express were becoming burdensome to work through by hand. In essence, Monte Carlo modeling automates this kind of task. These models do not eliminate the combinatorial explosion of interacting variables, but they help human analysts undertake more complex analyses than they can with pencil and paper.

Monte Carlo modeling was first used in the 1940s at the Los Alamos Laboratory. A group of famous physicists and mathematicians, including Enrico Fermi, Nicholas Metropolis, Stanislaw Ulam, and John von Neumann, employed it on the primitive computing devices of the time to work through mathematical problems in the development of atomic weapons. Ulam coined the name after the casino of Monte Carlo, where his uncle used to gamble with money borrowed from family members.[1]

Today, Monte Carlo modeling is used in molecular dynamics, physical chemistry, computational physics, aerodynamics, digital animation, and many other scientific and engineering fields. The techniques give useful estimates in problems whose underlying equations are so complex that finding the precise answer would be intractable. But Monte Carlo is more than brute-force number crunching: it can be thought of as a form of probabilistic reasoning. Artificial intelligence researchers consider it an effective technique for solving networks of probability trees, something that may eventually allow computers to reason much as humans do.[2]

The U.S. Navy uses Monte Carlo techniques in search-and-rescue operations to estimate the location of missing ships. In one of my favorite Monte Carlo stories, a team of recovery engineers borrowed Navy techniques to hunt for the SS *Central America*, a passenger ship carrying a cargo of gold that sank off the Carolina coast in 1857. The engineers researched data about the currents and weather conditions when the ship sank, cobbled together from historical accounts of survivors and crews of passing ships. Using a Monte Carlo model, the engineers projected 10,000 scenarios, which helped them map out the highest-probability locations for the sunken ship. The team located the vessel and recovered $50 million in gold.[3]

Those of us who are not quants might be tempted to dismiss Monte Carlo models as excessively abstract and complex—especially after seeing case studies where these models produced the wrong answers (Chapter 3). My skepticism dissipated when I saw the gold ingots recovered from the SS *Central America* on display at the American Museum of Natural History, seemingly tangible proof of the model's potential.

Figuring Legal Risk at American Express

Our first story shows how Monte Carlo models can help answer fundamental questions too complicated to work through with basic probability trees. In this case, my team built a Monte Carlo model to help explore litigation risk at American Express. Recall that in Chapter 7 we discussed litigation between the credit card industry and merchants. Visa and MasterCard were the primary targets, not American Express. But that did not mean American Express was immune: after all, it charged merchants the highest fees in the industry. This pricing power was not lost on litigators.

My research team had uncovered certain lawsuits aimed at American Express. In one case, *Marcus v. American Express*, a group of retailers claimed that American Express enjoyed market power with the charge cards it issued to corporate travelers and affluent consumers, for which merchants had to pay high fees. The plaintiffs complained that American Express forced them to pay the same fees for its credit cards, even though these cards were marketed to a lower-spending demographic. In the fall of 2005, the presiding judge denied American Express's motion to dismiss, allowing the case to move into discovery and setting the stage for possible class-action certification.[4]

A second issue for American Express was the legal defensibility of the so-called no-surcharge rules, by which the credit card industry forbade merchants from passing on to consumers the merchant discount associated with credit card usage (averaging around 2 percentage points of sales). If surcharges were legal, as the plaintiffs argued they should be, then merchants could add these fees onto the checkout bill. To be sure, cardholders valued the prestige, service, and membership benefits associated with American Express cards. But would they still use the card if a surcharge were added to the bill every time they swiped it?

Third, there was a question of "collateral damage." If the threat of litigation forced Visa and MasterCard to lower their merchant fees, would American Express have to follow suit? In Australia, financial regulators had ordered Visa and MasterCard to cut their merchant fees in half. American Express was not subject to this ruling. But over time, its merchant fees trended down in parallel with Visa and MasterCard's new pricing. Apparently, Australian merchants had forced American Express to adjust its fees to the new regulator-induced equilibrium. Merchant fees made up some 50% of American Express's revenues, and most of these fees came from the United States. Any pressure on U.S. fees could have devastating implications for the company's earnings.

To get my arms around the topic of legal risk, I came up with various scenarios for each of these 3 issues and estimated subjective probabilities for different outcomes. In principle, I could have created a set of probability trees to calculate American Express's exposure under the various permutations of these legal threats. But trying to keep track of large numbers of

EXHIBIT 8.1   American Express: Litigation Risk Scenarios by Percentile

Scenario Percentile (%)	Impact on Intrinsic Value per Share ($)
5	2.00
10	0.00
20	0.00
30	0.00
40	(0.15)
50	(2.15)
60	(2.15)
70	(3.23)
80	(4.45)
90	(7.67)
95	(12.00)

Source: Morgan Stanley Research.

branches gets confusing. It seemed easier to toss these variables into a Monte Carlo model, then see what came out.

The Monte Carlo output is shown in Exhibit 8.1. Just a quick glance reveals a highly asymmetric, nonnormal distribution. In many scenarios, the litigation fails and the company suffers no costs at all. Not until the 40th percentile do the scenarios start to produce measurable costs. By the 90th percentile, however, the costs are quite significant, almost $8 per share. The model's output was like a probability tree with 1,000 branches. Averaging across these scenarios produced an expected litigation cost of $3 per share.

At this time, I was valuing the company's stock at $58 per share, before considering legal risk. So I set my price target at $55, to account for the average $3 discount for litigation risk produced by the Monte Carlo model.

With the stock trading at $54, almost exactly in line with my target, the shares seemed fairly valued. I reasoned, however, that concerns about American Express's litigation exposure would intensify when MasterCard started its initial public offering road show in the next couple of months, in effect keeping a lid on appreciation in American Express shares, which looked fully valued in any case. There was much controversy surrounding MasterCard's exposure to litigation, which was sure to be the subject of pointed questioning during road-show investor meetings.

Other risk factors would keep American Express shares from rallying, I thought. The company was vulnerable to cyclical factors, such as rising interest rates. And I was skeptical that the partnership business (where banks issued credit cards that operated over the American Express network, as discussed in the last chapter) would produce material profits.

I came up with a short-term recommendation, selling a call option struck at $60 that would expire in October 2006. This recommendation was a variant of the confidence interval strategy presented in Chapter 3. The idea was to capture the premium from selling the call option, in the expectation that the stock would still be under $60 in 6 months, when the option expired. Of course, if the stock ended up above $60 at expiration, then the option holder would have to make a payout, rendering the strategy a money loser. I published this recommendation on March 14, 2006:

> A fresh analysis suggests less upside potential in American Express stock than the market appears to be anticipating. American Express boasts a tremendous franchise, and management deserves credit for setting strategy and delivering on execution. But so far as we can tell, these positives are fully discounted in the stock, which trades at a steep premium to other financials. Further, we see moderate pressure on earnings from the current interest rate environment and more serious risk in the nagging problem of merchant backlash against US payments industry pricing. The bulls appear to dismiss these risks and, at the same time, envision larger profits from the bank partnership strategy than we are able to model. Our concerns may not be serious enough to warrant shorting the stock or avoiding the debt, but, if we are right, they might serve to limit the upside appreciation potential in the stock. For qualified investors who agree with our analysis, a possible investment strategy would be to sell call options.[5]

About a month later, the stock had dipped down by a couple of dollars to $52 (Exhibit 8.2). Because the call option was sensitive to small movements in the stock price, it lost much of its value, and I recommended closing the position.[6]

"You were lucky," a client complained. True, I could not point to any reason for the $2 sell-off in the shares, which mattered for the option but was hardly a meaningful move in the stock. The thesis about MasterCard keeping a lid on the share price may have been correct. However, a few months later, investor thinking on MasterCard shifted from concern about legal risk

EXHIBIT 8.2 American Express Stock Price and Option Recommendation

Source: SNL Financial.

Arrows indicate timing of recommendation to sell option and close out trade. Line represents call option strike price and ends at expiration.

to enthusiasm for revenue growth and margin expansion. As MasterCard's stock started to rally, it appeared to lift American Express's stock as well. Investors started to wonder whether American Express's payments business might deliver explosive earnings growth similar to MasterCard's. The call sale strategy would have worked had the position been held until the option expired in October, although American Express's shares were closing in on the strike price.

As it turned out, even three years later, not much had happened on the legal front. The *Marcus* case slipped back into obscurity, and the merchants made little discernible progress in their high-profile claims against Visa and MasterCard. This outcome was consistent with the distribution produced by the Monte Carlo model, in which most scenarios ended without any material cost. The model had done exactly what it was supposed to do: help us quantify a serious and complicated risk, so that we could factor it into our calculations, neither ignoring nor overreacting to it.

Consequences of Misestimating Correlation

The whiff of correlation between the stock prices of American Express and MasterCard highlights a risk with Monte Carlo models: their results are highly sensitive to assumptions about correlation. In recent years, misestimating correlation has produced spectacular losses, in part because people relied on Monte Carlo models without understanding the causative forces at play.

One of the most notorious correlation disasters involved the hedge fund LTCM. In October 1998, the Federal Reserve Bank of New York organized a bailout of LTCM by a consortium of Wall Street investment banks because fear of its imminent collapse was contributing to a liquidity crisis in the capital markets. The firm's troubles had many causes, including excessive leverage, hugely concentrated positions, poor decisions about liquidity, and over-confident traders. Nonetheless, there was a common theme to many of its bad trades: inaccurate estimates of correlation.

For example, one of LTCM's most important trades was buying corporate bonds and shorting U.S Treasuries. Under this strategy, it pocketed the spread differential between corporate bonds and Treasuries as ongoing profits. Between 1993 and 1997, the correlation between corporate bonds and Treasuries was 0.9654, suggesting that the spread differential was a rock-solid relationship that could be counted on to persist. Under the assumption that this relationship would continue, and with a debt-to-equity ratio of 25:1, the firm stood to generate returns on equity of almost 40%.

The flaw in this strategy was that in a period of economic or financial stress, the risk of corporate defaults would rise, whereas presumably the risk of U.S. government default would not, thanks to the government's power to tax and print money. In this scenario, corporate bonds would lose value relative to Treasuries. Indeed, during the recession of 1991, the correlation between corporate bonds and Treasuries had dropped to 0.8. And when this pattern repeated itself during the global currency crisis of 1998, LTCM suffered massive mark-to-market losses, as the corporate bonds it owned lost value, while the Treasuries it had shorted, gained.

Most likely the principals recognized this risk, as the company had many other trades on its books, presumably to mitigate risk through diversification. However, in figuring the prudent amount of capital to hold, the company's principals apparently relied on historical levels of correlation between different assets. They must have neglected the fact that extra capital should be held for the risk that historical data may misstate correlations, especially in a crisis.[7] A 25:1 ratio of debt to equity did not leave enough cushion.

LTCM's failure drove home the point that correlations can change over time, especially during a crisis. Yet unstable correlation appears to be a subtle risk: within a few years, the mistakes of LTCM would be repeated on a far larger scale.

Correlation Trading

Around 2000, a new market called *correlation trading* emerged. This new market involved a variety of exotic structures, including such things as "*n*-to-default baskets" of loans as well as the collateralized debt obligations (CDO) that we met in passing in Chapter 2. At its simplest, a CDO was just a portfolio of fixed-income securities, typically a mix of corporate bonds and asset-backed securities (that is, securities backed by pools of credit cards, auto loans, student loans, and especially subprime mortgages).

What makes a CDO interesting is that to pay for the securities it purchases, the CDO issues its own set of securities (Exhibit 8.3). These securities come in different forms. The so-called equity tranches are the riskiest, as they have first-loss exposure to the CDO's assets. The senior tranches are the least risky: they are protected by the equity tranche as well as by a mezzanine tranche sandwiched between the equity and senior securities. Even more exotic were so-called CDO-squareds, which bought securities issued by other CDOs.

The fact that this market ended up failing does not mean that its premise was invalid. A CDO ought to be less risky than its individual assets, because the default risk for each asset is not completely correlated with the others; some should cancel out thanks to diversification. There was no reason to think that subprime mortgages, credit cards, and corporate bonds would all go bad at the same time. Thus the CDO should be able to use more leverage than would be appropriate for the individual assets. And higher leverage means higher returns. Of course, most loans are sensitive to the business cycle, so it would not be sensible to assume the individual assets' default risk was perfectly *uncorrelated*. How much leverage a CDO might prudently employ depended on an accurate estimate of the correlation among its assets.

EXHIBIT 8.3 Structure of CDOs and CDO-Squareds

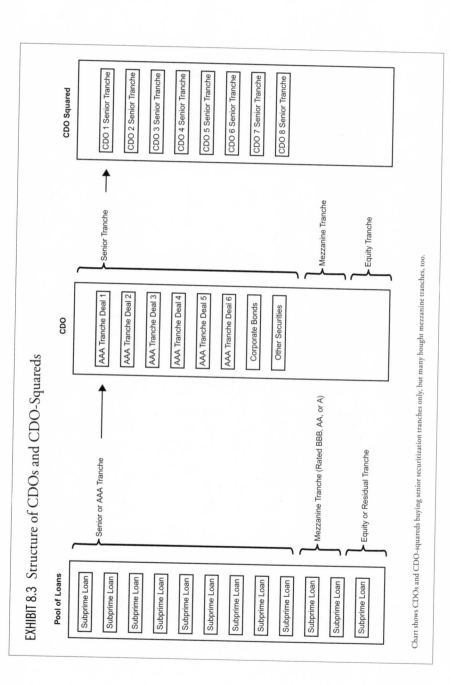

Chart shows CDOs and CDO-squareds buying senior securitization tranches only, but many bought mezzanine tranches, too.

An accurate sense of correlation was also necessary for pricing the different tranches of debt issued by the CDO. The senior tranches were potentially vulnerable to high levels of correlation: if defaults were highly correlated, a large number of loans might go bad at the same time, inflicting enough losses to imperil the senior tranches. However, if correlation stayed low, only a few loans would go bad at once, and the senior tranches would not be threatened.

For the equity and mezzanine tranches, exposure to correlation was just the opposite. If defaults turned out to be highly correlated, then either a large number of loans would go bad at once or the majority of loans would continue paying. If they went bad, the equity and mezzanine tranches would be wiped out. But if they all stayed good, those tranches would be in great shape. The expected value of this binary outcome was good enough to attract investors, because the profits in one branch of the tree outweighed the losses in the other.[8]

When a new CDO was created, the rating agencies established how much debt could be issued and determined the proportion of senior, mezzanine, and equity tranches. Rating agency analysts would review the CDO's proposed assets, consider the managers' track record, and estimate the correlation among its assets. These inputs were fed into a Monte Carlo simulation model. A properly structured CDO should survive all but a small handful of the thousands of scenarios produced by the Monte Carlo model.

Despite these analytics, investors were skeptical. AAA-rated CDO tranches traded with wider spreads than other AAA bonds, suggesting that investors thought rating agency correlation assumptions were too low.[9] As it turned out, investors' estimates were too low as well.

Correlation in the Housing Markets

The key to correlation among CDO assets lay with the housing markets, because mortgage-related securities made up a large share of CDO assets—in fact, as much as 90% of some CDOs.[10] One way to think about housing market correlation was to compare home price volatility at the national level with that in individual metropolitan areas. In studying this dynamic, I had found that local home prices had fallen by as much as 20% to 30% in some of the toughest regional downturns—for example, in Texas during the "oil

EXHIBIT 8.4 Normalized Home Price Distributions for the United
States and MSAs, 1975–2004

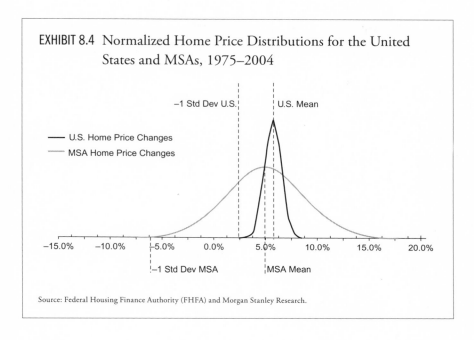

Source: Federal Housing Finance Authority (FHFA) and Morgan Stanley Research.

patch bust" of the late 1980s and in New England and California during the
early 1990s. The United States as a whole had not suffered such a severe
home price correction since the Great Depression, in part because the nation
as a whole had not suffered as harsh a labor market shock as those that had
characterized the regional downturns. Put differently, the United States was
a larger and more diversified geographic region than any local market—just
as a CDO portfolio was more diversified than each of its assets. Specifically,
data collected by Fannie Mae's and Freddie Mac's regulator showed that the
standard deviation of national home price changes since the 1970s was
around 4%, as opposed to a standard deviation of 11% for the average Metropolitan Statistical Area (MSA) (Exhibit 8.4).[11]

There was a weakness in this analysis—as well as a clue that many missed
(as did I, even though I had run the numbers). Exhibit 8.5 shows how the
standard deviation of MSA home prices changed over time. The clue was
that the standard deviation dropped meaningfully from the 1980s to the late
1990s.

With hindsight, we now know that a great liquidity cycle was pushing up
home prices across the country in a synchronized fashion. The correlation

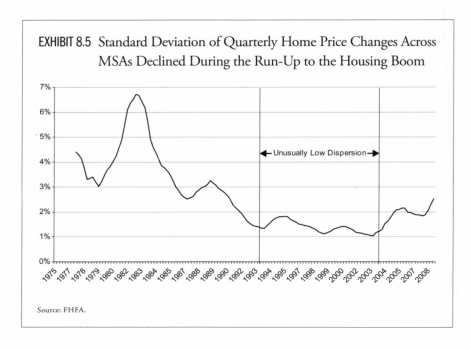

EXHIBIT 8.5 Standard Deviation of Quarterly Home Price Changes Across MSAs Declined During the Run-Up to the Housing Boom

Source: FHFA.

among home prices in different local markets had gone up under the influence of this underlying causative factor. In fact, so powerful had the global securitization markets become that correlations increased both among housing markets in different parts of the world and between housing and other securitization-funded markets, like commercial real estate.[12] In the United States, rising correlations across local markets meant that long-term volatility measurements for national home prices were no longer reliable. But few picked up on this.

As the liquidity cycle crested and then reversed, local home prices that had risen together began to fall together. By mid-2009, the U.S. average home price was already down 20%, according to Federal Housing Finance Authority (FHFA) data, and even further on other indexes. Based on the historical data, that crash represented a 3.5-standard-deviation event—quite improbable, according to the historical record, but understandable in light of the underlying force of the securitization markets. Needless to say, large numbers of subprime mortgages went bad in an extremely correlated fashion, much to the dismay of CDO investors.

Missing the Forest for the Trees

Getting correlation right depends on understanding causation. In the CDO and housing example, most analysts did not understand how the availability of mortgage credit was affecting the housing market. This "lurking" causative variable (Exhibit 8.6) was not directly apparent, but could be detected in the changing correlations between MSA-level home prices.

Humans have an inbuilt drive to search for causative variables. Some researchers believe we try too hard, as people sometimes insist they have found causal relationships even among random data. For example, in one famous study, test subjects imagined they could identify basketball players with a "hot hand," even when there was no statistical difference in the frequency of successful shots after a player had just made or missed the last few.[13] Missing causative relationships (as in the CDO market), or imagining ones that are not there (the hot hand), are both ways to go wrong. There is no magic answer to the search for causative drivers, but it helps to stick with the discipline of generating hypotheses, testing them, and learning from the results (Chapter 1).

Computers may help unearth some causal relationships, but they are no panacea. There are powerful computer techniques for measuring correlations. *Principal components analysis* can be used to map out the correlations in systems with large numbers of variables. When used to model interest rates,

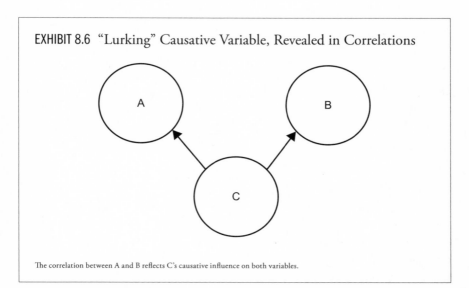

EXHIBIT 8.6 "Lurking" Causative Variable, Revealed in Correlations

The correlation between A and B reflects C's causative influence on both variables.

principal components analysis reveals that three variables—namely, the level of rates, the steepness of the yield curve, and the degree of curvature—explain anywhere between 95% and 99% of returns on Treasury securities over time.[14] Fixed-income analysts can build parsimonious models using these three variables, rather than trying to manipulate every point along the yield curve. The problem with applying these techniques to equities is that the range of causative factors is potentially unlimited. Further, an important variable in one time period may lose its relevance in the next. Until such time as computers can reason conceptually, the burden of identifying causative variables will fall on fundamental analysts.

Here are some practical suggestions for learning to recognize causal variables before it is too late:

- Allocate time, budget, or other resources to acquiring or developing expert knowledge about companies and industries of interest.
- Consider critical issues from the broader environment, such as macroeconomic, political, demographic, and social trends.
- Pay attention to intuitive responses, which are the way we typically recognize critical issues (Chapter 4).
- Search for possible linkages between critical issues by examining data or asking what-if questions.
- Watch how correlations change over time.
- Recognize that increasing volatility may signal the emergence of causative factors that were not previously apparent.

In a world of complexity and near-infinite information, understanding all causative variables is impossible, of course. That is why one should never lose sight of the importance of reacting quickly when conditions change.

Causation and Mapping

Understanding causation is crucial to mapping any problem, whether you are using a Monte Carlo model or the back of an envelope. If you do not understand the causal relationships, you will not be able to properly weight the important variables. Recall from Chapter 7 the process of decomposing a problem into smaller pieces, each of which is tackled individually and then recombined into a model to produce a more accurate estimate. The gain in

EXHIBIT 8.7 Effect on Volatility of the Number of Assumptions and the Correlation Between Assumptions

Volatility of Output

Correlation Between Assumptions	Number of Assumptions			
	2	3	4	5
0%	21%	17%	15%	13%
25%	24%	21%	20%	19%
50%	26%	24%	24%	23%
75%	28%	27%	27%	27%
100%	30%	30%	30%	30%

Figure assumes each input is described by a 30% standard deviation and has equal weighting.

accuracy occurs, in part, because some of the random error in the assumptions cancels out. But increasing the number of input variables will not reduce the model's aggregate volatility if those variables are correlated. As already noted here, Monte Carlo models can be extremely dangerous with the wrong correlation assumptions. Exhibit 8.7 illustrates this point. Suppose an analyst thought five input variables each had a 30% standard deviation but were uncorrelated with each other. In this case, he would come to a 13% estimate for the volatility of the output. But if those five variables were all influenced by an underlying causative factor (and were in actuality 100% correlated), then the correct volatility estimate would be 30%. This is one way in which analysts who undertake detailed research projects may become overconfident in their forecasts: they focus too much on each part of the analysis and not enough on the relations between the parts. Put more simply, they miss the forest for the trees.

We saw this mistake in the MasterCard case study, where I implicitly treated the six critical issues as uncorrelated, without recognizing that management incentives acted as an underlying causative driver. Similarly, in the Providian story, we discovered that competitive pressure underlay many of the critical issues. But not every situation is dominated by a single factor. In the Discover case study, several variables mattered: strategic considerations, credit risk, and interest rates.

In summary, when many variables are important, complex analytics like detailed scenario modeling and Monte Carlo simulation can help produce more accurate forecasts. But when one or two causative variables are dominant, the benefits of complex modeling are more questionable. The analyst or decision maker who understands the importance of the dominant variables will cut to the chase, focus resources on figuring them out, and more quickly recognize the potential for extreme outcomes than will analysts struggling to balance multiple variables in complex models. In a world where Black Swans come and go, it may be necessary to shift from complex analytics to simple decisions and back again.

Fannie Mae and the Mystery of the Missing Financial Statements

Our second story illustrates the power of the Monte Carlo model to produce accurate forecasts. Since this story involves Fannie Mae, we know that it ends in a situation where credit and liquidity risk became decisive. But the Monte Carlo model was appropriate for the time in question (2006), when many factors had to be considered—an example of the need for flexibility in picking one's tools.

After the revelation of Fannie's accounting problems in late 2004, sensible investors had all but given up trying to understand the company. The highly leveraged balance sheet was one problem. Another problem: Congress was threatening to enact stricter oversight rules, which might curtail growth. To top it all off, Fannie was not publishing timely financial statements. After its accounting debacle, the company had embarked on a multiyear project to redefine its accounting policies, retool its systems, and restate its financial results. It would not return to timely filing status until late 2007. In early 2006, the most recent full-year financial statements dated to 2003—and these had been discredited. The company's Web site warned investors not to rely on them.

A traditional value investor following the practices of Graham and Dodd would look for stocks with low price-to-book ratios. But what is book value without financial statements? To figure that out was our goal.

We started with four critical issues: the company's exposure to interest rate risk, credit risk, the possibility of new regulation, and—what we thought was the biggest question—the result of the accounting restatement, or what the books would look like once we finally got to see them. While the issues themselves were complicated, the causal relationships seemed straightforward, as pictured in the influence diagram in Exhibit 8.8.

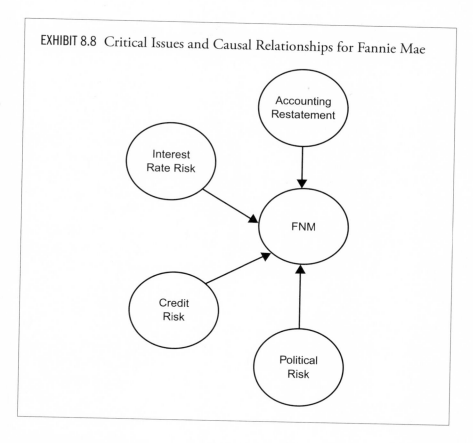

EXHIBIT 8.8 Critical Issues and Causal Relationships for Fannie Mae

Business Model Risk

By way of background, Fannie managed two sizable portfolios with different risks. Back in 2006, the more controversial of these was the "retained" portfolio, in which Fannie held mortgages and mortgage-backed securities for long-term investment. To fund new purchases, Fannie issued unsecured debt in the so-called government agency market, at spreads close to Treasuries. The retained portfolios at Fannie and its sibling Freddie Mac had grown at double-digit rates throughout the 1990s, and by 2006 each held $700 to $800 billion in assets. Critics saw this growth as an abuse of the companies' special charters, arguing that the low cost of agency debt reflected implicit government backing, an unfair advantage.[15]

Critics also warned of the perils of interest rate risk in Fannie's and Freddie's retained portfolios, which held mostly fixed-rate mortgages. Sudden shifts in interest rates affect the speed at which consumers pay off their mortgages, changing the expected duration of these assets and making it tricky to keep a stable margin. Fannie and Freddie's required equity cushion was only 2.5% of the retained portfolio balance, equivalent to a leverage ratio of 40:1 debt-to-equity—well above LTCM's leverage ratio of 25:1. Interest rate volatility could reduce the value of their mortgage investments, putting that small equity cushion at risk. To hedge this risk, Fannie and Freddie bought large volumes of interest rate derivatives. Critics worried that these derivatives might backfire.

My team had studied interest rate risk at Fannie and Freddie and had come to a more sanguine view of their risk management.[16] But that did not mean we could model earnings from this portfolio with any precision. We put our best guess of the portfolio's growth rate and margins into the Monte Carlo model, specified a range of variance around those assumptions, and made allowance for the possibility (remote, one hoped) of a major interest rate shock that could impair the portfolio. As it turned out, for all the controversy on this subject, interest rate risk was not to be a problem.

Fannie Mae was ultimately to go under because of its second portfolio, the so-called credit guarantee portfolio. Here the company guaranteed newly produced mortgages against default and repackaged them as securities that could be traded in the capital markets, thanks to the company's AAA-rated stamp of approval. Fannie collected guaranty fees from the mortgage companies servicing the loans; its main costs were occasional defaults on the mortgages it had guaranteed. In 2006, even the critics regarded this as a legitimate, low-risk business.

In the Monte Carlo simulation, we assumed a moderate growth rate for the credit guarantee portfolio. We thought credit losses would remain extremely low, on the order of 0.01% of the portfolio balance, although we allowed for some variance. Of course, today such loss rates seem ridiculously low. But in coming to this determination, we had studied nearly 20 years' worth of data. And we had cross-referenced our estimates against the assumptions underlying new capital standards for mortgages produced by staff economists at the Federal Reserve and by a roundtable of risk management experts from major commercial banks.[17] Put simply, prime mortgages historically had almost never defaulted. And Fannie and Freddie took the cream off the top, letting banks and finance companies compete for riskier loans. (In Chapter 9, we will discuss how things can go wrong when everyone draws the same conclusions from past data.)

Political Risk

If Fannie and Freddie's risks had been limited to just these two portfolios, then they might have been more popular stocks in early 2006. But investors were also concerned about reform legislation in Congress that might impose new costs and limit growth. Though the government-sponsored enterprises (GSEs) had been controversial for years, they could usually outmaneuver their political foes. Accounting scandals and management shake-ups eroded much of their credibility, however. The risk of unfavorable legislation could no longer be dismissed.

Two versions of GSE reform legislation were under discussion in 2006. Both the House of Representatives and the Senate would have created a new regulator with enhanced supervisory powers, including the authority to set higher capital standards. Higher capital would reduce the companies' leverage and depress their returns on equity. The Senate bill would have also required the GSEs to run off their retained portfolios, curtailing their ability to issue low-cost government agency debt and thus eliminating much of the value in this business.

Of course, we could not predict political outcomes precisely. Yet the Monte Carlo approach was meant to help us handle uncertainty. We set out to measure the range of informed opinion, reasoning that people in the know could make as good a prediction as anyone. To do this, we surveyed close GSE observers like consultants, lobbyists, journalists, and traders. We asked for their subjective estimates of whether reform legislation would pass and, assuming it did, the likelihood of higher capital standards and a requirement to run off the retained portfolios. These experts thought the writing was already on the wall: they foresaw an average 80% probability of reform legislation over the next few years and thought the firms would most likely face higher capital standards. But the retained portfolio runoff scenario seemed less credible; the odds here were only 25%.

We now had variables for political risk in the Monte Carlo model. They might not be perfect, but they were reasonable.

The Impact of New Accounting

We still lacked financial statements. But there was no shortage of information on which to base an estimate. Our strategy was much like that of the recovery team that located the sunken treasure ship: we would cobble together data from multiple sources into a format that fit the simulation model and see what came out.

First, we needed to define the question. Whatever the results of the financial restatement, they would show up as an adjustment to shareholders' equity. Instead of using the generally accepted accounting standards (GAAP) definition of equity, we decided to look at the "fair value" of equity, an estimate of the mark-to-market value of the company's assets and liabilities, which was disclosed in the footnotes to the annual report. We reasoned that investors would look through accounting distortions that might affect the company's GAAP results and focus instead on its economic value. By the time the company was seized in September 2008, mark-to-market accounting had become controversial, with some blaming it for exacerbating the global banking crisis. But these concerns were not on the radar screen in 2006.

Here were our clues:

• First, we had a long time series on both Fannie's and Freddie's book value (both accounting and fair value) dating back to the early 1990s. We observed a steady increase in accounting book value, consistent with the companies' stable earnings. The fair-value version of book value largely tracked the accounting results, although it bounced around during periods of capital-market volatility. This pattern made sense to us, and we figured it was a trustworthy starting point.

• High interest rate volatility made 2002 and 2003 difficult years for Fannie Mae. During 2002 the Federal Reserve lowered interest rates to offset the recessionary impact of the stock market crash. Then during the summer of 2003, interest rates shot back up. Skeptics thought Fannie's derivatives might not have sheltered its retained portfolio as intended. Some claimed that the company was economically insolvent. But Fannie disclosed measures of the interest rate risk in its portfolio each month, and using these figures, an outsider could make a fair guess as to the portfolio's gains and losses. Our calculations dovetailed with the company's annual disclosures, so we felt we were on relatively solid ground.

• For 2004 and 2005, we had no fair-value disclosures from Fannie. But its sister company Freddie Mac had already completed a similar accounting restatement. We knew how Freddie's fair value of equity had performed, and the two companies' business models were similar. So we used Freddie's results as a base case for Fannie, with the simulation model incorporating a band of variance around them.

• Finally, we reviewed reports on Fannie's capital published by its regulator, then called the Office of Federal Housing Enterprise Oversight (OFHEO). These reports deserved some weight, we reasoned, since the regulator had staff on site at Fannie with access to nonpublic data, such as weekly cash flow reports. Fannie's new auditors were examining the books as diligently as possible, given the high stakes of opining on a company emerging from scandal. If they found something amiss, they would report it to the company's board of directors, which would notify OFHEO. So when OFHEO issued a quarterly capital classification report indicating that Fannie had $29 per share in regulatory capital, we put a subjective 80% probability on that as a floor for its fair value, too.

After all these estimates and assumptions were translated into inputs, the Monte Carlo simulation model produced a distribution for the fair value of common equity that we expected the company eventually to report for restated year-end 2005.

We then ran the Monte Carlo model for the entire company, combining assumptions about the two portfolios' risk factors together with those for the political and accounting risks. The distribution appears in Exhibit 8.9. The mean, which corresponded to our best estimate of the value of the company, came to $72 per share, well above the stock price of $55 at the time. The standard deviation of the distribution was 23%, essentially the same as the implied volatility then discounted in Fannie Mae stock options. The options market seemed to be gauging the level of uncertainty accurately, but we thought equity investors were too conservative in valuing the stock. Out of all the risk factors in the model, the net interest margin was the largest source of volatility, reflecting no doubt the history of concern about interest rate risk. This variable was followed by political risk and credit risk. Exhibit 8.10 shows the contribution of each factor to the total volatility we estimated for the stock, revealing the weights that we had implicitly placed on the critical issues.

Based on this analysis, I recommended a strategy that combined ownership of the stock with the sale of a put option struck at $55 that expired in early 2007[18]—another variation of the option strangle (Chapter 3). Since we had studied the risk factors at great length, we believed we could accurately estimate a confidence interval around the stock price. The primary catalyst

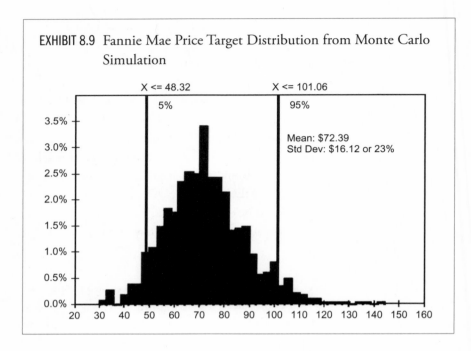

EXHIBIT 8.9 Fannie Mae Price Target Distribution from Monte Carlo Simulation

was to be completion of the restatement, at which point I expected the fair value of common equity per share to be disclosed in the mid-$30s. By selling the put, an investor would capture a premium of $4 per share, which added to the returns we envisioned if the stock moved toward our target price. The risk in selling the put was that the investor would be on the hook to buy more shares if the stock ended below $50 at the time of expiration. In other words, the put provided extra yield but doubled the downside risk of owning the shares.

Soon after my recommendation, Fannie stock dropped to $45 (Exhibit 8.11). Anyone following my strategy would have suffered a mark-to-market loss on the stock and the option. The financial research team of which I was a member had just launched a model portfolio. This trade dropped us into the red. Teammates eyed me with suspicion.

Within a few months, however, the stock recovered back into the $50s. We closed the put option recommendation at a profit without waiting for it to expire.

In December 2006, Fannie completed the first phase of its massive restatement, producing audited results for the years 2002 through 2004. Fair

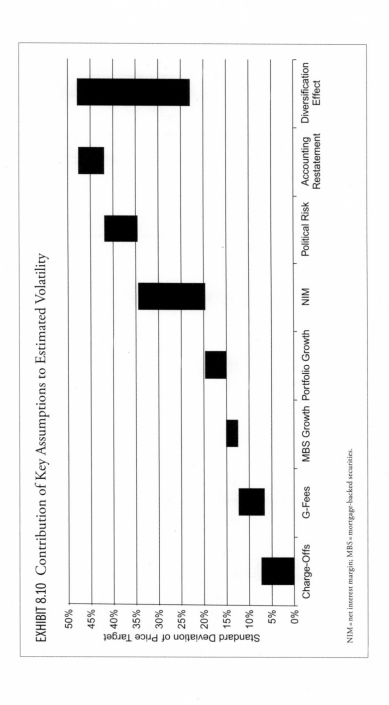

EXHIBIT 8.10 Contribution of Key Assumptions to Estimated Volatility

NIM = net interest margin; MBS = mortgage-backed securities.

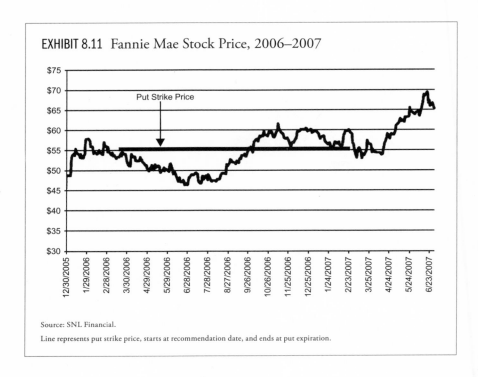

EXHIBIT 8.11 Fannie Mae Stock Price, 2006–2007

Source: SNL Financial.

Line represents put strike price, starts at recommendation date, and ends at put expiration.

value at the end of 2004 was $32 per share, slightly ahead of our estimate of $31.50.[19] The simulation model indeed put us in the right ballpark.

A Monte Carlo simulation can aggregate information from many sources to produce a probabilistic estimate, which, in this case, proved surprisingly accurate. But the Fannie Mae story does not end there. Although the volatility estimate that emerged from the simulation model was calibrated with the volatility implied in the options markets, in hindsight my team (and the markets) underestimated the risk. We did not appreciate the magnitude of the looming credit cycle, which was to break with full force in little more than a year.

Another factor we failed to fully grasp was the interaction between business model and political risk. As part of our modeling, we assumed zero correlation between political risk and interest rate or credit risk. But this was not a sound assumption. Politics was both the source of Fannie's strength and a cause of its demise. The perceived government backing indeed let the firm issue large quantities of low-cost debt. But to stay in good graces with politicians, who expected the GSEs to help support the housing markets, the companies appear to have loosened their underwriting standards too far. They guaranteed so-called alt-A loans (whose risk lay between subprime and prime) and bought AAA-rated tranches from subprime securitizations. Unfortunately, even small amounts of these assets were to contribute significant losses. It would not be right to blame political pressure for all of the GSEs' problems, but political risk contributed to credit risk. These two variables were not independent of one another.

Then credit risk exacerbated political risk. In the summer of 2008, investors began to fear that the GSEs would not be able to roll over their short-term debt as it matured. GSE debt spreads widened, despite the implicit government backing that investors had long regarded as a source of strength. Given the firm's credit problems, as well as questions about government policy (which was after all only implicit), investors would not inject the new equity necessary to get them back on their feet. For the government, letting the institutions fail was unthinkable, and with their size and importance in the mortgage market, letting them founder was not an option, either. Treasury secretary Hank Paulson decided to backstop the GSEs, but only after their regulator placed them in conservatorship, in effect wiping out the equity. This action was necessary, he stated, because of

ambiguities in the GSE Congressional charters, which have been perceived to indicate government support for agency debt and guaranteed MBS. Our nation has tolerated these ambiguities for too long, and as a result GSE debt and MBS are held by central banks and investors throughout the United States and around the world who believe them to be virtually risk-free. Because the U.S. Government created these ambiguities, we have a responsibility to both avert and ultimately address the systemic risk now posed by the scale and breadth of the holdings of GSE debt and MBS.[20]

Because of the "ambiguities" inherent in their special nature of their charters, the GSEs got harsher treatment than major banks like Citigroup, which received government insurance on their assets, guarantees of their debt, injections of preferred equity, and then the conversion of the preferred into common at favorable prices. The GSE charter, which had been for so long the company's most important asset, had become a fatal liability (Exhibit 8.12).

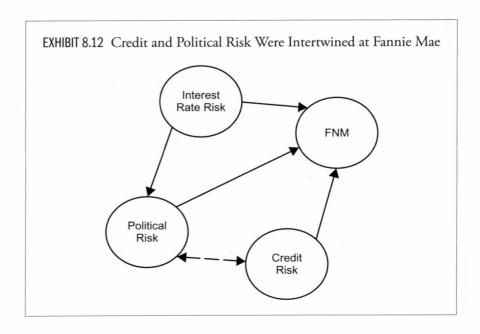

EXHIBIT 8.12 Credit and Political Risk Were Intertwined at Fannie Mae

Epilogue: In the End, Monte Carlo Models Could Not Save Fannie

Fannie Mae and Freddie Mac make an interesting case study in Monte Carlo modeling because simulation analysis was central to their operations and risk management. Because of their sensitivity to interest rates, mortgages are commonly valued using Monte Carlo models. In a typical model, valuing a loan requires something like 300 different interest rate "paths" (or scenarios). With around 12 million loans in the GSE portfolios, a full analysis would require 3.6 billion simulation paths. Testing how the entire portfolio might respond to shocks in interest rates, home prices, and unemployment (a typical risk management exercise) would call for, say, 10,000 economic scenarios, bringing us to a total of 36 trillion paths. Even with the ability to distribute complex calculations across extensive computer networks, full Monte Carlo simulations of certain types of fixed-income portfolios could take hundreds of machine days, according to risk management experts.[21] There are shortcuts to make this process more tractable. But perhaps there is a lesson—that is, financial services firms can reach only a certain size and complexity before their risks become, in practice, unquantifiable.

Interestingly, using Monte Carlo models to plumb the mysteries of the GSEs caught on with outside observers. The *Journal of Monetary Economics* published a Monte Carlo analysis of Fannie Mae and its sister Freddie Mac in 2006, written by Deborah Lucas and Robert McDonald of Northwestern University's Kellogg School of Management. They used the model to estimate both the probability that the companies would default and the resulting cost to the government, as a function of regulatory scrutiny, capital standards, growth rates, and other factors.[22]

In July 2008, the Congressional Budget Office used a Monte Carlo simulation to estimate the cost to the government of potential failure at Fannie Mae and Freddie Mac, which suddenly seemed more likely than my analysis or the Northwestern professors'. The CBO analysis concluded that the probability that the GSEs would need assistance from the government was less than 50%, that there was a 5% probability their losses would exceed $100 billion, and that the probability-weighted average across thousands of scenarios implied an expected cost to the government of $25 billion.[23]

As the crisis intensified during August 2008, the Treasury hired investment bankers to help it understand the GSEs' portfolios and advise it on possible options. The bankers planned to put information about Freddie Mac's portfolio into their own simulation model to provide an independent risk assessment. Unfortunately, this process was going to take several weeks.[24] How much time would have been required for computer calculations and how much for logistics, such as reading tapes and translating formats, I am not sure. In any event, the Treasury department believed that it could not wait this long to take action, so these calculations were in practice intractable. Within a few weeks, Fannie and Freddie were seized by their regulator. Even a year later, the ultimate loss content of their mortgage portfolios remained an unknown; I presume that the companies continue to run their Monte Carlo models, recalibrating as necessary.

Chapter 9

Judgment

When . . . difficult cases occur, they are difficult, chiefly because while we have them under consideration, all the reasons pro and con are not present to the mind at the same time, but sometimes one set present themselves, and at other times another, the first being out of sight. Hence the various purposes or inclinations that alternatively prevail, and the uncertainty that perplexes us.

—Benjamin Franklin,
The Complete Works of Benjamin Franklin, 1887

An enormous and almost unequivocal research literature implies expert judgments are rarely impressively accurate and virtually never better than a mechanical judgment rule. . . . The implication for practice seems clear: Whenever possible, human judges should be replaced by simple linear models.

—Reid Hastie and Robyn M. Dawes,
Rational Choice in an Uncertain World, 2001

This book has argued that fundamental research and analysis can improve decision making in volatile environments. But the analytic tools we have discussed—intuition, mental simulation, computer modeling—all share the limitation of any algorithmic routine: they cannot be counted on to solve every problem. For this reason, successful decision making requires something extra, which we will call *judgment.*

The textbook approach to judgment advises weighing the pros and cons. Though weighing is a necessary step, the advice nonetheless misses the bigger picture: judgment is a kind of recursive process, in which we turn our analytic tools on the very process by which we come to decisions. While the inner workings of the human mind are still veiled, one of the pioneers of artificial intelligence, Marvin Minsky of the Massachusetts Institute of Technology (MIT), conjectures that the brain selects among different ways to think, depending on the problem type and the pace of progress toward goals.[1] If so, this may be how judgment is hardwired in the brain. One sees judgment in action when a decision maker weighs different "ways to think"—for example, balancing the output of a sophisticated computer model against intuitive insights. Judgment is also practiced when executives evaluate their corporate strategy in the light of changing competitive conditions.

Judgment is a critical defense against the Black Swans that arise when too many people follow the same style of analysis and decision making without recognizing that their collective behavior can bring about a break with the past. We have already seen how this form of misjudgment contributed to the mortgage, housing, and capital-market crisis that erupted in 2007. This chapter has several stories that illustrate similar misjudgments with swanlike outcomes. In the "Quant Quake" of 2007, those who followed fully quantitative investment strategies suffered devastating losses, just like the traditional value investors profiled in Chapter 4. Sticking with a risk management strategy that worked in the past led to a fatal misstep for MBNA, the largest independent credit card issuer before its acquisition by Bank of America. On a larger scale, the banking crisis of 2008 revealed the enormous misjudgment implicit in the regulatory capital regime known as Basel II. And strategic misjudgments contributed to the 90% decline in the shares of Sallie Mae, the nation's largest student lender.

Introduction to Sallie Mae

Like Countrywide's, the story of Sallie Mae shows the importance of changing strategies and the consequences of missing opportunities to do so. The nation's largest student lender, Sallie Mae was formed in 1972 as a government-sponsored entity (GSE). Its mission was to help ensure a liquid secondary market for student loans, so that originators could access fresh capital to produce new loans. In the mid-1990s, under the leadership of chief executive officer (CEO) Al Lord, the company embarked on a different strategy. As a

GSE, it was limited to purchasing newly produced loans from banks and other originators. But Lord saw an opportunity to boost profits by bypassing the banks and originating loans directly from student borrowers, as well as undertaking other business activities not permitted under the GSE charter.

In 1997, Sallie started down the path to privatization. By 2004, it had weaned itself from the government agency debt market, turning instead to unsecured corporate debt and the securitization markets. Freed from the restrictions of its charter, it built up a sizable origination capacity, acquired smaller student lenders, hired a sales force to call on college financial aid offices, and developed technology that made it easy for schools and students to connect with the company. Along the way, Sallie diversified into new products, including so-called private (not government-guaranteed) student loans. As the company grew, established a dominant market share, and produced strong returns, its stock price soared. From the start of Lord's tenure as CEO in 1997 through the end of 2002, the stock rose almost 3.5 times, equivalent to an annual appreciation rate in excess of 20%. Switching strategies was an enormous success.

Taking note of the earnings growth, strong market position, and rising stock price, I began studying Sallie Mae in 2002. On the basis of my research into the education industry, I regarded government-guaranteed student lending as a steady business. But the stock looked expensive, trading at a lofty valuation of nearly 10 times tangible book value (a measure of shareholders' equity that excludes goodwill). Also, I was concerned about political support for the government program: Democrats preferred direct lending by the government, Republican support had wavered in the past, and schools thought students were graduating with too much debt.

Sallie Mae's high leverage also gave me pause. With capital less than 3% of assets, or a debt-to-equity ratio in excess of 33:1, its leverage was higher than that of Long-Term Capital Management (LTCM). To be fair, the vast majority of its assets were government-guaranteed student loans, which do not need much capital since Washington takes on nearly all the credit and interest rate risk. But the company had little cushion for other kinds of risk, like operating, political, legal, or reputational risk. Such a thin capital ratio may have made sense for a GSE that benefited from implicit government backing, as Fannie and Freddie did for many years (until their final crisis). But as a private entity, Sallie Mae was at the mercy of financial markets for its funding needs.

Further, as Roger Lister, a colleague in the fixed-income department, pointed out to me, Sallie Mae had entered into "forward repurchase commitments," contracts with broker-dealers under which Sallie arranged to buy back its own stock in the future at a specified price. Plenty of companies buy back stock when cash builds up without investment opportunities. But a forward commitment at a fixed price is a relatively unusual transaction, and it raises the stakes. If the stock rallies, the company makes a profit because it buys back its stock at a price that has ended up below market. But if the stock price were to fall, then the company would have to buy it back at an above-market price. This scenario would not only produce a loss, but it could also mean a cash drain at an inopportune time. In magnifying the positive and negative outcomes, the forward commitment was just like extra leverage. At Sallie, the forward commitment signaled management's confidence that the stock would continue to rise. Recall that Professor Sydney Finkelstein had found that managers of dominant companies sometimes became overconfident, overestimated their control of the environment, and underestimated the role of chance and circumstance (Chapter 6).

Thinking the stock overvalued, I initiated coverage in 2003 with an underweight rating.[2] Over the next three years, earnings per share would come in just slightly ahead of my forecast (finishing 2006 at $2.80, as opposed to my original forecast of $2.70). But the stock continued to rally: my underweight rating was an unsuccessful call (Exhibit 9.1). In 2006, the company lost the joint venture with JP Morgan (Chapter 6), but it responded by cutting prices, boosting market share, and accelerating the growth of its private student loan portfolio. On further investigation into the private loan market, the reason for the growth seemed legitimate: students needed private student loans to fill the widening gap between rising education costs and stagnant federal aid programs. I thought private student lending might be a risk to my negative stance on the stock. In May 2006, I upgraded Sallie Mae to equal-weight.[3] It was time to take a fresh look at the stock and reassess my strategy.

My analysis focused on the 4 critical issues in the influence diagram in Exhibit 9.2. As I studied the company's business, I found the government-guaranteed business had become something of a loss leader. Its real value seemed to lie in positioning lenders to compete for private loans. Indeed, I concluded that private loans would generate most of Sallie's profit growth.

When Sallie reported its 2006 fourth-quarter results, the net interest margin was weaker than analysts expected, and earnings were hurt by unexpected write-offs. The stock sold off.

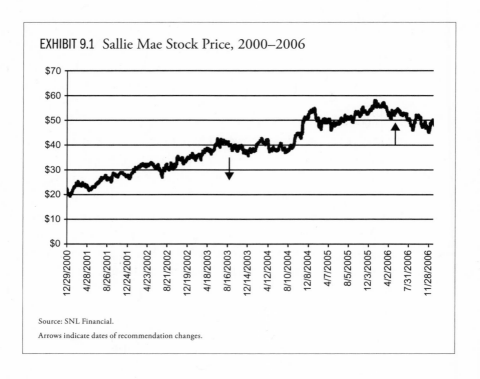

EXHIBIT 9.1 Sallie Mae Stock Price, 2000–2006

Source: SNL Financial.

Arrows indicate dates of recommendation changes.

Meanwhile, investors had become anxious about the government-guaranteed lending program because of mounting pressure on the Federal budget. While the Republicans continued to defend the student lending program, the Democrats pushed ever more assertively to cut subsidies for lenders. Whether anything substantive would happen was not clear, but the risk did not faze me because I viewed guaranteed lending as a loss leader. Cutting subsidies would force out smaller and less efficient firms, and Sallie would pick up market share, thanks to its size and cost structure.

With the stock now at $45, and my analysis indicating a fair value of $50, I saw an opportunity to bet on a rebound. Rather than buying the shares for only moderate upside (from $45 to $50), I recommended a strategy involving call options that would produce a higher return if the stock rebounded.

We see a buying opportunity in SLM shares. Last week, the shares sold off in the wake of disappointing 4Q results and the passage in the House of Representatives of HR 5, which would curtail subsidies for student lenders like Sallie. With the stock now below our intrinsic value estimate of $50, we hy-

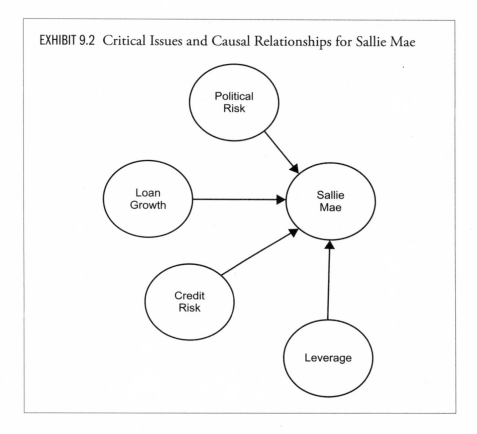

EXHIBIT 9.2 Critical Issues and Causal Relationships for Sallie Mae

pothesize that investors have over discounted for political and balance sheet risk and may have lost sight of the significant growth opportunity in private loans.[4]

My timing was unfortunate. The Bush administration's budget for 2007, released a few weeks later, contained a bombshell: the administration had decided to side with the Democrats and call for significant cutbacks in guaranteed student loans. (According to a source, the president had "flip-flopped" out of political necessity, needing support from Democrats to continue funding the war in Iraq.) The implications were unsettling: lenders were going to face a severe shakeout, much worse than what investors had previously feared. While Sallie was certainly going to be a survivor, that did not mean its earnings would be unaffected. The stock slid toward $40.

Now another problem surfaced. The repurchase forward commitment—that unusual transaction with which management had signaled its confidence in a rising stock price—suddenly became a liability. With a forward buyback price of roughly $45 per share, the contract was going to produce a mark-to-market loss in the next quarter, resulting in a hit to equity. Further, if the stock continued to fall, the liability would become ever larger, putting more pressure on Sallie's thin capital base and leaving the company vulnerable to a positive feedback loop with its own stock price.

My recommendation had proved a bust, as the falling stock price quickly wiped out the value of the call option I had recommended. It was once again time to reevaluate my strategy. Little did I know it, but the company was reevaluating its strategy, too.

The Practice of Judgment

Under the textbook approach, judgment is considered *a process of weighing the evidence before coming to a decision*. Experts often cite the advice of Benjamin Franklin, who came up with a simple method for weighing the pros and cons over 200 years ago:

> My way is to divide half a sheet of paper by a line into two columns; writing over the one Pro, and the other Con. Then, during three or four days of consideration, I put down under the different heads short hints of the different motives, that at different times occur to me, for or against the measure.
>
> When I have thus got them all together in one view, I endeavor to estimate their respective weights; and where I find two, one on each side, that seem equal, I strike them both out. If I find a reason pro equal to some two reasons con, I strike out the three . . . and thus proceeding I find at length where the balance lies . . . .
>
> And, though the weight of reasons cannot be taken with the precision of algebraic quantities, yet when each is thus considered, separately and comparatively, and the whole lies before me, I think I can judge better, and am less liable to make a rash step, and in fact I have found great advantage from this kind of equation. . . .[5]

Franklin's approach has many merits—for example, reducing the load on working memory, as most people have trouble focusing on more than a handful of variables at once. Some experts would replace the pros and cons with numerical quantities and use a linear model (like a spreadsheet) to add them up. They argue that using linear models leads to a significant improvement in accuracy over intuitive judgments.[6] Models are not only more precise in their calculations, but they eliminate emotion, bias, and other forms of human error.

But there is a major problem with any process of weighing or adding up multiple factors, regardless of whether the process is conducted intuitively, more deliberately (with pen and paper, as Franklin suggested), or using high-powered computer models. I have pointed out different aspects of this problem throughout this book. To summarize:

• The analyst must zero in on critical issues, or be forced to weigh an infinite number of factors (Chapter 4).
• In practice, we may assign weights to variables on the basis of confidence as an emotional signal, which does not always reflect the accuracy of the analysis (Chapter 3).
• We need to be careful not to overweight the critical issues that we study most carefully, ignoring or underweighting other variables in the environment, a sign that we may have fallen into the representativeness trap (Chapter 3).
• In an uncertain world, we may need to consider multiple outcomes for critical issues so that we recognize the full range of the risks. We cannot add up the variables properly if we miss asymmetries (recall Jensen's inequality from Chapter 2). That is why the weighing-up process must often be conducted using probability trees.
• The process of adding up can become intractably complex because of the combinatorial explosion of interactions between variables. For this reason, analysts must map out the problem, seeking to balance gains in accuracy against the costs of complexity (Chapter 7).
• Analysts cannot add up variables properly without grasping the correlations among them, which requires a sound understanding of the causative drivers (Chapter 8).
• Finally, all these weighing processes are essentially algorithmic in nature. Algorithms cannot solve all problems, because for some, calculations will never stop—this is the "halting problem" identified by Alan Turing in the 1930s

(Chapter 4). For this reason, some kind of oversight, which we are calling judgment, is necessary to assess whether an analytic process is producing useful results, or whether some other process should be used instead.

Sometimes judgment is seen in the imposition of a seemingly arbitrary constraint on the output of a sophisticated computer model. For example, portfolio managers often use statistical models to search for the "efficient frontier," where they hope to maximize risk-adjusted returns by optimally allocating capital across a portfolio of investments. These kinds of optimization models have a tendency (no doubt mathematically correct) to concentrate portfolios in a small number of assets with high expected returns. But portfolio managers are rarely comfortable with such concentrated allocations. More often they spread their bets, even at the cost of earning suboptimal returns. In doing so, they are acknowledging the presence of what Martin Leibowitz calls "dragon risk," a reference to the practice of medieval mapmakers, who labeled uncharted territories as places where dragons might dwell. Leibowitz uses the term dragon risk to refer to the possibility that the statistical model might be invalid, or that if many managers allocate assets similarly, the returns might become correlated with the broader market and collapse in a downturn.[7]

Judgment may also be recognized in a give-and-take debate, where decision makers weigh computer models against other factors. Goldman Sachs was one of the few financial institutions that profited from the subprime mortgage meltdown, and part of the difference was the judgment exercised by its leaders. The company shorted the ABX index just like the hedge fund in Chapter 4, earning more than $1 billion in profits during 2007. During this period, senior executives were monitoring the value-at-risk (VaR, a statistical measure of potential loss) associated with the firm's mortgage position, as well as grilling the mortgage traders on the rationale for their bets. On separate occasions, the executives forced the traders to downsize their positions, even though the trades were profitable, in order to keep the VaR in check. At other times, they allowed the VaR to rise to an all-time high.[8]

Thinking About Competitors

The traditional definition of judgment ignores the competitive dynamic, a serious risk when other decision makers are analyzing the same historical data and possibly coming to similar conclusions (Exhibit 9.3). Recall the

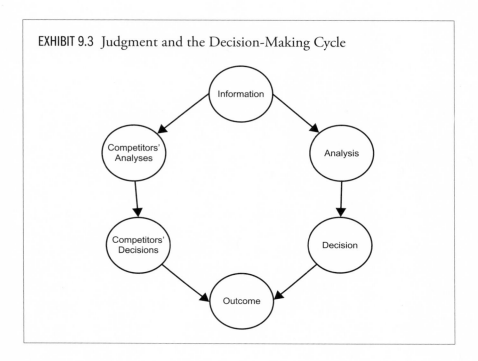

EXHIBIT 9.3 Judgment and the Decision-Making Cycle

subprime mortgage debacle. Mortgage underwriting models were based on a statistical analysis of credit scores, loan characteristics, and past loss rates. (No doubt the psychology researchers quoted at the start of this chapter would have nodded in approval at the use of "mechanical judgment rules.") On the basis of the statistical analysis, it was perfectly rational for lenders to loosen underwriting standards when loss rates came in so far below expectations. But when the entire market loosened standards, the result was a massive increase in subprime lending, big enough to affect home prices. Ultimately the outcome shifted from better-than-expected loss rates to much worse. Computerized decision-making models had produced the wrong answers, albeit with greater speed and consistency than human analysts.

Strategy requires judgment. A strategy simplifies organizational decision making, providing leaders and staff with a set of rules to follow. But like any checklist approach, a strategy is at heart just an algorithm: it cannot be counted on to give the right answer (or any answer) for every problem. When the competitive environment changes, the strategy will need rethinking. Recognizing these situations is an act of judgment. Shifting strategies is difficult enough for investors; it must be one of the greatest challenges for corporate decision makers, especially when a strategy has produced excellent results in the past. What makes judgment so difficult is that the actions of competitors are paramount, yet rarely do decision makers have detailed information about their peers. Life-or-death decisions may turn on anecdotal impressions, guesswork, or intuitive hunches—hardly grist for the mill of formal decision making.

Value Investing Reduced to Algorithms

The premise of an investment strategy or "style" is that following a set of rules will produce superior returns. Styles economize on investors' computational resources, that is, their time and mental effort. But styles miss the importance of judgment, and this shortcoming renders them unreliable. Value investing is a case in point. Not only did traditional value managers suffer poor results during the crash of 2007 (like the mutual fund managers from Chapter 4), but so did fully quantitative strategies that had replicated many principles of value investing with computer algorithms.

Value investing is based on a set of simple rules, such as selecting stocks that look cheap under traditional valuation metrics. Exhibit 9.4 summarizes a popular book by Chris Browne, a respected value manager, as an algorithmic procedure. The process starts by screening for stocks with low valuations. Then the analyst runs the companies through a series of filters, looking to pull out those with unacceptable risks.

Joel Greenblatt, a noted hedge fund manager, offers an even simpler approach to value investing. He recommends a "magic formula" as a strategy for sorting stocks. The idea behind the formula is to buy stocks with high returns on capital and low valuations. Based on back-testing, he claims that the magic formula would have outperformed the market (some are skeptical of his calculations).[9] An even more efficient approach, sparing the investor the trouble of calculating formulas, would be the "The Buffett System," which I happened upon while surfing the Internet. This system tells investors "exactly how to invest like Warren Buffett":

> With The Buffett System, you punch in a few quick numbers, answer a few simple questions about your stock and poof: you're told right away whether or not that particular stock is a "Buffett stock" worth investing in. . . . Never again waste precious hours analyzing balance sheets and income statements. Instead,

EXHIBIT 9.4 Value Investing Style, Represented as an Algorithmic Process

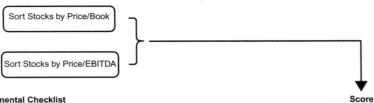

Sort Stocks by Price/Book

Sort Stocks by Price/EBITDA

Fundamental Checklist   **Score**

1. What is the outlook for raising prices?

2. Can the company sell more?

3. What is the outlook for gross profit margin?

4. Can the company control expenses?

5. If the company raises sales, will extra profits fall to the bottom line?

6. Can the company be as profitable as its competitors?

7. Does the company have one-time expenses that will not need to be paid in the future?

8. Does the company have unprofitable operations that can be shed?

9. Is the company comfortable with Wall Street's earnings estimates?

10. How much can the company grow over the next 5 years?

11. What will the company do with excess cash generated by the business?

12. What does the company expect its competitors to do?

13. How does the company compare financially with competitors?

14. What would the company be worth if it were sold?

15. Does the company plan to buy back stock?

16. Are insiders buying or selling the stock?

Sum Scores

Rank Stocks

Based on C. Browne, *The Little Book of Value Investing* (Hoboken, NJ: Wiley, 2007).

EBITDA = earnings before interest, taxes, depreciation, and amortization.

The Buffett System does this for you and shows you exactly how to find the few numbers that actually matter when it comes to investing in a stock.[10]

There is much experience, common sense, and wisdom embedded in Browne's rules and Greenblatt's formula. But these are algorithmic approaches, and they omit the critical aspect of human judgment: the need to ask whether the analysis or algorithm or style is producing the right answer, or whether it needs to be adjusted to take into account new factors, such as the effect of competition. This shortcoming became evident during 2007, not only to traditional value managers, but also to the new breed of ultrasophisticated quant investors.

The Quant Quake of August 2007

One of the most profitable and fastest-growing investment niches, fully quantitative strategies had amassed at their peak in June 2007 some $205 billion in equity assets under management, accounting for more than 20% of hedge fund holdings and 1% of total equity market capitalization.[11]

Early quant investors used computers to exploit small discrepancies in the trading patterns of pairs of similar stocks. When one of the two stocks moved more than the other, the variance might reflect the execution of a large block trade, in which case the two stocks ought to subsequently converge.[12] This strategy, which has come to be known as "statistical arbitrage," has evolved to include larger baskets of stocks and faster execution times. Quant investors have also developed many other strategies.

Certain quant strategies resemble traditional value investing. Value investors love Benjamin Graham's description of "Mr. Market" as a "manic-depressive."[13] Their goal is to buy stocks when Mr. Market is depressed, a situation in which traders all hold bearish views, and they are willing to wait over many years for valuations to revert to normal. Under quantitative mean-reversion strategies, computer algorithms buy stocks that have gone down and sell those that have risen, seeking to exploit microshifts in Mr. Market's mood over holding periods measured in minutes. Some quant shops run "fundamental" strategies that trade stocks on the basis of statistical relationships with macrofactors, company data, or valuation indicators. Some of these strategies have a "value bias" in that they favor stocks with low price-to-book multiples.

Because of the high velocity with which algorithmic strategies generate buy and sell orders, these computer models operate without human intervention. However, human judgment becomes necessary when the strategy stops performing. Then the human principals must decide whether to recalibrate the model, abort the strategy, or stay the course.

Quant strategies had produced steady profits—with moderate volatility and low correlation to the broad market—for at least five years before they were finally tested in early August 2007 (Exhibit 9.5). In the course of two days, the median quant investor suffered an unprecedented –14% return, before considering leverage, which would have significantly amplified losses. According to media reports, some of the best-known quant investors suffered devastating losses: Renaissance Technologies reported a 9% loss, Highbridge Capital lost 18%, and Goldman Sachs Global Equity Opportunity Fund was down 30%. The firms' principals had to make crucial decisions about reducing positions or sticking with their strategies. Those who stuck to their guns recovered much of their gains. But many chose to deleverage. By December 2007, total quant equity holdings had dropped from the prior $205 billion peak to $130 billion because of deleveraging and redemptions.[14]

Because of the secretive nature of hedge fund investing, no one knows exactly what happened to trigger this crash. However, a recent study by Amir Khandani and Andrew Lo of MIT sheds some light on the events of early August. In a minute-by-minute analysis of stock prices and quant strategy returns, they found signs that fundamental quant strategies with a bias to value factors started to underperform on August 1. Negative returns may have been triggered when multistrategy hedge funds that had taken large losses on holdings of subprime securities began to liquidate their equity holdings. Recall that this was when Countrywide was struggling with deteriorating liquidity in the mortgage securitization market. Khandani and Lo found that on August 6, underperformance for value factor strategies was especially severe in financial stocks. By August 8, underperformance had spread to stocks in all industry groups. They hypothesize that hedge funds following statistical arbitrage strategies predicated on daily mean reversion withdrew liquidity from the market, exacerbating losses for those that remained.

This was the crucial juncture. The decision to stay the course or fold would have a major impact on returns. For these kinds of decisions, the statistical models were of no help—after all, these models had just produced enormous losses. Rather, the decision had to turn on judgments about the competitive

EXHIBIT 9.5 The Quantitative Shock of August 2007

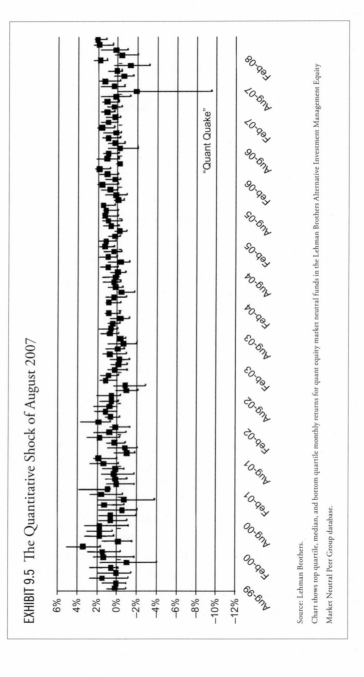

Source: Lehman Brothers.

Chart shows top quartile, median, and bottom quartile monthly returns for quant equity market neutral funds in the Lehman Brothers Alternative Investment Management Equity Market Neutral Peer Group database.

landscape, based on whatever scraps of information or anecdotal impressions the fund managers had of their peers.

Khandani and Lo quote a quant analyst: "By and large, [quant models] understated the risks as they were not calibrated for quant managers/models becoming our own asset class, creating our own contagion." Khandani and Lo conclude that "industry participants directly involved in the Quant Meltdown may not have been fully aware of the broader milieu in which they were operating."[15]

The lesson of this story is that algorithmic models of any kind—whether checklist rules, investment styles, or the most sophisticated quantitative modeling—are at risk once competition replicates their strategies. Decision makers must pass judgment on the efficacy of their models in a continual process of learning about, adapting to, and—where possible—anticipating the impact of competitive forces.

The dean of fundamental research, Benjamin Graham, would not have been surprised by the Quant Quake of 2007. He had developed a numerical system to predict the stock market, but after some initial success, he noticed that its accuracy had faded with time. Writing in the late 1940s, decades before the advent of quantitative investing, he observed:

> [The decline in efficacy of this system] demonstrates an inherent characteristic of forecasting and trading formulas in the fields of business and finance. Those formulas that gain adherents and importance do so because they have worked well over a period, or sometimes merely because they have been plausibly adapted to the statistical record of the past. But as their acceptance increases, their reliability tends to diminish. This happens for two reasons: First, the passage of time brings new conditions which the old formula no longer fits. Second, in stock-market affairs the popularity of a trading theory has itself an influence on the market's behavior which detracts in the long run from its profit-making possibilities. . . . The advent of popularity marked almost the exact moment when the system ceased to work well.[16]

MBNA's Risk Management Stumble

Strategies consist of rules that simplify decision making. Judgment requires considering the possible shortcomings of these rules, especially given the effects of changing competition. The story of MBNA illustrates how failure to factor in the competition led a tried-and-true risk management strategy to backfire, with unfortunate results. Once the leading independent credit card issuer, MBNA was famous for marketing "affinity" credit cards, which carry the imprint of not-for-profit associations, schools, sports teams, or other organizations. Over the years, the company had issued thousands of affinity cards, building a large base of loyal customers. MBNA's success also reflected a cultlike devotion to customer service among its thousands of employees. Visitors to its headquarters encountered the mantra "Think of yourself as a customer" carved over every single doorway throughout the facility (even washrooms). With a unique strategy and strong execution, MBNA produced growing profits and a rising stock price for many years.

MBNA also followed a unique risk management strategy. It made a practice of borrowing short and lending long. According to the belt-and-suspenders approach to risk management, companies are supposed to match the duration of assets and liabilities. This sensible precept sprang up in the aftermath of the savings and loan crisis. Savings institutions (or "thrifts") had traditionally borrowed short (overnight deposits) and lent long (fixed-rate mortgages). When interest rates soared in the early 1980s, thrift deposit costs went through the roof, but yields on their mortgages did not change, as they were fixed. Margins were crushed, and thrifts went bust by the thousands.[17]

The reason for MBNA's unconventional strategy was a shrewd judgment about the correlation between credit losses and interest rates. If the economy went into recession and people lost jobs, the company would suffer a spike in credit losses. But the Federal Reserve would probably cut interest rates to revive economic growth, or so MBNA's managers reasoned. By borrowing short and lending long, MBNA would capture a benefit in its net interest margin at an opportune time, when it could use some help offsetting higher credit losses. When the cycle turned the other way and the Federal Reserve raised rates, then the company's margin would suffer, just like the thrifts', but it would get a break on credit losses. What's more, credit card issuers enjoy the contractual right to raise interest rates on existing accounts at any time; this is an extra lever to pull in order to sustain the net interest margin during this part of the cycle. (Thrifts did not have the ability to raise the rates on their mortgages.) MBNA had refined its repricing tactics over the years by carefully testing and measuring the price sensitivity of different classes of cardholders in its large customer base. CEO Bruce Hammonds explained the company's strategy on a conference call with analysts to review fourth-quarter 2004 results:

> For more than 30 years, two things are happening at different times: Credit losses are moving up, interest rates are moving down; or interest rates are moving up and credit losses are moving down as they are now. They work in tandem and then you've got a third lever here and that is pricing to the customer to be able to make sure that you can have a very, very consistent net interest margin.[18]

Recall that Discover Financial Services followed a similar approach, which helped sustain its earnings during 2008, as was related in Chapter 7. (CEO David Nelms had been a senior executive of MBNA before moving to Discover.) But most other card issuers followed the traditional risk management approach, matching the duration of assets and liabilities. As a result, their net interest margins were steadier than MBNA's, but their earnings were more volatile, as they had no way to offset fluctuations in credit losses.

From 2001 to 2003, MBNA's strategy worked like a charm. The net interest margin expanded thanks to large interest rate cuts by the Federal Reserve. The wider margin more than offset a moderate increase in credit losses produced by rising unemployment and the turn in the bankruptcy cycle. (Providian collapsed at this time, as discussed in Chapter 2).

The problem came in early 2005. The economy was growing again, and the Federal Reserve began to raise interest rates back to normal levels. MBNA's credit losses were improving, but its net interest margin came under pressure, so it began repricing its customer accounts. At the company's first-ever analyst day, management guided to a stable net interest margin in coming quarters, counting on a successful repricing campaign. But just a few weeks later when it released first-quarter 2005 results, it reported a shocking surprise: instead of remaining stable, its net interest margin had tumbled—from 7.12% in the prior quarter to 6.80%. The stock plummeted, losing 20% in a single day (Exhibit 9.6). Its credibility in tatters, MBNA sold itself to Bank of America a short time later, sacrificing its independent identity and ending a 20-year run of growth and profits.

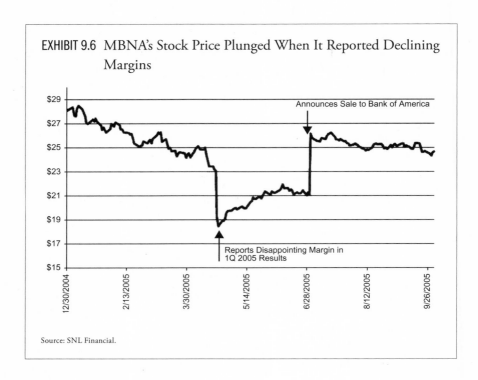

EXHIBIT 9.6 MBNA's Stock Price Plunged When It Reported Declining Margins

Source: SNL Financial.

In early 2005, the volatility implied in MBNA options was about 25%, equivalent to market expectations of a one-standard-deviation one-day move in the stock of roughly 1.7%. In this light, the 20% move would theoretically count as an 11-standard-deviation surprise, another example of a Black Swan afflicting a single stock.

Because the other card issuers had matched asset and liability durations, their net interest margins were not under pressure. At the same time, they too were benefiting from lower credit losses. Rather than needing to raise prices like MBNA, they had room to cut prices. Many used 0% teaser rates to lure new accounts, including thousands of MBNA's historically loyal customers, some of whom had just received notices that they would have to pay higher interest rates on their MBNA balances. MBNA's estimates of customer price sensitivity had come from periods when the competitive dynamic was different. MBNA had not allowed for the possibility that its risk management strategy might be sensitive to the behavior of competitors.[19]

Basel II: The Failure of Algorithmic Capital Standards

When MBNA's strategy misfired, the consequences were serious: the company forfeited its independence. The consequences of Basel II were bigger: it helped unleash a systemic crisis. The problem was that Basel II had allowed some of the world's largest financial institutions to operate with excessive leverage, specifically, capital ratios of 4% or lower, which were weak compared even with LTCM's (Exhibit 9.7). Such thin cushions left them ill prepared for the subprime mortgage crisis, especially when many had bulked up on subprime-related securities—another consequence of Basel II's new rules. Named for the town in Switzerland where the Bank for International Settlements makes its headquarters, Basel II was an ambitious program meant to reduce systemic risk in the global banking system by standardizing capital requirements. Yet its authors failed to recognize how collective dynamics might render invalid a strategy based on historical data.

The Bank for International Settlements promulgated its first set of regulatory capital standards in the early 1990s. Called Basel I, these rules were based on the sensible premise that riskier assets warranted more capital. Previously, bank capital regulations had applied a fixed ratio to all bank assets, irrespective of risk. The problem was that a fixed ratio penalizes banks with safe assets by making them hold just as big a cushion as competitors with risky loans. The fixed ratio, regulators worried, created an incentive for banks to bulk up on risky assets, as the wide margins that accompany dicey loans would generate high returns and fast earnings growth (as long as the loans paid off). If those risky loans went bad, that was likely to be the regulators' problem—the familiar situation of "heads, managers win; tails, regulators lose."[20]

To counter this misalignment of incentives, Basel I introduced different capital ratios for different assets. Low-risk securities like government obligations would require much lower capital ratios than risky assets like commercial loans or credit cards. Since residential mortgages had historically enjoyed low default rates, they would require less capital than riskier commercial loans, although more than government securities.

So far, so good. But during the 1990s, financial innovation accelerated, as did the complexity of large bank organizations. Basel I was not designed with derivatives, securitization, credit default swaps (CDSs), or subprime mortgages in mind. The answer was Basel II. Ten years in the making, these new rules had the same premise of matching capital to risk—but the authors of Basel II

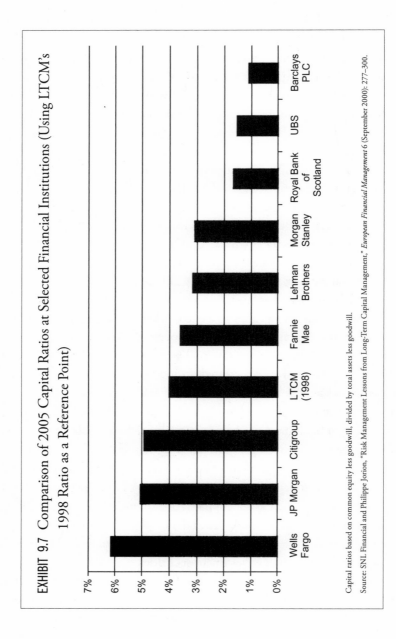

EXHIBIT 9.7 Comparison of 2005 Capital Ratios at Selected Financial Institutions (Using LTCM's 1998 Ratio as a Reference Point)

Capital ratios based on common equity less goodwill, divided by total assets less goodwill.

Source: SNL Financial and Philippe Jorion, "Risk Management Lessons from Long-Term Capital Management," *European Financial Management* 6 (September 2000): 277–300.

were more ambitious and their rules, more complex. Basel II established a broader range of capital ratios for a wider set of assets. For certain risks, the rules specified complicated mathematical formulas for calculating capital levels. And the program encouraged large, sophisticated banks to set their own capital ratios based on statistical analysis of their own historical credit data. Collecting details of past loan performance became a priority for large banks, which stored this information in vast data warehouses. As one might guess, this information was fed into Monte Carlo simulation models, the application of choice for estimating capital standards for large portfolios of complex instruments. By 2007, the cost of implementing Basel II in Europe alone was running well over $10 billion, according to consultant Oliver Wyman.[21]

Fundamentally, Basel II was an algorithmic approach to risk management, based on the view that calculations of past data could serve as a strategy for setting capital. By emphasizing the math, Basel II ignored the role of judgment.[22] In hindsight, it is now clear why it was doomed. First of all, when all major banks based their analyses on similar data, they made similar decisions. Everyone's historical data showed that mortgages and AAA-rated securities had low default rates. Low default rates translated into low capital standards for these assets, and this encouraged the flow of capital into subprime and other nontraditional mortgages, AAA-rated mortgage securities, and collateralized debt obligations. But these capital flows distorted the performance of the underlying real estate markets, leading first to the housing boom, then to the crash, and finally to an unprecedented surge in defaults, in a complete break with the past data.

Second, the capital standards focused too much on institution-specific risk factors, such as the nature of a bank's assets, and ignored the possibility that other variables in the environment might affect the risk profile. In this way the Basel II formulas embedded the "representativeness" error (Chapter 3) by overweighting the variables regulators had studied in great depth (historical credit losses) relative to other factors in the environment (housing booms, liquidity cycles, and other macroeconomic disturbances).

A concept in financial regulation called the "macroprudential" orientation recognizes that focusing exclusively on the financial strength of individual institutions may overlook common or correlated exposures across financial institutions that could cause them to fail in large numbers.[23] Avinash Persaud, a consultant and professor of economics, points out that trying to make the system as a whole safe by ensuring that individual banks are safe "represents a fallacy of composition. In trying to make themselves safer, banks and other highly leveraged financial intermediaries can behave in ways that collectively undermine the system."[24] Caught up in the search for ever more precise measurements, the authors of Basel II lost sight of this concept.

A final problem is the possibility that regulated institutions might find ways to counteract the new safeguards. After all, Basel II did not change banks' appetite for risk taking. The rules merely added certain constraints. That regulatory goals may be frustrated by the regulated entity's offsetting behavior is known as "The Peltzman effect," after University of Chicago economist Sam Peltzman, who first observed this phenomenon in studying traffic safety laws in the 1970s. Introducing seat belts and other safety standards, he found, did not reduce the rate of accidental vehicular death from its long-term trend. Instead, as drivers felt safer, they drove faster, resulting in a higher frequency of accidents. The new standards did not change drivers' tolerance for risk.[25]

The likelihood that regulated entities will take offsetting actions argues for simpler rules and a greater role for judgment and action. For example, in the early 1990s, when U.S. banks were in the process of adopting Basel I, U.S. regulators introduced a supplemental capital standard based on the old-fashioned fixed ratio; it was called the "leverage ratio." Bill Seidman, then head of the Federal Deposit Insurance Corporation, explained the rationale for this standard:

> Unless the new risk standards were overridden by a leverage standard demanding a ratio of at least six percent of capital to loans, about nine out of ten small banks across the country would be allowed to reduce their capital cushion at precisely the time when the entire banking industry was being threatened by a rising level of risk.[26]

There was no formula behind the 6% standard. It was simply a judgment about what the situation demanded.

Good judgment has informed other effective actions by U.S. regulators over the years, such as imposing a capital surcharge for subprime loans, standardizing rules and disclosures for credit card portfolios, and eliminating the agent bank model for payday lending. The emergency recapitalization of the banking industry in the crisis of 2008 involved ad hoc measures, such as injecting government preferred stock and implementing a forward-looking stress test. While these measures were controversial at the time, they helped restore stability to the U.S. financial system, preventing the risk of a much deeper crisis.

Clearly there is a place for analysis of past data, and rules will need to be specific and in some cases complicated. But in a dynamic environment, where innovation and competition continually alter the landscape, regulators will need judgment to recognize when rules are being end-run or just not working. In these cases, decisive action will trump the benefits of ever more precise rules. One cannot proscribe Black Swans.

Sallie Mae: The Denouement

Picking up the story where we left off, the budget surprise in early February 2007 meant that student lenders were going to face a tougher shakeout than I had anticipated. The idea that Sallie Mae's stock would rebound to $50 no longer seemed like an easy bet. I had to adjust my strategy once again. Yet I still thought the company was better positioned than its peers to exploit growth in private student lending. So I decided to recommend a so-called relative value trade, which included buying Sallie's shares and simultaneously selling short shares of two competitors, Nelnet and First Marblehead. Nelnet focused only on government-guaranteed loans, with no real capability to penetrate the private student loan market. First Marblehead produced only private student loans, but lacked Sallie Mae's scale and infrastructure; without government-guaranteed loans, it had a hard time establishing a presence on campus. My thesis was that the market had lost sight of Sallie's competitive advantage relative to these smaller, weaker institutions.

I still worried about Sallie's stock repurchase forward. To be sure, in the scenarios I was considering, the contract was not going to break Sallie's bank. But I was receiving a constant stream of calls from worried clients. I feared these investors would flee if Sallie's shares dipped any further, as a lower stock price would produce additional losses on the repurchase contract, eat deeper into shareholders equity, and leave the company even more levered— potentially triggering further pressure on the stock in a dangerous, circular process. This risk might jeopardize the relative value strategy, because Nelnet and First Marblehead did not have stock repurchase forward commitments.

An idea came to mind: since Sallie's debt traded at tight levels, I might recommend a CDS contract that would pay off in the event that Sallie's debt spreads widened. If the stock sold off, I reasoned, debt holders would worry about the stock repurchase mark-to-market losses eroding the company's equity cushion (which was after all there to protect the debt). So I added the CDS protection to the relative value recommendation.[27]

I mentioned that Sallie was reconsidering its strategy. A few weeks after my relative value recommendation, the company announced that it had agreed to sell itself for $60 per share in a leveraged buyout (LBO) transaction to a consortium of buyers led by private equity investor J.C. Flowers & Co. and including Bank of America and JP Morgan. This event produced a highly positive outcome for my recommendations. The options recovered their value as the stock shot past the strike price, and the relative value trade worked because the other student lenders did not receive private equity bids. What is more, the CDS contract also produced a large profit: in agreeing to an LBO bid that would heap additional debt on the company, Sallie Mae took on a much riskier profile, and its debt spreads widened dramatically. Although I had not anticipated an LBO as a catalyst, members of the consortium did speak of the growth opportunity in private student loans and Sallie Mae's competitive advantages, in ways similar to my thinking.

What did not make sense to me was the $60 per share price tag, or the idea of further leveraging a company that had only the thinnest of capital cushions to start with. As Sallie reported results for the first and second quarters, credit losses in the private student loan portfolio came in above my expectations. The company had warned investors of back-office operational problems. However, I was starting to hear skepticism about the quality of its underwriting from sources in the securitization markets. That credit was already under pressure seemed to undermine my ideas about the size of the growth opportunity. I was not ready to throw in the towel on the private loan thesis, but I could not understand how the consortium had valued Sallie at $60.

Moreover, in taking on the additional debt contemplated in an LBO, Sallie would be operating with *negative* equity. This seemed consistent with its strategy of maximizing leverage. But was it prudent? In making its capital structure riskier, Sallie had disadvantaged its existing debt investors, whose claims on the company's assets were now second to those of the new LBO debt. Spreads on Sallie's unsecured bonds widened, inflicting sizeable mark-to-market losses on debt holders, and making it unlikely the company would access the unsecured market again. The company would now be totally dependent on the financing package offered by Bank of America and JP Morgan as part of the deal, as well as continued access to the securitization markets. Ominously, this was the time when liquidity in the securitization markets was just starting to falter.

To an outside observer, paying top dollar for a company dependent on securitization funding might have looked questionable. In due course, it became apparent that the buyers' consortium was having second thoughts. But the buyers had signed a binding contract. They tried to argue that changes in the political outlook for government-guaranteed student lending had triggered a so-called material adverse change, a clause in the buyout agreement that would let them rescind the offer. Investors were skeptical about the legal merits of this claim, since the Bush administration's stance toward student lending was public well before the acquisition was announced. Nonetheless, the buyers returned to the negotiating table with a revised offer of $50 per share plus warrants whose value would equal $7 if Sallie hit its projections and as much as $10 if it exceeded them.

Sallie was in an awkward position. It had burned bridges with unsecured debt investors. The securitization markets were starting to wobble. Its credit quality was deteriorating. To some extent, the LBO seemed like a continuation of its past strategy of maximizing leverage. In late 2007, this was no longer the right game plan. In hindsight, Sallie ought to have taken the revised offer and run. My sources are split on whether the revised offer was sincere or a public relations ploy. In any case, the two parties did not come to terms and ended up in litigation.

As the litigation dragged on, Sallie's stock fell to $20 per share. Desperate for financing, Sallie settled the litigation and waived the $500 million break-up fee it was entitled to in exchange for a new line of credit from Bank of America and JP Morgan. At the new lower stock price, Sallie's forward commitment had become a $900 million liability. To pay for it, Sallie issued new equity, diluting the ownership stake of its existing shareholders. In due course, management acknowledged that it had been too aggressive in marketing private loans at certain nontraditional schools, where loss rates turned out to be an order of magnitude higher than expectations. But bad luck continued. Financing for private student loans dried up. Then in early 2009, the Obama administration proposed shifting the guaranteed loan program to a government operation, cutting out lenders like Sallie, whose future was left in limbo. As of mid-2009, Sallie's shares were trading under $10 (Exhibit 9.8).

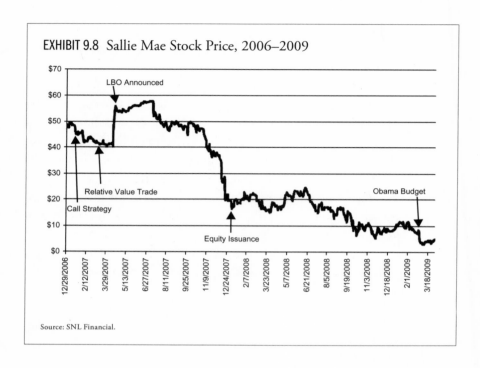

EXHIBIT 9.8 Sallie Mae Stock Price, 2006–2009

Source: SNL Financial.

Lessons Learned

Sallie Mae and its shareholders had 3 swans to blame for the 90% decline in the stock. First, the company's challenges were part of the bigger swan that emerged from the mortgage credit cycle and wrought chaos across the financial sector. Second, the government student loan program lost out in the ever-shifting political landscape. Third, some of the company's problems were self-inflicted, as its management team missed the opportunity to modify strategies as conditions changed. I think Sallie Mae struggled with the transition from growth to maturity. Had the company tightened underwriting standards and strengthened its balance sheet, rather than continued to chase growth and maximize leverage, it would have been better positioned to face the turbulence of 2007. Instead, it pushed too aggressively for private student loans, leveraged its balance sheet excessively, and grasped for a highly levered transaction that was not soundly conceived.

For analysts, there is another lesson here about the importance of understanding causal relationships. Three critical issues—loan growth, credit quality, and leverage—were all reflections of the company's strategy of

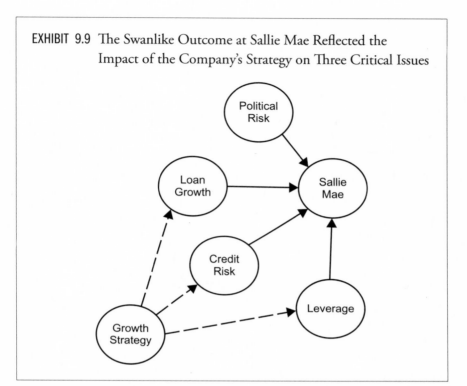

EXHIBIT 9.9 The Swanlike Outcome at Sallie Mae Reflected the Impact of the Company's Strategy on Three Critical Issues

growth and leverage, and thus all three ended up with correlated outcomes. Until 2007, Sallie grew aggressively, enjoyed good credit, and maximized its leverage. One reason my early underweight rating on the stock did not work was that the market expected this combination of positives to continue producing strong results. But the good times could not last forever. The simultaneous shift in these three variables from positive to negative contributed to the swanlike outcome in its stock (Exhibit 9.9).

Conclusion: The Hunt Goes On

In wrapping up, I want to leave the reader with two thoughts. First, what can we say about the causes of the great capital-market crash of 2007–8, which swept aside many of the financial services firms whose stories are chronicled in this book? Common explanations focus on the greed of market participants, the foolishness of investors, and the lack of sound regulation. There is some merit in these explanations, but they do not provide much explanatory power. After all, greed and foolishness are constants, and regulation is never perfect. The more convincing explanation for the crash, in my view, was the collective failure of market participants to recognize that the securitization markets had become so powerful as to affect the assets they financed, creating the circular relationship between markets and fundamentals that characterizes all credit cycles. In this case, the boom was especially big because it was fueled by advances in computer technology and the growing interconnectedness of the global capital markets, which together produced a financing capability of a magnitude never seen before.

But the lesson is not just about credit cycles, as these are but one example of the unpredictability of collective action. Given the size of the global securitization markets, it is hard to believe any person, firm, or regulatory agency could ever comprehend their full scope and power. There would be too much information, but not enough computational resources. Even with more resources, forecasting would be stymied by the sensitivity of consensus opinions to feedback, feedforward, and phase shifts. We cannot fully understand the markets, and the markets cannot fully understand their impact on the fundamental world, because that would require groups of people to operate with complete and instantaneous self-knowledge, a physical impossibility. For this reason, I do not think we can ever banish the Black Swan.

The more constructive attitude, in my view, is to learn to live with the phenomenon of extreme volatility. This means allocating resources to predicting swanlike outcomes where feasible, and remaining ready to react quickly and accurately when surprises emerge. Being quick on your feet requires many of the techniques discussed in this book:

- Focus on critical issues.
- Think probabilistically.
- Study the diagnostic power of new information.
- Mitigate cognitive dissonance.
- Drop complex models when environments turn volatile.
- Be ready to adjust decision-making rules and shift strategies.

In the next cycle, we will all be better off if regulators, policymakers, and company executives move just a little bit faster. For investors, it is a zero-sum game, and the spoils will go to the swift.

This brings me to my second point. Most of the valuation, investment, and decision-making books I have seen offer a set of rules to follow. This volume provides a number of suggestions, too. In concluding, however, I would like to emphasize that rules produce positive results only for limited periods, especially when competitors are following similar strategies. The essence of judgment is the recognition that analytic tools and decision-making strategies must be continually examined and adjusted, in an ongoing cycle of learning.

Most of the stories in this book ended badly for the companies involved because of the risky nature of specialty finance and the timing of my experience as an analyst, which ended with the great downturn. Yet Black Swans do not have to be negative. Recall the stunning performance of Master-Card's IPO and the early days at Countrywide, Providian, and Sallie Mae. Before long a new flock of cygnets will be stretching their wings, and as the system eventually finds a new equilibrium, a series of more positive surprises may appear. Analysts, investors, and other decision makers will need to shift strategies once again. Undoubtedly, the sharpest are trying even now to anticipate the next surprise.

Introduction

1. Nassim Nicholas Taleb, *The Black Swan: The Impact of the Highly Improbable* (New York: Random House, 2007). Regarding Taleb's criticism of value at risk, a statistical risk management metric, see "The Jorion-Taleb Debate," April 1997, at http://DerivativesStrategy.com.

2. As Malcolm Gladwell puts it, "I think that the task of figuring out how to combine the best of conscious deliberation and instinctive judgment is one of the great challenges of our time." Gladwell, *Blink: The Power of Thinking Without Thinking* (New York: Little, Brown, 2005), 269.

3. Because of accelerating capacity growth in processors, memory, and bandwidth, futurologist Ray Kurzweil predicts that the computational power of a typical personal computer will match that of the human brain sometime around 2020. Kurzweil, *The Singularity Is Near: When Humans Transcend Biology* (New York: Viking Penguin, 2005), 70.

Chapter 1

1. James Gleick, *Chaos: Making a New Science* (New York: Viking, 1987), 11–31.

2. William A. Sherden, *The Fortune Sellers: The Big Business of Buying and Selling Predictions* (New York: Wiley, 1998), 31–54.

3. American Meteorological Society, "Weather Analysis and Forecasting," *Bulletin of the American Meteorological Society* 88 (August 8, 2007).

4. A. J. Simmons and A. Hollingsworth, "Some Aspects of the Improvement in Skill of Numerical Weather Prediction," *Quarterly Journal of the Royal Meteorological Society* 128 (2002): 647–77.

5. Ibid., 648–52.

6. Sherden, *Fortune Sellers,* 61–72. For a more recent discussion with similar conclusions, see Michael F. Bryan and Linsey Molloy, "Mirror, Mirror, Who's the Best Forecaster of Them All?" *Federal Reserve Bank of Cleveland Economic Commentary,* March 13, 2007.

7. Tonis Vaga, *Profiting from Chaos: Using Chaos Theory for Market Timing, Stock Selection, and Option Valuation* (New York: McGraw-Hill, 1994), 33–37.

8. Robert J. Geller, David D. Jackson, Yan Y. Kagan, and Francesco Mulargia, "Earthquakes Cannot Be Predicted," *Enhanced Perspectives* 275.5306 (1996): 1616.

9. Robert J. Shiller, "From Efficient Market Theory to Behavioral Finance," *Cowles Foundation Discussion Paper,* no. 1385 (October 2002): 4, 14, 21. Shiller's arguments may seem convincing, but there are other potential explanations for why stock prices are more volatile than dividends. One is that stock prices fluctuate because of changes in the risk premiums with which investors discount future dividends to present value. These risk premiums could change as investors continually reassess the probability of economic downturns or stock market crashes. See Jessica A. Wachter, "Can Time-Varying Risk of Rare Disasters Explain Aggregate Stock Market Volatility?" draft Working Paper, October 8, 2008, Wharton School of Business, at http://finance.wharton.upenn.edu/~jwachter/.

10. The classic formula is spelled out in Charles P. Kindelberger, *Manias, Panics, and Crashes* (New York: Wiley, 1996).

11. Edward Chancellor, *Devil Take the Hindmost* (Basingstoke, UK: Macmillan, 1999), 58–95.

12. Gustave Le Bon, *The Crowd: A Study of the Popular Mind* (1895), 1, 2, 14, 22. Contrarian investor David Dreman cites Le Bon's observations as an accurate description of market dynamics. See Dreman, *Contrarian Investment Strategies: The Next Generation* (New York: Simon & Schuster, 1998), 356–57.

13. Solomon Asch, "Opinions and Social Pressure," 1955, at www.panarchy.org/asch/social.pressure.1955.html.

14. S. Bikhchandani, D. Hirshleifer, and I. Welch, "A Theory of Fads, Fashion, Custom, and Cultural Change as Informational Cascades," *Journal of Political Economy* 100 (October 1992).

15. For a description of Ising models, see Philip Ball, *Critical Mass: How One Thing Leads to Another* (New York: Farrar, Straus and Giroux, 2004), 87–93. Didier Sornette, in *Why Stock Markets Crash: Critical Events in Complex Financial Systems* (Princeton, NJ: Princeton University Press, 2003), extends the Ising model approach (pp. 123–30) to predict the exponential shapes characteristic of market bubble episodes.

16. Walter Bagehot, *Lombard Street: A Description of the Money Market* (1873).

17. Ball, *Critical Mass*, 156–77.

18. Herbert Simon, *The Sciences of the Artificial* (Cambridge: Massachusetts Institute of Technology Press, hereafter referred to as MIT Press, 1996), 36–37.

19. For example, Richard W. Roll, "The International Crash of October 1987," in *Black Monday and the Future of Financial Markets*, ed. Robert W. Kamphuis and Roger C. Kormendi (Chicago: Mid America Institute for Public Policy Research, 1989).

20. Fischer Black, "An Equilibrium Model of the Crash," in *National Bureau of Economic Research Macroeconomics Annual*, ed. Stanley Fischer (Cambridge: MIT Press, 1988).

21. George Soros, *The Alchemy of Finance: Reading the Mind of the Market* (New York: Simon and Schuster, 1994), 27–80.

22. Morris A. Davis and Michael G. Palumbo, "A Primer on the Economics and Time Series Econometrics of Wealth Effects," Finance and Economics Discussion Series 2001–09, Divisions of Research & Statistics and Monetary Affairs, Federal Reserve Board, Washington, DC.

23. Hyman Minsky, *Stabilizing an Unstable Economy* (New Haven, CT: Yale University Press, 1986).

24. Ben S. Bernanke, *Essays on the Great Depression* (Princeton, NJ: Princeton University Press, 2000), 25–27, 42, 89–107.

25. Ibid., 108–56.

26. Michael Pettis, *The Volatility Machine: Emerging Economies and the Threat of Financial Collapse* (New York: Oxford University Press, 2001).

27. Avanidhar Subrahmanyam and Sheridan Titman, "Feedback from Stock Prices to Cash Flows," Anderson Graduate School of Management, Paper 23 (1998).

28. This is an extremely simplistic synopsis of the Merton model for treating debt under an option valuation approach. See Robert C. Merton, "On the Pricing of Corporate Debt: The Risk Structure of Interest Rates," *Journal of Finance* 29 (1974): 449–70.

29. Quoted in Peter J. Tanous, *Investment Gurus* (New York: Prentice Hall Press, 1997), 353.

30. Judea Pearl, *Probabilistic Reasoning in Intelligent Systems: Networks of Plausible Inference* (San Francisco: Morgan Kaufmann Publishers, 1988), 381–82.

31. University of Chicago researchers Lubos Pastor and Pietro Veronesi argue that "learning is facilitated by the existence of vast quantities of financial data, but it is also hampered by the large amount of randomness pervading financial markets." They describe how valuation models that incorporate Bayesian updating and uncertainty can explain seemingly irrational phenomena, like the high valuations of technology stocks (a rational function of uncertainty, in their view) or the subsequent crash (when investors learn of the true profitability of the firms). They point out that the stocks of younger firms have higher volatility and prices than those of older firms; a phenomenon that they conjecture reflects greater initial uncertainty about the business models, which diminishes as investors learn about the firms over time. Learning may explain why individual investors trade excessively (it helps them learn about their stock-picking skills) or why venture capital firms' performance is persistent (they may learn valuable information from their investments). See Pastor and Veronesi, "Learning in Financial Markets," *Annual Review of Financial Economics* (2009), and Andrew W. Lo, "Reconciling Efficient Markets with Behavioral Finance: The Adaptive Markets Hypothesis," *The Journal of Investment Consulting* 7:2 (2005).

32. This terminology comes from Philip Tetlock, who studied the forecasting accuracy of a panel of political experts. Tetlock uses the term *calibration* to refer to the degree to which subjective probabilities (forecasts) were aligned with objective frequencies. *Discrimination* measures the ability of forecasters to do better than predicting base rates by assigning high probabilities to events that actually occur and near-zero probabilities to events that do not. See Tetlock, *Expert Political Judgment: How Good Is It? How Can We Know?* (Princeton, NJ: Princeton University Press, 2005), 47–49.

33. J. Edward Russo and Paul J. H. Schoemaker, "Managing Overconfidence," *Sloan Management Review* 33:2 (1992), 10–11. The authors argue that in order to learn from experience (and thus improve calibration and forecasting accuracy), forecasters must get feedback on and be held accountable for their predictions.

34. Christopher Cherniak describes the "minimal rationality" that characterizes human cognition as evolving in a social context, where people vet what they know not only against their own beliefs but also against the shared knowledge of the community. "Doctrines like 'Ignorance of the law is no excuse' indicate that the agent is held to a standard of care that includes responsibility for collecting information by consulting appropriate experts in the community" (Cherniak, *Minimal Rationality* [Cambridge: MIT Press, 1986], 115).

35. Risk premiums cannot be directly observed. They can be estimated as the difference between equity returns and U.S. Treasury bond returns, but equity risk premiums have fluctuated across different periods, and there has been enormous variability in the risk premium from year to year. See Bradford Cornell, *The Equity Risk Premium: The Long-Run Future of the Stock Market* (New York: Wiley, 1999).

36. The concept of the "null hypothesis" is commonly used in statistical hypothesis testing. Bayesian statisticians prefer to think of new evidence modifying the "prior distribution" (or theory) before conducting the experiment. For the Bayesian point of view, see Colin Howson and Peter Urbach, *Scientific Reasoning: The Bayesian Approach*, 3rd ed. (Chicago: Open Court, 2006).

37. John Maynard Keynes, *The General Theory of Employment* (New York: Harcourt, Brace, 1912).

38. Karl Popper, *Conjectures and Refutations* (New York: Basic Books, 1963). While some argue that Popper's approach is too strict, there is a great deal of wisdom in his definition of a scientific proposition. The U.S. courts have adopted falsifiability as a standard for vetting expert witnesses and other presumed scientific evidence. See Kenneth R. Foster and Peter W. Huber, *Judging Science: Scientific Knowledge and the Federal Courts* (Cambridge: MIT Press, 1997).

39. Kenneth A. Posner and Vivian Wang, "In the Long Term, Pricing Trumps Losses, but the Short Term Could Still Be Volatile," Morgan Stanley Research, October 26, 2007.

40. Kenneth A. Posner and Vivian Wang, "Prime Mortgage Credit Now Deteriorating Rapidly—Reiterate FNM Underweight," Morgan Stanley Research, February 8, 2008.

41. Kenneth A. Posner and Vivian Wang, "Downgrading FNM to Underweight on Risk of Higher Losses," Morgan Stanley Research, January 18, 2008.

42. Kenneth A. Posner and Vivian Wang, "Upgrading FNM to Equal-weight: Waiting for Credit to Stabilize," Morgan Stanley Research, March 5, 2008.

Chapter 2

1. Nassim Nicholas Taleb draws a distinction between totally unpredictable Black Swans and what he calls "near-black" or "gray" swans that may be predictable. He also acknowledges that "severe Black Swans" may occur when surprises could have been predicted but people misunderstood the sources of uncertainty or "lack imagination" in their forecasts. Taleb, *The Black Swan: The Impact of the Highly Improbable* (New York: Random House, 2007), 36–37.

2. Kenneth A. Posner and Athina Meehan, "Providian Corp: Betting on Legal/Regulatory Resolution," Morgan Stanley Dean Witter Research, April 5, 2005.

3. John C. Hull, *Options, Futures, and Other Derivatives,* 5th ed. (Upper Saddle River, NJ: Pearson/Prentice Hall, 2003), 392–94. In this example, we assumed no rate of growth in the stock price.

4. Robert T. Clemen, *Making Hard Decisions: An Introduction to Decision Analysis* (Boston: South-Western College Publishing, 1996), 70–74. See also Judea Pearl, *Probabilistic Reasoning in Intelligent Systems: Networks of Plausible Inference* (San Mateo, CA: Morgan Kaufmann Publishers, 1988), 13, 306–12.

5. There are plenty of examples in Keith M. Moore, *Risk Arbitrage: An Investor's Guide* (New York: Wiley, 1999).

6. Richard Berner, "US Economics: Recession in Smokestack America," Morgan Stanley Dean Witter Research, November 24, 2000.

7. Richard Jeffrey, *Subjective Probability: The Real Thing* (New York: Cambridge University Press, 2004), 76.

8. I first encountered the idea of calibrating a valuation model to current market prices in Alfred Rappaport and Michael J. Mauboussin, *Expectations Investing: Reading Stock Prices for Better Returns* (Cambridge: Harvard Business Press, 2001).

9. Thomas M. Cover and Joy A. Thomas, *Elements of Information Theory,* 2nd ed. (Hoboken, NJ: Wiley-Interscience, 2006), 25–27.

10. Kenneth A. Posner, Mita Nambiar, and Athina Meehan, "Consumer Credit Cycle: Sweet Spot to Persist," Morgan Stanley Dean Witter Research (September 8, 2000), 3.

11. Kenneth A. Posner, Michael D. Courtian, and Athina Meehan, "Introducing the Weekly Pulse," Morgan Stanley Dean Witter Research, October 26, 2000.

12. Kenneth A. Posner, Athina Meehan, and Mita Nambiar, "Flying by the Numbers," Morgan Stanley Dean Witter Research, January 8, 2001.

13. Kenneth A. Posner and Athina L. Meehan, "Surfing the Loss Wave," Morgan Stanley Dean Witter Equity Research, April 2, 2001.

14. Kenneth A. Posner, Athina Meehan, and Mita Nambiar, "Surfing the Loss Wave III: Time to Trim," Morgan Stanley Dean Witter Research, June 14, 2001, and "Providian Corp.: Industry Risk Intensifying; Downgrade to Neutral," June 12, 2001.

15. Kenneth A. Posner and Athina Meehan, "Providian Corp.: All the King's Horses," Morgan Stanley Research, March 27, 2002.

Chapter 3

1. For references, see Paul J. Healey and Don A. Moore, "Bayesian Overconfidence," Working Paper, available at http://cess.nyu.edu/exp_seminar/fall_08_papers/Healy_Moore-Overconfidence.pdf.

2. CIT model portfolio short position contained in Kenneth A. Posner and Andy Bernard, "Specialty Finance: Betting on the Tortoise: Upgrading DFS to Overweight-V," Morgan Stanley Research, February 22, 2008, 14.

3. For an example of one of these tests, see Max Bazerman, *Judgment in Managerial Decision Making*, 6th ed. (Hoboken, NJ: Wiley, 2006), 34. For a survey of results across a range of experiments that measured overconfidence on the part of test subjects, see Sarah Lichtenstein, Baruch Fischhoff, and Lawrence D. Phillips, "Calibration of Probabilities: The State of the Art to 1980," in *Judgment Under Uncertainty: Heuristics and Biases*, ed. Daniel Kahneman, Paul Slovic, and Amos Tversky (Cambridge, UK, and New York: Cambridge University Press, 1982).

4. Some researchers have argued that overconfident traders are more aggressive than rational traders at exploiting mispricings caused by liquidity or noise traders; thus they expect to find in long-run equilibrium that overconfident traders make up a substantial fraction of the trading population. Other reasons cited in the academic literature for overconfident traders to persist include the tendency of rational traders to cut back on their own trades when they realize that overconfident traders are buying or selling aggressively. See Guo Ying Luo and David A. Hirshleifer, "On the Survival of Overconfident Traders in a Competitive Securities Market," *Journal of Financial Markets* 4:1 (January 2001).

5. Robert A. Burton, M.D., *On Being Certain: Believing You Are Right Even When You're Not* (New York: St. Martin's Press, 2008), 11, 16–17, 22–27, 39, 114–19, 134–35.

6. Quoted in Thomas Kida, *Don't Believe Everything You Think: The 6 Basic Mistakes We Make in Thinking* (Amherst, NY: Prometheus Books, 2006).

7. Gary Klein, *The Power of Intuition: How to Use Your Gut Feelings to Make Better Decisions at Work* (New York: Broadway Books, Random House, 2008), 68, 92.

8. The horse racing study is discussed in Richard J. Heuer, Jr., *Psychology of Intelligence Analysis* (New York: Novinka Books, 2006), 68. The study on predicting suspects' guilt is discussed in Carol Tavris and Elliot Aronson, *Mistakes Were Made (But Not By Me): Why We Justify Foolish Beliefs, Bad Decisions, and Hurtful Acts* (Orlando, FL: Harcourt, 2007), 145. The reference to clinical psychologists comes from David Dreman, *Contrarian Investment Strategies: The Next Generation* (New York: Simon & Schuster, 1998), 80. Also see, for example, Stuart Oskamp, "Overconfidence in Case-Study Judgments," in *Judgment Under Uncertainty*.

9. Malcom Gladwell, *Blink: The Power of Thinking Without Thinking* (New York: Little, Brown, 2005), 139.

10. Don A. Moore and Paul J. Healy, "The Trouble with Overconfidence," *Psychological Review* 115:2 (2008).

11. Ibid.

12. Brett N. Steenbarger, *The Psychology of Trading: Tools and Techniques for Minding the Markets* (Hoboken, NJ: Wiley, 2002).

13. Perry Mehrling, *Fischer Black and the Revolutionary Idea of Finance* (Hoboken, NJ: Wiley, 2005), 283.

14. Kent Daniel, David Hirshleifer, and Avanidhar Subrahmanyam, "A Theory of Overconfidence, Self-Attribution, and Security Market Under- and Overreactions," Working Paper, February 19, 1997.

15. For example, during the Cold War, roughly 80% of information about the Soviet Union came from classified sources and only 20% from open sources. Today, 80% is open source. The data are taken from Mark M. Lowenthal, *Intelligence: From Secrets to Policy*, 3rd ed. (Washington, DC: CQ Press, 2006), 102. The importance of open-source information is one of the key themes of Gregory F. Treverton, *Reshaping National Intelligence for an Age of Information* (Cambridge, UK, and New York: Cambridge University Press, 2003). For example (p. 10), "The more-open world is blurring the distinction between collection and analysis. The best looker is not a spymaster, much less an impersonal satellite, but someone steeped in the substance at hand—in short, an analyst." Also, see Robert M. Clark, *Intelligence Analysis: A Target-Centric Approach*, 2nd ed. (Washington, DC: CQ Press, 2007), 87, 124.

16. Kahneman and Tversky, "On the Psychology of Prediction," in *Judgment Under Uncertainty*, 49.

17. Kenneth A. Posner, Tony Kim, and David Brown, "Countrywide Financial Corp.: Market Misprices Risk—Upgrade/Option Strategies," Morgan Stanley Research, May 11, 2006.

18. Kenneth A. Posner, "Countrywide Financial Corp.: Countrywide's Liquidity Having Become an Issue, We Downgrade to Equal-Weight," Morgan Stanley Research, August 17, 2007.

19. For a discussion of why loan level models are not suitable for aggregate forecasting, see Tony Hughes and Robert J. Stewart, "Forecasting and Stress Testing Using Model Pool Level Data," *Moody's Economy.com Regional Financial Review*, August 2008. For a description of micro-macro calibration, see Cris DeRitis and Tony Hughes, "The Moody's CreditCycle Approach to Loan Loss Modeling," *Moody's Economy.com Regional Financial Review*, March 2009.

Chapter 4

1. Christopher H. Browne, *The Little Book of Value Investing* (Hoboken, NJ: Wiley, 2007), 149.

2. This estimate is based on 10^{25} atoms in a kilogram of matter and the ability to store 1,024 bits of information in the magnetic interactions of the protons of a single molecule containing 19 hydrogen atoms, which has apparently been demonstrated by researchers at the University of Oklahoma. See Ray Kurzweil, *The Singularity Is Near: When Humans Transcend Biology* (London: Penguin Books, 2005), 131.

3. A point made by Nassim Nicholas Taleb in *Fooled by Randomness: The Hidden Role of Chance in the Markets and in Life* (New York: Texere, 2001), 165–66.

4. For example, in one study, researchers found a correlation between public opinion about the problem of illegal drugs and the number of media stories on the subject. See Thomas Kida, *Don't Believe Everything You Think: The 6 Basic Mistakes We Make in Thinking* (Amherst, NY: Prometheus Books, 2006), 178.

5. John Maynard Keynes, *The General Theory of Employment* (New York: Harcourt, Brace, 1912). For a discussion of infinite recursion, also see Didier Sornette, *Why Stock Markets Crash: Critical Events in Complex Financial Systems* (Princeton, NJ: Princeton University Press, 2003), 99–103.

6. The theoretical minimum cost of computing is quite low, especially if you could operate the computer at a temperature close to absolute zero and harness futuristic technologies like reversible and quantum computing. However, even with these technologies, there is in practice a limit to how powerful a computer could become, because transient fluctuations in energy at the subatomic level would introduce occasional mistakes into the calculations. Thus the device would need some kind of routine to check for and correct errors. The amount of energy dissipated in the processing of a single bit of information is kT, where k refers to Boltzman's constant and T to the ambient temperature in degrees Kelvin. See Kurzweil, *Singularity*

Is Near, 130–31, and R. Landauer, "Irreversibility and Heat Generation in the Computing Process," *IBM Journal* (July 1961). The amount of energy required to perform an elementary logical operation in time t is equal to or greater than $\pi h/2t$, where h refers to the quantum scale. See Seth Lloyd, "Ultimate Physical Limits to Computation," *Nature* (August 31, 2000): 1047. For a basic introduction to thermodynamics, see Peter Atkins, *Four Laws That Drive the Universe* (Oxford and New York: Oxford University Press, 2007) or Arieh Ben-Naim, *Entropy Demystified: The Second Law Reduced to Plain Common Sense* (Hackensack, NJ: World Scientific, 2007).

7. John Haugeland, *Artificial Intelligence: The Very Idea* (Cambridge: Massachusetts Institute of Technology Press, hereafter referred to as MIT Press, 1985), 65.

8. Roger Penrose, *The Emperor's New Mind* (New York: Penguin, 1998), 40–97. For a more technical discussion, see Thomas M. Cover and Joy A. Thomas, *Elements of Information Theory*, 2nd ed. (Hoboken, NJ: Wiley-Interscience, 2006), 463–90.

9. The "halting problem" and intractability are some of the problems that lead philosophers to consider minimal rationality as a characteristic of human cognition, rather than the perfect rationality assumed in classic economics. See Christopher Cherniak, *Minimal Rationality* (Cambridge: MIT Press, 1986), 77–81.

10. Penrose, *Emperor's New Mind*, 181–89. For an example of problems that cannot be solved even with an ideal computer, see Cherniak, *Minimal Rationality*, 93–94. The reference to chess is from Herbert A. Simon, *The Sciences of the Artificial*, 3rd ed. (Cambridge: MIT Press, 1996), 118.

11. Michael E. Porter, "What Is Strategy?" *Harvard Business Review* (November–December 1996).

12. The term *critical uncertainty* comes from the literature on scenario analysis in strategic planning. See Peter Schwartz, *The Art of the Long View: Planning for the Future in an Uncertain World* (New York: Doubleday, 1996), 115, and Kees Van Der Heijden, *Scenarios: The Art of Strategic Conversation*, 2nd ed. (Hoboken, NJ: Wiley, 2005), 248. Critical uncertainties are called "load-bearing, vulnerable assumptions" in James A. Dewar, *Assumption-Based Planning: A Tool for Reducing Avoidable Surprises* (Cambridge, UK, and New York: Cambridge University Press, 2002), 64–90. Ben Gilad uses an "impact matrix" with one axis for uncertainty and the other for potential impact (which I have borrowed in my exhibit) to quantify the risk associated with "change drivers" in *Early Warning: Using Competitive Intelligence to Anticipate Market Shifts, Control Risk, and Create Powerful Strategies* (New York: AMA COM, 2004), 82.

13. Simon, *Sciences of the Artificial*, 51–58. Similarly, "the main reason to focus attention on a select set of target hypotheses is to economize the acquisition of new data . . . [and] to confine inferences to pertinent regions of the network," making propagation of new information through the entire network unnecessary (thus economizing on computational time). See Judea Pearl, *Probabilistic Reasoning in Intelligent*

Systems: Networks of Plausible Inference (San Mateo, CA: Morgan Kaufmann, 1997), 318–19.

14. Neuroscientists view our ability to pay attention as a limited resource that one allocates to an object or a location in order to enhance the speed or accuracy of sensory perception. Experiments with monkeys and humans that involve the monitoring of a random selection of visual cues show that the subjects' ability to systematically focus their attention at locations was consistent with the probability of the cues appearing there. See Paul Glimcher, *Decisions, Uncertainty, and the Brain: The Science of Neuroeconomics* (Cambridge: MIT Press, 2003), 323–28.

15. Van Hecke cites one study where researchers observed that law students failed to consider both sides of an issue before writing an essay that required them to do so. In another, a researcher studying Fortune 100 employees identified failure to stop and think as a greater barrier to intelligent behavior than either limited motivation or ability. See Madeleine L. Van Hecke, *Blind Spots: Why Smart People Do Dumb Things* (Amherst, NY: Prometheus Books, 2007), 37–39.

16. Gay Klein, *Power of Intuition* (New York: Currency Books, 2003), 270.

17. Mark Bowden, *Black Hawk Down* (New York: Atlantic Monthly Press, 1999), 175.

18. Quoted in Peter J. Tanous, *Investment Gurus* (New York: Prentice Hall Press, 1997), 353.

19. If 50,000 chunks of knowledge define expert knowledge (of the sort acquired over a decade's study), then it would take about 16 dichotomous tests to identify the relevant information. At about 10 milliseconds per test, the act of identification would take less than 200 milliseconds. Apparently it takes in practice a few hundred milliseconds to 1 or 2 seconds for memory to produce results. See Simon, *Sciences of the Artificial*, 88, 90.

20. See Klein, *Power of Intuition*, 13–29, for his theory of recognition-primed decision making and a case study.

21. William Duggan, *Strategic Intuition: The Creative Spark in Human Achievement* (New York: Columbia Business School Publishing, 2007). Napoleon's *coup d'oeil* is discussed on pp. 55–67.

22. See Simon, *Sciences of the Artificial*, 193–200, for a discussion of the trial-and-error approach to searching and the near decomposability of certain kinds of problems.

23. Pearl, *Probabilistic Reasoning in Intelligent Systems*, 107.

24. Gilad, *Early Warning*, 131.

25. Rob Johnston, *Analytic Culture in the U.S. Intelligence Community: An Ethnographic Study* (Washington, DC: Central Intelligence Agency, 2005), 25–27.

26. David Hirshleifer and Ivo Welch, "An Economic Approach to the Psychology of Change: Amnesia, Inertia, and Impulsiveness," Yale Cowles Foundation Discussion Paper No. 1306, June 2001.

27. Because of the "combinatorial explosion" entailed in trying to search through all branches of a decision tree, searching must be *"selective*, that is, partial and risky" (Haugeland, *Artificial Intelligence*, 178).

28. Kenneth A. Posner, Camron Ghaffari, and David Brown, "Advance America: Initiating with an Underweight-V Rating," Morgan Stanley Research, January 25, 2005.

Chapter 5

1. Quoted in Christopher Cherniak, *Minimal Rationality* (Cambridge: Massachusetts Institute of Technology Press, hereafter referred to as MIT Press, 1986), 108.

2. In a report downgrading CIT to neutral on the heels of the announcement, I wrote that the transaction rationale was unclear: "The real issue at CIT, in our view, is the company's high cost of capital and low returns on equity. Until CIT improves its funding costs, we think it will have trouble competing with bank-owned finance companies, not to mention the likes of GE Capital, especially given the thin margins characteristic of vendor finance and other commercial finance businesses. We don't see Tyco's purchase of CIT as providing any benefit to CIT's funding costs. In fact, CIT's corporate debt spreads widened 2 bps yesterday on news of the deal, while TYC's were unchanged. CIT's corporate debt is ranked by the fixed-income rating agencies several notches better than Tyco's (A1/A+ versus Baa1/A-). Moody's has indicated it will review CIT's ratings for possible downgrade, although Standard & Poor's has reaffirmed its current ratings. CIT's recent 5-year bond issuance ('06 maturity) is currently trading at 165 bps over Treasuries, 10 bps lower than Tyco's 10-year debt ('11 maturity) at 175 bps." See Kenneth A. Posner and Athina Meehan, "The CIT Group: Downgrading to Neutral," Morgan Stanley Dean Witter Research, March 14, 2001.

3. Kenneth A. Posner and Athina Meehan, "CIT Group: A Long Way to Go," Morgan Stanley Research, July 5, 2002.

4. Kenneth A. Posner and Athina Meehan, "The CIT Group: Rebalancing Our Ratings," Morgan Stanley Research, September 8, 2003.

5. Carol Tavris and Elliot Aronson, *Mistakes Were Made (but Not by Me): Why We Justify Foolish Beliefs, Bad Decisions, and Hurtful Acts* (New York: Houghton Mifflin Harcourt, 2007), 10. See also Eddie Harmon-Jones and Judson Mills, eds., *Cognitive Dissonance: Progress on a Pivotal Theory in Social Psychology* (Washington, DC: American Psychological Association, 1999).

6. Tavris and Aronson, *Mistakes Were Made*, 19.

7. For examples of studies on this topic, see Max Bazerman, *Judgment in Managerial Decision Making*, 6th ed. (Hoboken, NJ: Wiley, 2006), 35–36.

8. Tavris and Aronson detail many of these bad decisions in *Mistakes Were Made*.

9. Uri Bar-Joseph, "Intelligence Failure and the Need for Cognitive Closure: The Case of Yom Kippur," in *Paradoxes of Strategic Intelligence: Essays in Honor of Michael I. Handel*, ed. Richard K. Betts and Thomas G. Mahnken (Portland, OR: Frank Cass, 2003), 166–89.

10. Ward Edwards, "Conservatism in Human Information Processing," in *Judgment Under Uncertainty: Heuristics and Biases*, ed. Daniel Kahneman, Paul Slovic, and Amos Tversky (Cambridge, UK: Cambridge University Press, 1982), 359–69.

11. The other explanation comes from prospect theory, according to which people are willing to take greater risk to avoid a loss than they are to sustain a gain. See Andrea Frazzini, "The Disposition Effect and Under-Reaction to News," *The Journal of Finance* LXI.4 (August 2006): 2017–46.

12. Richard J. Heuer, Jr., *Psychology of Intelligence Analysis* (New York: Novinka Books, 2006), 28. Tavris and Aronson have a similar thought: "Becoming aware that we are in a state of dissonance can help us make sharper, smarter, conscious choices instead of letting automatic, self-protective mechanisms resolve our discomfort in our favor" (Tavris and Aronson, *Mistakes Were Made*, 226).

13. Bazerman, *Judgment in Managerial Decision Making*, 172–74.

14. Heuer, *Psychology of Intelligence Analysis*, 24–25.

15. The need for "mettle" comes from Christopher H. Browne, *The Little Book of Value Investing* (Hoboken, NJ: Wiley, 2007), 149.

16. Some practitioners have come to the same conclusion. For example, the CIA conducted case studies on how its analysts gauge diagnostic power when they update their subjective probability assessments. In a declassified study conducted in the early 1970s, a group of analysts was polled on their changing views of the odds of hostilities between the Soviet Union and China. The study revealed that the analysts' judgments about probabilities were inconsistent with their assessment of the diagnostic power of new information—a troubling inconsistency. See Charles E. Fisk, "The Sino-Soviet Border Dispute: A Comparison of the Conventional and Bayesian Methods for Intelligence Warning," originally published in *Studies in Intelligence*, 1972, reprinted in *Inside CIA's Private World: Declassified Articles from the Agency's Internal Journal 1955–1992*, ed. H. Bradford Westerfield (New Haven, CT: Yale University Press, 1995).

17. The suggestion is taken from Heuer's *Psychology of Intelligence Analysis*, which in turn quotes a study by Daniel J. Isenberg, "How Senior Managers Think," in *Decision Making: Descriptive, Normative, and Prescriptive Interactions*, ed. David Bell, Howard Raiffa, and Amos Tversky (Cambridge, UK, and New York: Cambridge University Press, 1988).

18. James A. Dewar *Assumption-Based Planning: A Tool for Reducing Avoidable Surprises* (Cambridge, UK, and New York: Cambridge University Press, 2002),

91–107, and Peter Schwartz, *The Art of the Long View: Planning for the Future in an Uncertain World* (New York: Doubleday, 1996), 198.

19. Kenneth A. Posner, "Discover Financial Services: Market May Be Overlooking Value of Network 'Put' Option," Morgan Stanley Research, August 14, 2007.

20. Kenneth A. Posner, "Discover Financial Services: To Underweight-V on Risk of Consumer Credit Recession," Morgan Stanley Research, October 31, 2007. Betsy Graseck's report calling for a consumer credit recession, "Large Cap Banks: Consumer Contagion Coming," was published on the same day (Morgan Stanley Research).

21. Kenneth A. Posner and Andy Bernard, "Betting on the Tortoise: Upgrading DFS to Overweight-V," Morgan Stanley Research, February 22, 2008.

Chapter 6

1. Peter J. Tanous, *Investment Gurus: A Road Map to Wealth from the World's Best Money Managers* (New York: Prentice Hall Press, 1997), 38.

2. Alice Schroeder, *The Snowball: Warren Buffett and the Business of Life* (New York: Bantam, 2008), 598.

3. For a high-level summary of the development of information economics, as well as a brief discussion of asymmetric information and strategies for overcoming it, see Joseph E. Stiglitz, "Information and the Change in the Paradigm in Economics," *The American Economic Review* (June 2002).

4. Kenneth A. Posner, Camron Ghaffari, and David Brown, "Specialty Finance: Student Lending Survey II: Underweight SLM, Overweight NNI," Morgan Stanley Research, September 13, 2005.

5. Sallie Mae, Q3 2005 Earnings Call Transcript, CallStreet, October 20, 2005.

6. Ben Gilad, *Early Warning: Using Competitive Intelligence to Anticipate Market Shifts, Control Risk, and Create Powerful Strategies* (New York: AMACOM, 2004), 101.

7. Ibid., 7, 8.

8. Sydney Finkelstein, *Why Smart Executives Fail: And What You Can Learn From Their Mistakes* (New York: Penguin, 2003), 165, 169, 214.

9. Wachovia Corp., Q2 2008 Earnings Call, CallStreet (July 22, 2008), 14.

10. For those unfamiliar with the term, a *deferred tax asset* reflects the value of tax deductions that have run through the generally accepted accounting principles (GAAP) income statement but have not yet been taken in the tax returns. Freddie had established reserves against future credit losses in its financial statements under GAAP, even though it would not deduct those reserves for tax purposes until it wrote off the loans. If a company cannot demonstrate that it will have sufficient taxable income in future periods to use those tax deductions, then its auditors may force the

company to write off a portion of the deferred tax asset, a move that would impair its capital. For this reason, regulators limit the size of deferred tax assets that banks can count as capital. The regulatory guidelines for Freddie and Fannie Mae did not address deferred tax assets, but the companies were still vulnerable to their auditors' determination.

11. Federal Home Loan Mortgage Corp., 2008 Q2 Earnings Conference Call, CallStreet (August 6, 2008), 20.

12. Undoubtedly, part of the reason for the deferred tax write-down was the auditors' concern that the government would have the company take actions to benefit public policy, such as reducing its guarantee fees, rather than maximize profits. Whether the company would have been forced to write off its deferred tax asset if it had remained private is an open question.

13. Rakesh Khurana, *Searching for a Corporate Savior: The Irrational Quest for Charismatic CEOs* (Princeton, NJ: Princeton University Press, 2002), 79, 156.

14. Adapted from Judea Pearl, *Probabilistic Reasoning in Intelligent Systems: Networks of Plausible Inference* (San Mateo, CA: Morgan Kaufmann Publishers, 1988), 58–59.

Chapter 7

1. In computational theory, *mapping* is another term for a mathematical function that produces an output for one or more inputs. See Michael Sipser, *Theory of Computation* (London: Springer, 2007), 15.

2. According to Metcalfe's Law (named after Bob Metcalfe, the coinventor of the Ethernet), the value of a network increases with the square of the number of connected users. For a discussion of network economics, see Carl Shapiro and Hal R. Varian, *Information Rules: A Strategic Guide to the Network Economy* (Boston: Harvard Business School Press, 1999), 173–225.

3. Kenneth A. Posner and Athina Meehan, "Attacking the Death Star," Morgan Stanley Research, April 15, 2004.

4. Marcia Vickers, "Plastic Under Attack," *Fortune* (May 17, 2006).

5. Gary Klein, *Source of Power: How People Make Decisions* (Cambridge: Massachusetts Institute of Technology Press, hereafter referred to as MIT Press, 1998), 45–74. Keith E. Stanovich and Richard F. West draw a similar distinction between what they call "system 1" (or heuristic-based reasoning) and "system 2" (or conscious, analytic reasoning). See Stanovich and West, "Individual Differences in Reasoning: Implications for the Rationality Debate," in *Heuristics and Biases: The Psychology of Intuitive Judgment*, ed. T. Gilovich, D. Griffin, and D. Kahneman (New York: Cambridge University Press, 2002), 421–40.

6. Robert T. Clemen, *Making Hard Decisions: An Introduction to Decision Analysis* (Pacific Grove, CA: Duxbury/Thomson Learning, 1996), 285–94.

7. John Haugeland, *Artificial Intelligence: The Very Idea* (Cambridge: MIT Press, 1985), 178.

8. Kenneth A. Posner, "MasterCard: Litigation and Other Risks May Be Less Severe Than Market Expects; Initiate with Overweight-V," Morgan Stanley Research, June 22, 2002.

9. Kenneth A. Posner and Andrew Chen, "MasterCard: Market Responding Accurately to Upside Surprise; Downgrade to Equal-weight-V," Morgan Stanley Research, November 2, 2006.

10. Kenneth A. Posner and Betsy Graseck, "The Coming Battle for the Affluent Cardholder," Morgan Stanley Research, August 11, 2006.

11. Kenneth Posner and Camron Ghaffari, "American Express: Giving More Credit to Operating Leverage: Upgrade," Morgan Stanley Research, August 10, 2005.

12. Kenneth A. Posner and Charles Murphy, "Long MA, Short AXP—A Strategy Levered to Payments Pricing That Hedges US Consumer Risk," Morgan Stanley Research, November 21, 2007.

13. Charlie Murphy, "MasterCard: Quick Comment: MA Raising Cross-Border Fees in 2008, Industry Source Suggests; Confirming Data Point for Our Pricing Power Thesis," Morgan Stanley Research, December 10, 2007.

14. Kenneth A. Posner and Andy Bernard, "American Express: Cutting 2008 EPS by $0.16 on Higher Funding Costs, Lowering Price Target to $39—Remain Underweight," Morgan Stanley Research, March 17, 2008.

Chapter 8

1. N. Metropolis, "The Beginning of the Monte Carlo Method," *Los Alamos Science*, Special Issue 1987.

2. Judea Pearl, *Probabilistic Reasoning in Intelligent Systems: Networks of Plausible Inference* (San Mateo, CA: Morgan Kaufmann Publishers, 1988), 211.

3. Gary Kinder, *Ship of Gold in the Deep Blue Sea* (New York: Atlantic Monthly Press, 1998), 215–18, 228–29.

4. Kenneth A. Posner and Camron Ghaffari, "American Express Co.: Legal Risk to Partnership Strategy," Morgan Stanley Research, July 11, 2005.

5. Kenneth A. Posner and Camron Ghaffari, "American Express Co.: Risk Factors Limit Upside; Consider Selling Volatility," Morgan Stanley Research, March 14, 2006.

6. Kenneth A. Posner and Camron Ghaffari, "American Express Co.: Repurchase Calls," Morgan Stanley Research, April 11, 2006.

7. Philippe Jorion, "Risk Management Lessons from Long-Term Capital Management," *European Financial Management* 6 (September 2000): 277–300. For a more general background, see Roger Lowenstein, *When Genius Failed: The Rise and Fall of Long-Term Capital Management* (New York: Random House, 2000).

8. Atish Kakodkar, Barnaby Martin, and Stefano Galiani, "Correlation Trading: A New Asset Class Emerges," Merrill Lynch, November 26, 2003.

9. "Who's the More Foolish? The Fool, or the Fool Who Follows Him?" June 28, 2007, at www.accruedint.blogspot.com.

10. Gary B. Gorton, *The Panic of 2007* (Hoboken, NJ: Wiley, 2007), 190.

11. Kenneth Posner, Melini Jesudason, Armando Lopez, Robert Stevenson, "Housing Market Downside," Morgan Stanley Research, February 5, 2003, 8.

12. Christopher Mayer and R. Glenn Hubbard, "House Prices, Interest Rates, and the Mortgage Market Meltdown," draft Working Paper, Columbia Business School, October, 2008.

13. Reid Hastie and Robyn M. Dawes, *Rational Choice in an Uncertain World* (Thousand Oaks, CA: Sage, 2001), 156–62.

14. Bennett W. Golub and Leo M. Tilman, *Risk Management Approaches for Fixed Income Markets* (Hoboken, NJ: Wiley, 2000), 56–62 for key rate durations, 95–123 for principal components analysis.

15. For the classic critique of the GSE model (albeit a bit early), see Thomas H. Stanton, *A State of Risk: Will Government-Sponsored Enterprises Be the Next Financial Crisis?* (New York: HarperBusiness, 1991), and Stanton's updated *Government-Sponsored Enterprises: Mercantilist Companies in the Modern World* (Washington, DC: AEI Press, 2002).

16. Kenneth A. Posner, "Fannie Mae, Freddie Mac, and Interest Rate Risk," Morgan Stanley Research, September 9, 2002, and Kenneth A. Posner and David Brown, "Fannie Mae, Freddie Mac & the Road to Redemption," Morgan Stanley Research, July 6, 2005.

17. Diana Hancock, Andreas Lehnert, Wayne Passmore, and Shane M. Sherlund, "An Analysis of the Potential Competitive Impacts of Basel II Capital Standards on U.S. Mortgage Rates and Mortgage Securitization," Federal Reserve Board, April 2005, Figure 5.1. See also "Retail Credit Economic Capital Estimation—Best Practices," The Risk Management Association, February 2003, 54.

18. Kenneth A. Posner, Tony Kim, David Brown, and Drew Uher, "Fannie Mae Cross-Asset Insights: Equity Discounting Too Much Risk, While Sub-Debt Appears Complacent," Morgan Stanley Research, February 2, 2006.

19. Kenneth A. Posner and Tony Kim, "Fannie Mae: Restatement Shows Strong Balance Sheet," Morgan Stanley Research, December 6, 2006.

20. Statement by Secretary Henry M. Paulson, Jr. on Treasury and Federal Housing Finance Agency Action to Protect Financial Markets and Taxpayers, September 7, 2008, at www.treas.gov/press/releases/hp1129.htm.

21. Golub and Tilman, *Risk Management Approaches*, 203.

22. Deborah Lucas and Robert L. McDonald, "An Options-Based Approach to Evaluating the Risk of Fannie Mae and Freddie Mac," *Journal of Monetary Economics* 53 (2006): 155–76.

23. CBO's Estimate of Cost of the Administration's Proposal to Authorize Federal Financial Assistance for the Government-Sponsored Enterprises for Housing, Letter to the Honorable John M. Spratt Jr., July 22, 2008.

24. Charles Duhigg, Stephen Labaton, and Andrew Ross Sorkin, "As Crisis Grew, a Few Options Shrank to One," *New York Times* (September 8, 2008): A1.

Chapter 9

1. Marvin Minsky, *The Emotion Machine: Commonsense Thinking, Artificial Intelligence, and the Future of the Human Mind* (New York: Simon & Schuster, 2006).

2. Kenneth A. Posner and Athina Meehan, "SLM Corporation: Great Expectations," Morgan Stanley Research, September 8, 2003.

3. Kenneth A. Posner, "SLM Corporation: Increasing PT to $54.50, Upgrading to Equal-Weight," Morgan Stanley Research, May 8, 2006.

4. Kenneth A. Posner and Andrew Chen, "SLM Corporation: Stock Now Discounts Political, Balance Sheet Risk; Potential for Rebound," Morgan Stanley Research, January 23, 2007.

5. Quotation referenced in Richard J. Heuer, Jr., *Psychology of Intelligence Analysis* (New York: Novinka Books, 2006), 82.

6. For a general discussion, see Reid Hastie and Robyn M. Dawes, *Rational Choice in an Uncertain World* (Thousand Oaks, CA: Sage Publications, 2001), 47–98.

7. Martin Leibowitz and Anthony Bova, "Portfolio Analysis: Beyond Diversification: 'Dragon Risk'," Morgan Stanley Research, July 21, 2004. Leibowitz attributes the term "dragon risk" to Cliff Asness.

8. Kate Kelly, "How Goldman Won Big on Mortgage Meltdown," *Dow Jones Financial News Online* (December 17, 2007).

9. Joel Greenblatt, *The Little Book That Beats the Market* (Hoboken, NJ: Wiley, 2006). For an analysis critical of Greenblatt's back-testing claims, see Bill Alpert, "The Little Book's Little Flaw," *Barron's Online*, Wednesday, March 27, 2006, at http://online.barrons.com/article/SB114325090789508133.html.

10. www.buffettsystem.com/.

11. Brian T. Hayes, PhD, "August 2007 Quantitative Equity Turbulence: An Unknown Unknown Becomes a Known Unknown," Lehman Brothers, November 2007.

12. Richard Bookstaber, *A Demon of Our Own Design* (Hoboken, NJ: Wiley, 2007), 182–90.

13. Graham's image of Mr. Market is "probably the most brilliant metaphor ever created for explaining how stocks can become mispriced" (Jason Zweig, commentary to chapter 8 of Benjamin Dodd's *The Intelligent Investor* [New York: Harper-Business, 2005], 213).

14. Hayes, "August 2007 Quant Equity Turbulence," Presentation to New York Academy of Sciences, April 17, 2008. See also Amir E. Khandani and Andrew W. Lo, "What Happened to the Quants in August 2007? Evidence from Factors and Transactions Data," Working Paper, October 23, 2008.

15. Khandani and Lo, "What Happened to the Quants in August 2007? Evidence from Factors and Transactions Data," 3. The Lehman analyst quoted was M. Rothman, "Turbulent Times in Quant Land," U.S. Equity Quantitative Strategies, Lehman Brothers Research, 2007.

16. *The Intelligent Investor*, 191–92, 194.

17. George J. Benston, *An Analysis of the Causes of Savings and Loan Association Failures*, Salomon Brothers Center for the Study of Financial Institutions, 1985.

18. MBNA Corp., Q4 2004 Earnings Call Corrected Transcript, CallStreet (January 21, 2005), 8.

19. It was thought that MBNA's largest investors were interested in monetizing their stakes, so perhaps management had to push for growth as aggressively as possible if it wanted a chance to maintain the company's independence.

20. For example, see Laurence H. Meyer, "Supervising Large Complex Banking Organizations: Adapting to Change," in *Prudential Supervision: What Works and What Doesn't*, ed. Frederic S. Mishkin (Chicago: University of Chicago Press, 2001), 97–98.

21. Oliver Wyman, "Payback Time for Basel II," 2007.

22. "The growing fashion in risk management, supported by the Basel Committee on Banking Supervision, is a move away from discretionary judgments about risk and a move to more quantitative and market-sensitive approaches" (Avinash Persaud, "Sending the Herd off the Cliff Edge: The Disturbing Interaction Between Herding and Market-Sensitive Risk Management Practices," Bank for International Settlements Papers, No 2 [2000]).

23. Claudio Borio, "The Macroprudential Approach to Regulation and Supervision," VOX—Research-Based Policy Analysis and Commentary from Leading Economists, April 14, 2009, at www.voxeu.org/index.php?q=node/3445.

24. Avinash Persaud, "Macro-Prudential Regulation: Fixing Market (and Regulatory) Failures," Policy Brief, undated.

25. For a quick summary, see Sam Peltzman, "Regulation and the Natural Progress of Opulence," 2004 Distinguished Lecture, AEI-Brookings Joint Center for Regulatory Studies, American Enterprise Institute for Public Policy Research,

Washington, DC. For a discussion of how risk management systems encourage financial institutions to take on more risk, see Kent Osband, *Iceberg Risk: An Adventure in Portfolio Theory* (New York: Texere, 2003).

26. L. William Seidman, *Full Faith and Credit: The Great S&L Debacle and Other Washington Sagas* (New York: Times Books, 1993), 133–34.

27. Kenneth A. Posner and Andrew Chen, "SLM Corporation: Seeking Relative Value," in *North American Financials US Financials Model Portfolio*, Morgan Stanley Research, February 15, 2007.

New Century Financial, 76
Newcourt, 111–112
nonlinear fundamentals, 7
normalized distributions, 189
no-surcharge rules, 181
null hypothesis, 24–25

OCC. *See* Office of the Comptroller of
the Currency
Office of Federal Housing Enterprise
Oversight (OFHEO), 199
Office of the Comptroller of the
Currency (OCC), 35
OFHEO. *See* Office of Federal Housing
Enterprise Oversight
one-to-many mapping, 173–174
one-to-one mapping, 173–174
option adjustable-rate mortgages (option
ARMs), 144
option ARMs. *See* option adjustable-rate
mortgages
option market's view, 38
options market, 60–61
output variable, 172
overconfidence. *See also* confidence: in
action, 65; Bank of America, 77–78;
Countrywide, 72–78; Golden West
stock volatility, 76; loan-level loss
models, 80–81; mapping, 163; model
related, 72–79; New Century
Financial stock volatility, 76; properly
specified loss models, 82–83; share of
origination market, 74; standard
deviation, 79–80; stock volatility, 76;
subprime mortgage collapse, 76–84;
vs. underconfidence, 59–60;
Washington Mutual stock volatility,
76; Wells Fargo stock volatility, 76

paradox of the three prisoners, 148–150
Pastor, Lubos, 22–23
payday lender, 106
peer pressure, 15
Peltzman, Sam, 228

"The Peltzman effect," 228
phase shifts, 16–17, 21
physical limits, 96–97
political risk, 119–120, 197, 204
Porter, Michael, 99
practical techniques, 130–131
premium customer base, 170
price target distribution, 199
pricing power, 170
principal components analysis, 191–192
probabilistic estimate, 202
probability trees: accurate updating, 133;
American Express stock price
1999–2000, 36; American Express
stock price 1999–2002, 52;
asymmetric outcomes, 44–48;
Bayesian networks, 39; Capital One
Financial Corporation stock price
1999–2000, 36; Capital One
Financial Corporation stock price
1999–2002, 52; CIT Group, 114;
correlations, 48–49; credit card
companies, 33–34; critical issues, 40;
Discover Financial Services, 133;
discrimination, 43; expected value,
38; influence diagrams, 39; Jeffrey,
Richard, 41; Jensen, Johan, 46;
Jensen's inequality, 46–47; market
price and volatility, 42; OCC, 35;
option market's view, 38; Providian,
36–54; Providian, conclusions, 49–52;
Providian, influence diagram, 41, 53;
Providian, lesson learned, 52–54;
research, 45; risk factors, 47–48;
volatility, introduction to, 35–39
properly specified loss models, 82–83
Providian: Black Swan, 33–39, 51;
conclusions, 49–52; conditional
probabilities, 126; critical issues, 40;
decision tree for new information,
127; decision-making, real-time,
126–128; expected value, 38;
influence diagram, 41, 53; information
asymmetry, 151–153; lesson learned,